Who Translates?

Who Translates?

Translator Subjectivities Beyond Reason

Douglas Robinson

STATE UNIVERSITY OF NEW YORK PRESS

Published by
State University of New York Press, Albany

For information, address State University of New York Press,
State University Plaza, Albany, N.Y., 12246

Production by Kelli Williams
Marketing by Dana E. Yanulavich

Library of Congress Cataloging-in-Publication Data

Robinson, Douglas.
    Who translates? : translator subjectivities beyond reason / Douglas
Robinson.
        p.cm.
    Includes bibliographical references and index.
    ISBN 0-7914-4863-0 (alk. paper)—ISBN 0-7914-4864-9 (pbk. : alk. paper)
    1. Translating and interpreting. 2. Subjectivity. I. Title.

P306 .R644 2001
418'.02–dc21   00-057354

10 9 8 7 6 5 4 3 2 1

Contents

Acknowledgments vii

Introduction: Who Translates? 1

*Preliminary Questions 1   Channeling 7   Rationalism, Pre- and Post- 12
Part One: The Spirit-channeling Model 16   Part Two: Ideology 17
Part Three: Transient Assemblies 17*

PART ONE: THE SPIRIT-CHANNELING MODEL

1 Reason and Spirit 21

*The Translator as Spirit-channel 21   "Reason"? "Spirit"? 26
Logologies of Reason and Spirit 30*

2 The Divine Inspiration of Translation 36

*A Short History of Spirit-channeling 37   Socrates and the Art of the
Rhapsode 43   Philo and Augustine on the Legend of the Septuagint 48
Joseph Smith and* The Book of Mormon *54   Paul on Glossolalia and Interpreting 61*

PART TWO: IDEOLOGY

3 Ideology and Cryptonymy 69

*Logology of Ideology 69   Heidegger on Spirit 77   Cryptonymy: Abraham/
Torok and Freud 82   Heidegger's Crypt 94   First Translation 96
Second Translation 104   Third Translation 113*

4 The (Ideo)logic of Spectrality 116

*Shakespeare's Permission 116   (In)visibilizing Lear 124
Marx and Schleiermacher on Spirits and Ghosts 129*

PART THREE: TRANSIENT ASSEMBLIES

5 The Pandemonium Self   141

Rationalist and Postrationalist Theories of the Self 141   *Lacan's Schema L* 148
Pandemonium 151   *The Invisible Subject* 156   *The Translator's Objects* 164
Fidus interpres *and the Double Bind* 170

6 The Invisible Hand   180

Invisible and Hidden Hands 180   *Translation Agencies* 186

Conclusion: Beyond Reason   193

Works Cited 197

Index 203

Acknowledgments

Here are some of the people who contributed to whatever kind of "success" this book ends up having out there in the real world: Bill Kaul, Joanna Sheldon, Bob Ashley, Fred Will, Anthony Pym, Daniel Simeoni, Marcella Alohalani Boido, Michael Cronin, Sean Golden, the participants in the translation colloquium at the Universitat Autónoma de Barcelona where I presented some of these ideas in March 1997, Don Robinson, Don Kartiganer, Dena Shunra, Jussara Simões, Chris DeSantis, Marilyn Gaddis Rose and the four other unnamed readers who read the manuscript for SUNY Press (Marilyn twice) and made useful comments. James Peltz at SUNY Press continued to believe in the project over the long haul, and for that I am grateful.

Bill Kaul says he thinks Shakespeare's spirit probably helped me some too. But then he's been wrong before.

Introduction:
Who Translates?

Preliminary Questions

Who translates?

Silly question: the translator translates. The translator is s/he who translates. Translating is what is done by the translator.

What could be simpler?

But read through the following exchange, taken off the translators' online discussion forum LANTRA-L:

PAUL MERRIAM: The American Translator's Association has in their Translators' Code of Professional Conduct and Business Practices in part 1A: "I will endeavor to translate with utmost accuracy and fidelity, so that I convey to the readers of the translation the same meaning and spirit the original conveyed to me." As I read this, if the original was sexist, the translation should be as well. I don't see any problem, however, with getting with the client and making a new product. (Isn't this called "localization"?)

CARLOS MAYOR: I agree with what someone said about changing examples in a text so that people featured in them are not WASP every time, *if and only if* the customer agrees. Let's not forget translating can look like writing, but it's not.

DOUG ROBINSON: Translating IS writing. When I translate I sit at the computer and form sentences in my head and my fingers move across the keyboard and words appear on the screen. Same thing I do when I "write"—i.e., write "original" things, or write postings to lantra. There are differences, of course—my imagination is more constrained by someone else's words when I translate than when I write articles or books or postings to lantra—but they aren't absolute. My imagination has to be hard at work when I translate, too; and since I am choosing the target-language words, everything I write has to be filtered through my experience, my interpretations.

ALEX RYCHLEWSKI: That's a very interesting and largely pragmatic approach to translating. My only quarrel with it (well, I had to quarrel with *something,* didn't I?) is that you seem to minimize the constraint of sticking to the other person's words when translating. This constraint is in fact terribly weighty.

GISSELLE BERTOLA: Don't you think that "sticking to the other person's words" is the same thing as "let's not forget translating can look like writing, but it's not"? If you have to stick to the other person's words then it's not writing, and here comes the ability of us translators to make it look as if it was written by the original author. So, is it writing or not?;) What I usually do is to sit down in front of my computer and let my imagination flow just like Doug's, but it's not me who's *writing,* it's (or at least I try to be) the original author (my own thoughts don't play).

(From the LANTRA-L archives for August 14–16, 1996)

Who translates here? Who is the translator who translates? Is the translator a writer? Why or why not? What does the translator become if s/he is or is not a writer? If it is essential for the translator not to be a writer, does the translator then simply disappear, or become transparent or empty?

Gisselle Bertola writes "it's not me who's *writing*"—what does this mean, exactly? What does she mean by "me," and what does she mean by "*writing*"? By "*writing*" she presumably does not mean typing, since her body is almost certainly doing that (but does "me" *mean* her body?). She means something else, something transcendental, ideal, mental, something creative in a quasimystical sense. The original author writes through her typing. Writing is done by writers, not translators—even, it seems, when what a given translator is typing, and to all outward appearances writing, is a translation. Does this mean that the writer translates too—through the translator? Writers are those who write, but it does not follow from morphological parallelism that translators are those who translate. Writers write and writers translate.

Translators type. Translators serve as "borrowed bodies" for the writing of writers. But if this is the case, who is the "I" that, as Gisselle writes, tries to "be" the original author? Presumably the translator; but that translator clearly stands in a very problematic relation to the author s/he is trying to become. "My own thoughts don't play"—except in their attempts to become someone else?

In my own contribution to the debate I argue a position that is philosophically opposed to Gisselle's, and one that at first blush appears radical: the translator is a writer. The translator does not become *the* writer; s/he becomes *a* writer, one very like the original author, but only because they both write, and in much the same way, drawing on their own experiences of language and the world to formulate effective discourse. This position appears radical, and draws somewhat uneasy responses from Alex and Gisselle, because it seems to jettison the traditional safeguard of equivalence: a translator who is a writer might just write any old thing, without subordinating his or her imagination to the authority of the original text. "My imagination has to be hard at work when I translate, too; and since I am choosing the target-language words, everything I write has to be filtered through my experience, my interpretations." In the normative tradition of Western translation theory, this sounds like giving the translator license to impose his or her experiences and interpretations onto everything s/he "writes". . . or translates . . . or writes/translates.

But all you have to do to convert my apparently radical position into the more traditional claims Paul and Carlos and Alex and Gisselle are making is to add subordination to the original author's authority. "My imagination has to be hard at work *in the original author's service;* and since I am choosing the target-language words *in the original author's service,* everything I write *in the original author's service* has to be filtered through my experience, my interpretations." Put this way, my claim is perfectly orthodox.

Even so, my idea of writing/translating being filtered through the translator's experience and interpretations still fills other translators and translation scholars with unease.

Who translates? Who is the subject of translation? Is the translator allowed to be a subject, to have a subjectivity? If so, what forces are active within it, and to what extent are those forces channeled into it from without? That is the main concern of this book—with special focus on the translator's selfhood or individual agency in chapter five.

In virtually the same keystrokes as my paean to the translator's experiences and interpretations I also work in what seems to be a very different direction: I deliberately empty the act of writing (whether by

an "original author" or a translator) of authority, specifically the authority of intentionality. "When I translate I sit at the computer and
form sentences in my head and my fingers move across the keyboard
and words appear on the screen." This would make of both the translator and the writer automata; of their writing, automatic writing. They
move their fingers and words appear. But whose words? Whose intentionality controls the act of writing?

The traditional wisdom would tell us that the author's intentionality
controls both: the author as sovereign subject intends the original text,
and leaves that intention lying immanent in the text; the translator oc-
cupies that intention and "writes" the target text—and is a "writer"
only in this sense.

But what of writers who claim to be inspired by God, or the muse?
Must we discredit their claims? They say they were inspired, they say
they surrendered their will to the speaking of a higher voice from
within or above, but of course *we know* that that is merely a figure of
speech, a metaphor, a primitive or perhaps even superstitious way of
saying that they were geniuses whose creative subjectivity so far exceeds our own as translators that we might even be inclined to believe
them when they speak of divine inspiration—if we didn't already
know better.

And if we don't take this demystifying rationalist tack, must we then
think of these "inspired" authors as translators too? Just as we are possessed by the spirit (or intention, or meaning) of the original author,
they too were possessed by the spirit of something higher, a god or a
muse. In translating them we are simply reenacting the spirit-
channeling that created the source text in the first place.

Or is it enough to say that the intentionality of any piece of writing
comes from *somewhere*, we know not where? Writing about the transla-
tor/writer as personally and experientially creative, I seemed in the
first part of that 1996 lantran post close to the spirit of my book *The
Translator's Turn;* writing about the writer/translator as automaton, I
seemed in its second part closer to the spirit of *Who Translates?* Reading
those words today, just a few months after they were written, I honestly
don't know where they came from and how such different conceptions
of the translator managed to "possess" my writing fingers in such rapid
succession.

Who translates? Who writes? Who controls the act of writing/trans-
lating? Whose voice speaks when "we" write or translate?

And what of those translators whose writings/translations have
also been regarded as divinely inspired—indeed, more inspired than
the originals? The Hebrew Bible was written by many hands, over

many centuries; the Septuagint, according to the legend propagated by Philo Judaeus and accepted by every major Church Father except Jerome until the Renaissance, was written by God Himself through the collective instrument of 72 translators in 72 cells—proof positive of the inspired nature of what they wrote being that all 72 translations were verbatim identical. The monks were God's automata; their writing/translating was automatic. They channeled the Septuagint to the Hellenized Jewish community in Alexandria—not from the *human* original authors, but from the divine one. Jerome ridicules this notion, which we will be taking a closer look at in chapter two, in 401 in his *Praefatio in Pentateuchem:*

I know not who was the first lying author to construct the seventy cells at Alexandria, in which they were separated and yet all wrote the same words, whereas Aristeas, one of the bodyguard of the said Ptolemy, and long after him Josephus have said nothing of the sort, but write that they were assembled in a single hall and conferred together, not that they prophesied. For it is one thing to be a prophet, another to be an interpreter. (Moses Hadas' translation, in Robinson *Western* 30)

And ironically enough, the same fate befell Jerome himself: the Bible translation he cobbled together from existing Latin versions by revising and checking them against the original languages became for the medieval Church not a Latin translation of the Bible but *the Bible.* Erasmus was attacked by conservative churchmen in 1518 for making a new Latin translation of the Bible from the original Greek—as if Jerome's Vulgate were nothing! Assaulted in print by the Scottish theologian Edward Lee, Erasmus wrote (an open letter, probably with the idea of having it published, which he did) to his friend Maarten Lips:

Meanwhile he dreams up the idea [as if Lee had invented what the Church had been saying for centuries!] that the Latin translator [Jerome] produced what we now have under the inspiration of the Holy Spirit, though Jerome himself in his preface openly testifies that each translator renders to the best of his ability what he is capable of understanding. Otherwise, Jerome himself would be grossly irreligious, in that he is not afraid to find fault sometimes with what we have in this [the Vulgate] edition. (R.A.B. Mynori and D.E.S. Thomson's translation, in Robinson *Western* 67)

Just a few years later, in the 1520s, Martin Luther too drew conservative fire for "adding" a word to his 1522 German New Testament that was not in Jerome's Latin. "Adding to" or "subtracting from" the Bible in a German or other vernacular translation constituted distorting the

Vulgate; and distorting the Vulgate was distorting the Bible. In his 1530 *Sendbrief vom Dolmetschen* Luther defended his translation by reference to Jerome's own sense-for-sense translation method, the "modern" rationalist notion that "the Bible" consists not of divinely inspired Latin *or* Hebrew/Aramaic/Greek words but of transcendental meanings, and noted that Jerome faced the same kind of criticism in his day as well:

> They say when you work in public, everybody's a critic, and that's certainly been true for me. All these people who can't even talk right, let alone translate, try to teach *me* how to do it! And if I'd asked them how to translate the first two words of Matthew 1:1, *Liber Generationis*, not one of them could've said jack, yet these fine journeymen would pronounce judgment on the whole Bible. St. Jerome faced the same thing when he did his Latin translation: everybody knew better than him how to do it, and people bitched and moaned about his work as weren't fit to shine his shoes. It takes a heap of patience to try to do any public service; everybody's got to be Mister Knowitall and get everything bass-ackwards, teaching everyone and knowing nothing. That's just the way they are; a leopard can't change his spots. (My translation, in Robinson *Western* 85)

Note, however, that like his critics Luther too quotes here from "the Bible" not in the original Greek but in Jerome's Latin: *Liber Generationis.*
    The Rheims-Douai Bible, the first full English translation approved by the Catholic Church, was a literal translation from the Vulgate; and with the notable exception of Erasmus, Catholic translators continued to translate literally from the Vulgate rather than the original Hebrew, Aramaic, and Greek texts until the twentieth century. Jerome channeled the Source Author of the Bible, and so displaced the "originals" that he himself so venerated. The intensely and irascibly subjective translator who gleefully itemized all the mistakes made by the Seventy became the voice of the Lord for well over a thousand years.
    Who translates, then? God? The Holy Spirit?
    Or do we have to discount these stories too, scoff at them just as Jerome did, laugh (un)easily at them, call them naive superstitions that mask a more obvious truth (because more rational, and hence more in line with our own belief structures): that Jerome submitted his subjectivity to the authority not of some supernatural being (as if!) but of the original texts?
    And if we do that, in what sense are we not merely secularizing the notion of channeling? Jerome channels the Source Author of the Bible; Jerome channels the source authors of the Bible. The verb "channels" remains tendentious in that latter proposition, because it continues to imply some sort of spiritual or mystical access to discarnate sources of

meaning; but secularize "channels" one tiny step further and say that Jerome lets the source authors of the Bible speak through him, and hardly anyone would argue.

Channeling

That the territory loosely marked off by this series of questions is a heavily invested one for translators, and for translation theorists, should be clear. The socioemotional origins of that investment in medieval dogma and ancient mystical taboos were central concerns in my earlier books *The Translator's Turn* and *Translation and Taboo*, respectively; I am not going to be exploring those origins further here. What I propose to do instead is to map out the complexly crisscrossing byways of thought about the translator's normative or "desirable" subordinated or instrumentalized subjectivity, through the powerful analogue I raised above, channeling.

What forces or voices or intentionalities or subjectivities—what "spirits" or "ghosts" or "demons"—does the translator channel? Who (all) is the translator when s/he translates? How does the translator negotiate the different types and conceptions of channeling in translating, and in presenting him/herself as a translator? Just what sorts of channel is the translator allowed to be, encouraged to be, expected to be, required to be? Are any specific forms of channeling expressly off-limits to translators?

Presumably a translator in the present who claimed to be psychically channeling the dead spirit of Homer, for example, and thus to know exactly what Homer wanted to say in the target language, would be looked on with a certain amount of suspicion or contemptuous amusement. And yet the famous debate in the early 1860s between Francis Newman and Matthew Arnold over the former's Homer translations revolves around almost identical claims to know exactly what Homer wanted to say in English—only in a slightly secularized form that make those claims palatable to a rationalist age.

This is not, let me make plain at the outset, a book about translation as spirit-channeling. It is a book about the complex forces impinging, from "within" and "without" (as if we knew what that distinction meant), on the translator's subjectivity. My argument is grounded historically, specifically in chapter two on the most famous "spirit-channeled" translations I know of, the Septuagint, the Book of Mormon, and St. Paul's call for spirit-channeled interpreters in 1 Corinthians 14. I do believe, in other words, that some conception of translation as spirit-channeling lies historically behind many of our deepest and most normative beliefs about translation, especially the insistence that it is the translator's task to step aside and let the source author speak through him or her. But I am not interested in developing that historical argument at full length here; as I say, my main focus in the book is not really spirit-channeled translation. Spirit-channeling will operate primarily as a heuristic, or as I say in the title of part one a "model," a collection of recorded or reported mystical experiences that we can employ metaphorically to complicate our sense of what is going on in the "other-directed" act of translation:

- philosophically, psychoanalytically, and politically in part two through explorations of the intertwining of ideology and translation in Freud's *Wolf Man* and Heidegger's *Der Satz vom Grund* (chapter three), and in two Finnish texts based on *King Lear,* a translation and a poem, and a reading of Friedrich Schleiermacher and Karl Marx on translation, spirits, and ghosts (chapter four); and

- psychosocially and socioeconomically in part three, through investigations into the multiplicity of subjective agents in the individual, drawing on the work of Jacques Lacan and Daniel Dennett (chapter five); and through explorations of Adam Smith's "invisible hand," the mysterious force that guides economic systems, to exfoliate a postrational theory of economic agents (chapter six).

    Another way of putting this is that I'm much more interested in using the notion of spirit-channeled translation to ask *questions* about translation than in building a coherent historical argument about displacements of mystical thinking in translation across the centuries. My title is a question: who translates? And this introduction in particular, and more generally the book as a whole, are strings of unpacked versions of that question. Rhetorically, of course, questions complicate existing answers; questions are a theorist's most powerful weapons against petrified assumptions and entrenched dogmas. What is *really* going on here? "A person who possesses the art of questioning," as Hans-Georg Gadamer writes, thinking of his own Heidegger-influenced hermeneutical practice, "is a person who is able to prevent the suppression of a question by the dominant opinion" (quoted in Fiumara 37).

    But there is also a potential hitch here. Gemma Corradi Fiumara reminds us in *The Other Side of Language: A Philosophy of Listening* that "it might also be the case that the dominant role of the question can suppress any kind of understanding that goes beyond the limited amount it prepares us to receive" (37). In other words, the idiot questioner role, one of my personal rhetorical favorites—"But why isn't the emperor wearing any clothes?"—may be conditioned by the same will to power as the calm and confident knower role to which it poses a pointed challenge. By questioning established answers I open up new possibilities for seeing; but the specific questions I ask also close down other possibilities for seeing, simply by dint of their being *directed*. A dialogue (talking *and* listening, as Fiumara would insist) is far more fruitful for this sort of open questioning-and-answering than a monologue; and while an academic book is a difficult place to stage a dialogue, I will be insisting throughout, even if only implicitly, that this book should be thought of as merely a single utterance in an ongoing dialogue that also involves you talking and me listening. And in any case my revisions of this book between "completing" it and publishing it have been conditioned by repeated listenings to the suggestions and criticisms of readers (this paragraph and the one before it, for example, were suggested by a middle-aged undergraduate student who read the book for me).

As I interrogate the notion of channeling analogically, then, moving into the operation of ideology in part two and of inner demons and economic agents in part three, I will be pushing it way beyond the popular image of the psychic medium twitching in a trance, possessed by the spirit of a dead person. But in fact this extended use of the word "channel" has strong precedents in the channeling literature. The paranormal use of the word was coined by the twentieth-century American psychic Edgar Cayce, who insisted that it not be thought of narrowly as contact between the living and the dead; as Henry Reed writes in *Edgar Cayce on Channeling Your Higher Self* (one of a series of books published by the Association for Research and Enlightenment, founded by Cayce himself and headed today by his grandson Charles Thomas Cayce):

A channeler receives something that might otherwise be invisible to others, shapes it into a transmittable form, and presents it to others. With our lives, for example, we make visible our thoughts and motivations.

A channel also involves a specific form of application. We may experience our love for a person in the form of good feelings. When we channel those feelings, however, they may manifest in something specific, such as making dinner for that person, or helping someone with a problem.

Channeling has the special implication of transmitting something from beyond the channeler's personal self. A channeler brings forth information that's not part of the channeler's own learning or experience. . . .

A channeler may receive communications from a disembodied spirit, from God, from an angel, from plants or animals. The channeler may simply have an intuition. The channeler may then transmit what's received verbally, in writing,

by painting or other artwork, by actions, through community work, or by a
smile. The channeler may be asleep, in meditation, in a trance, or awake while
channeling. (17)

"From the perspective of the Cayce material," Reed continues, "the
type of channeling that's a fad today, the kind that's shown on TV, is
but one special instance of a very general phenomenon. Speaking with
the voice of a spirit is only one example of channeling. . . . Every day, in
countless ways, you and I are channels of spirit, of ideas, and of resources that come from beyond our conscious personalities" (18).

In this broad sense, clearly, translators are invariably, by definition,
channels or channelers. Translators channel the words and ideas of
their source authors. Indeed, as the wording of the ATA translator's
code (quoted above by Paul Merriam) makes clear, they channel the
"spirit" of their source authors: "I will endeavor to translate with utmost accuracy and fidelity, so that I convey to the readers of the translation the same meaning and *spirit* the original conveyed to me." As
long as we read that "spirit" in a figurative or abstract sense, as long as
we keep the supernatural out of it, this characterization of the profession is unlikely to raise eyebrows. But I do plan to raise some eyebrows,
both by pushing dead metaphors like the ATA's "spirit" heuristically
into the realm of the supernatural and by expanding even Reed's or
Cayce's broad conception of channeling into areas that they did not envision, especially ideology, the channeling of the political unconscious,
in part two, and various fragmented agents in part three.

I'm going to be arguing, in fact, that translators channel a wide variety of Other voices, using "Other" in the broadest sense possible to include everything vaguely indicated by Henry Reed's claim that "Every
day, in countless ways, you and I are channels of spirit, of ideas, and of
resources that come from beyond our conscious personalities." Whatever seems to come to us from the outside, or from beyond the realm of
our conscious awareness or control, is Other—even when, as for
Jacques Lacan and other twentieth-century theorists of Otherness, it
speaks to us from "inside our heads." As we'll see in chapter five, Lacan
wants to draw clear distinctions among the various types of Otherness:
the "objects" we choose, including love objects (other people and
things as invested by and with our needs); idealized forms of our ego,
or our "self" as ego-ideal, modeled on parents and other authority figures; and large social-unconscious forces such as nations, genders,
races, classes, age groups, professions, political and economic systems,
scholarly disciplines, metaphysical traditions, and so on. All of these
Others come from outside but speak (to) us from the inside; and without

sticking to Lacan's typologies of Otherness (except briefly, heuristically, in chapter five) I want to explore the ways in which translators channel, and especially how translators become and remain and present themselves as translators by channeling, all these Others, all these becoming-internalized forces, all these voices outside-and-inside our heads.

Another way of putting all this is to say that I am interested in exploring the gray area between the translator as a rational, fully conscious subject who is completely in control of all his thoughts and actions (this rationalist ideal is normatively male) and the translator as a mystical void filled with other voices, a channel or medium for the speech of others. Both ideals exist for translation, often in the same breath, the same sentence. That they are radically opposed to each other should go without saying, but *has* gone without saying for a long, long time. One of the things that the rational translator-subject is supposed to control, in fact, is the interference of his own control in the process of channeling the source author directly and immediately to the target reader. I want to argue that this dualism, like most dualisms, is harmful and limiting for the study of translation; and that what Jacques Derrida in *Specters of Marx* calls "spectrality" or "the logic of the ghost" (traced in some detail in chapter four) is a powerful crowbar for opening that dualism up to real-world complexity.

The forces that "shape" or "speak" or "wield" the translator, from within or without, have been one of the recurrent themes of my theoretical work over the past decade. The ideosomatics of *The Translator's Turn* was an exploration of the ideological regulation of individual behavior through the somatic imprinting of collective norms on the autonomic nervous system. The double binds that I elucidated in *Ring Lardner and the Other* and have been developing for translation studies and publishing elsewhere (one appears in chapter five, in somewhat fragmented form) are attempts to articulate the inward regulatory "speaking" of ideology, in all its paralyzing conflictuality, through our bodies—what I called in *Lardner* the "esemphonic" shaping of individual and collective behavior through the speaking-us of various sociopolitical Others. My tracing in *Translation and Taboo* of the displacements of taboo in the schizoid/ascetic/metempsychotic intellectual/religious traditions of the West was an attempt to narrow in on a single powerful strand of ideological regulation. My "abusanalysis" of translation in the "(Dis)Abusing Translation" chapter of *What Is Translation?*—my discussion of the dynastic culture of abuse in the context of Philip Lewis's Derridean concept "abusive fidelity"—was likewise an attempt to untangle the complex webs by which we are taught to submit to and be shaped by abuse, both as abusers and as abuse victims (typically, and complexly, both at once).

And my initial interest in spirit-channeling as this book was taking shape in my mind derived from precisely this three-way isomorphism: the possession of channels by discarnate spirits, the possession of the translator by the source author, and the possession of ideological subjects by collective forces. The first had always seemed to me a rather boring fraud, not even worth looking into; the second, a normative idealization that represented everything I hated most about traditional assumptions, worth taking seriously only long enough to launch an effective counterattack. But since the third was one of my most abiding scholarly interests, the parallels between it and the other two made me take another look at them, and generated this book.

Rationalism, Pre- and Post-

In my subtitle I promise an investigation into "translator subjectivities beyond reason," a phrase that does not seem at first particularly forthcoming. Beyond what reason? Are we talking irrationality? Irrationalism? Rationalism does mark anything beyond reason as irrational, and I have long been interested in that particular borderland, in its shifting landscapes, in the history of rationalist attempts to police it, in the rich history also of cop-eluding crossings. What it means to be "beyond reason" is always mind-numbingly contingent on a welter of conflicting factors and forces, some controlled by rationalist tradition, most not.

Rationalism is the dominant philosophical movement of Western civilization. Rationalism has shaped the West not only philosophically, of course, but politically, culturally, ideologically. Calling it a philosophical movement is in this sense misleading, as if it were merely a trend or camp of interest only to a few philosophy professors. Rationalism constitutes a kind of ideological operating system for the West, the internalized programming that provides norms and values for virtually every aspect of psychosocial life. Arising in ancient Greece, finding its first great proponents in Plato and Aristotle, and taking hold on a large social and political scale in classical Rome, it swept Europe in the Renaissance and after, becoming the dominant form of all thought, pushing mysticism to the peripheries in every way, branding it insanity, stupidity, evil, sin . . . until the primary forms of mysticism in our day have become schizophrenia, drug highs, and sex.

But in fact in our ideological climate, saturated by reason, it makes

no sense to speak of mystical experience at all; everything that bears any degree of thematic resemblance to mysticism comes to us down rationalist channels, so that numb unthinking mysticism becomes *irra*tional, determined mystical resistance becomes *anti*rational, a mystical past in our historical reconstructions becomes *pre*rational, and our imagination of a utopian mystical future becomes *post*rational. Even our power to envision alternatives to rationalist life is handed to us by reason, decked out in dualism, lashed to the mast of logic.

And it is in this severely compromised sense, with only the most self-consciously hobbled attempt at an antirationalist myth—a fall from some golden age of mystical holism into reason's atomism, the glorious return of the golden age after the fall of reason—that I put forward my tentative speculations on "translator subjectivities beyond reason," specifically pre- and postrationalist translator subjectivities. Was there ever a time when translators *preceded* reason? Perhaps; but if there was, we have no access to it. We can only imagine it, and that only by subtracting from what we know of translation today everything we associate with rationalist regimes: no analysis, no planning, no use of dictionaries, surrender to mystical forces coming from somewhere "outside" the reasoning mind.

And is there any realistic sense in which it is viable to speak of postrationalist translation, or postrationalist translator subjectivities? The term taken at face value makes us think of a changing of the guard, an end to rationalism and a wholly new beginning, cleansed of all contaminating rationalist elements. A silly, puerile thought.

I intend pre- and postrationalist in more or less the same radically mixed and imperfect sense as postcolonial scholars speak of pre- and postcolonialism: not as pure states that ever did or could exist, but rather as imaginary ciphers that mark off the boundaries of what we thematize as reason and empire—which are, in any case, powerfully congruent terms, the one more philosophical, the other more political, but together forming a Janus mask of control, reason's face on the inside, empire's out. Certainly reason has never perfectly controlled any human activity; and in a strict sense that "failure" to achieve perfect rational control would make everything we do incipiently prerationalist and always already postrationalist. Even the present, in other words, can be construed as prerationalist (just before the onset of rational control) and postrationalist (just after the failure of rational control). In this perspective, pre- and postrationalist become shorthand for a mixed, compromised, impure environment, a hybrid of the controlled and the uncontrolled, the unified and the fragmented, the becoming-rational and the becoming-mystical.

Nudging this hybridity in the direction of a temporal myth, from prerationalism through rationalism to postrationalism, then, gives it the form of activism. Just as postcolonialists struggle toward decolonization without any sense that the better world toward which their activism tends will be magically purified of the colonial legacy, so too would a postrationalist approach to translator subjectivities imagine a therapeutic *decrease* in rationalist control over the theory and practice of translation without necessarily positing an *end* to such control. (I am not, for example, an irrationalist celebrant of mystical surrender to monistic experience; even in my attacks on dogmatic rationalism I am thoroughly rationalistic.)

A prerationalist approach to translator subjectivities in turn might begin by positing a mythical prerational origin for translation, translation as spirit-channeling, translation as divine inspiration, translation as prophecy, translation more generally as complete surrender to forces beyond the translator's control or ken . . . and then determinedly *not* mythologize that origin, not insist that it existed in some pure historical state prior to the onslaught of reason and can yet be recuperated in some viable form today. Whatever prerationalist origin we can imagine will always be an activist construct, useful perhaps in guiding our thoughts and actions to those aspects of translation that have never been successfully controlled by reason and continue to thwart attempts to subject them to a perfected rationalist regime, but utterly useless as an ontological representation.

To make an argument like this work (as writer *or* reader) one would of course need a fine sense of complexity—a knack for teetering on the verge of several things at once. And it may be that my ability to teeter is inadequate, that in my attempts to stay in flux with hybridity I will lean too strongly in one direction or another and overly simplify my argument. I would, however, for the record, much rather be perceived as attempting pre- or postrationalist complexity and falling short—toppling into simplified rationalist structures (especially dualisms)—than as attempting to construct a nice tidy bivalent framework (down with rationality, up with irrationality!) and failing.

Indeed in the process of constructing my hybrid argument I am going to be moving through realms that are likely to generate massive anxieties in bivalent readers. This book is very similar to *Translation and Taboo* in its attempt to straddle the various shifting historical and ideological lines between mysticism and rationalism, and I expect some responses to my argument here to be at least similar to the ones I got to that earlier book. One bivalent rationalist reader of *Taboo*, for example, called it a mystical attack on reason; a bivalent Christian reader called it intellectual scoffing at religion. Both were right, but only taken together. It was an attack on reason and an attack on mysticism. But it was also a celebration of the two. Most of all, however, it was a tracing of the complex interminglings of the two in their effects on translation. The same is true of this book as well. I'm hoping readers will not assume, just because I am not entirely complimentary to some position they hold dear, that I am arguing simply its binary opposite. I am probably somewhere in between the binaries.

Some other misconceptions that arose when I presented some of the material from this book in an online colloquium based at the Universitat Autónoma de Barcelona in March, 1997 (the proceedings are currently stored at http://cc.uab.es/~iuts0/colloquium.htmlx):

- *How can you talk about translation as spirit-channeling, when rational people don't even believe spirits exist!* The dualism is clear, here: rational people don't believe in spirits, and therefore don't talk about them; if you talk about them, you must not be a rational person; in fact you must believe in them. In a rationalist regime, spiritualist phenomena accrue such a powerful charge of disreputability that even discussing them taints you: if you were a *serious* person you would pretend that there are no words, even, for such things; that no one ever talked about them. Readers inclined to protest along these lines should imagine me saying not "there are spirits and translators channel them" but "some people have *claimed* that there are spirits and translators channel them" as well as "some of the things translators are traditionally supposed to do are strikingly similar to some of the things that spirit-channelers are traditionally supposed to do." If the talk of spirit-channels bothers you, think of this book as a study of reported speech on them—a kind of scholarly "as if."

- *Modern translation theory has discredited the idea of the translator as passive conduit or vessel.* It has tried to, certainly. Mine has been one of the voices raised against that notion, in *The Translator's Turn* and elsewhere. But the notion still persists today among many; and historically it is stronger still. In any case, my brief is not that the translator *is* a passive conduit or vessel, and certainly not that the translator *should be* a passive conduit or vessel. In fact it is not even that the translator has been *thought of* as a passive conduit or vessel—for spirit-channels are never perfectly passive. Spirit-channels contribute to the channeling process too. Channeling in the spiritualist literature is much more of a meeting of minds than it is the total possession of a living body by a discarnate mind. As spirit-channels describe themselves, they are never the mere helpless instruments of the discarnate spirit; they are often highly active, engaged in interpreting the sights and sounds and feelings sent to and through them from what they describe as the spirit world. So far from being passive invisible conduits, in fact, spirit-channels in many cultures have been feared and revered as shamans, priests, even as gods and goddesses. And in any case, again: I am *not* equating translation with spirit-channeling in any ontological, let alone prescriptive way. I'm exploring a connection that is partly historical (some translators in some ages, of some texts, *have* been seen as spirit-channelers), partly metaphorical or analogical (ideological isomorphisms between the ancient and largely discredited notion of translation as spirit-channeling and more secular aspects of translation can yield useful heuristics).

Nor (let me reiterate) is the book entirely, or even primarily, about spiritualist phenomena. Spirit-channeling is the originary prerationalist construct that I employ to set up my explorations of what I take to be postrationalist moments in contemporary translator subjectivities. My focal concern is not with spirits dictating to translators but with secularized forms of alterity, forces of "otherness" that wield the "self" from within or without: ideology in chapters three and four, the "demons" of individual subjectivity in chapter five, and economic agents in chapter six. My idea is to explore several different forms of secular alterity that (are thought to) influence or shape translators' work *in terms of* spirit-channeling—not exactly as if they were forms of spirit- channeling, but as if they might take on new significance and import if viewed through that particular imagistic or metaphorical lens.

Part One: The Spirit-channeling Model

Chapter one, "The Philosophical Background," sets the theoretical stage for the postrationalist study of translator subjectivities. What are the stakes in such an approach? What are the implications or consequences of thinking about the translator as someone who is not entirely in control of his own work—as someone who is wielded by spiritualist or ideological or neurological or economic forces beyond his count or ken? (Note: whenever I use generic "he" in this book, I am attempting to project myself into traditional conceptions of translation and other human activities.) Why should we find such a notion attractive, and why should we oppose or resist it? What can it tell us about our unexamined assumptions regarding translation?

Chapter two is the "spiritualist" part of my argument. I begin with a short history of spirit-channeling, to give you some sense of the historical scope of the phenomenon, and segue from there into a reading of Plato's *Ion* as a theory of spirit-channeled literary "rewriting" (to use Lefevere's term) that at least implicitly contains or reflects translation as well. Then follow three famous cases of "divinely inspired" translation or interpretation: Philo Judaeus's legend of the Septuagint, *The Book of Mormon*, and Paul's instructions to the Corinthian congregation regarding interpreting for glossolalists. This is the ground zero for the historical argument that I will *not* be pursuing after this chapter: people really have seen translators as taken over by spiritual forces outside themselves. As the title of part one says specifically, I want to use the idea of translation as spirit-channeling as an explanatory model, not as a myth of origins.

Part Two: Ideology

Chapters three and four move us from spirit into the secularized but still analogous or "logologous" realm of ideology, taking two very different approaches to the impact of ideology on translation. In chapter three, "Ideology and Cryptonymy," I use (and partly critique and reformulate) the cryptanalytical method developed by Nicolas Abraham and Maria Torok in their book on Freud's Wolf Man to explore the ideological regulation of that method's very use, in Freud, Abraham and Torok, and the remarks on translation of Martin Heidegger. That chapter concludes with a series of translations of those remarks (from *Der Satz vom Grund*) into English, along with extensive (auto)cryptonymic commentary. Chapter four, "The (Ideo)logic of Spectrality," revolves loosely around William Shakespeare and Karl Marx: one Finnish Marxist translator/poet's ideologically charged versions of *King Lear*, Jacques Derrida's remarks on Marx and the logic of spectrality, and the telling convergences and divergences between Marx and Friedrich Schleiermacher on translation, spirits, and ghosts.

Part Three: Transient Assemblies

Chapter five, "The Pandemonium Self," goes inward (although, as we will see, that is a problematic way of describing it) to explore the "pandemonic" construction of the individual translator-subject. Drawing on Jacques Lacan's Schema L and the *summa neurophilosophica* of Daniel

Dennett, *Consciousness Explained*, I trace the inner multiplicity and fragmentariness of human subjectivity as it operates in the process of translation.

And finally, chapter six on "The Invisible Hand" uses Robert Nozick's Dennettian reading of Adam Smith's famous references to the invisible hand (which somehow mysteriously intervenes in economic processes from the "inside") to explore the operation of loose "translation agencies" in the economic marketplace: disjointed collections of economic agents (freelance translators, editors, proofreaders, project managers, etc.) who somehow collectively manage, in more or less unstructured ways, to produce competent professional-quality translations.

PART ONE

The Spirit-channeling Model

Chapter One

Reason and Spirit

The Translator as Spirit-channel

Let me begin by phrasing it as carefully as I can: in many significant ways translating resembles, or has been commonly thought of in terms that resemble, spirit-channeling—communicating with and/or mediating for others the spirits of dead people, or, as spiritualist writers like to put it, "discarnate spirits." I'm going to want to push on this analogy fairly hard in the course of this book, in several different directions at once, but for now let's take it slowly: when translators say that their job is to "step aside and let the original author speak through them," that is close enough to what is traditionally thought of as spirit-channeling or psychic communication with the dead to make the analogy potentially worth exploring. The translator is a "medium" or mediator who channels the "spirit" or voice or meaning or intention of the source author across linguistic and cultural and temporal barriers to a new audience that could not have understood that source author without such mediation. The translator does not speak in his own voice; he speaks in the voice of the original author. The translator does not convey to the target audience her own ideas, meanings, arguments, images; she is a neutral and noncommittal conduit to the target audience of the ideas and meanings of the original author. "How then," Alexander Frazer Tytler asked in 1797, "shall a translator accomplish this difficult union of ease with fidelity? To use a bold expression, he must adopt the very soul of his author, which must speak through his own organs" (Robinson *Western* 211). The translator, to use Patrick Mahoney's spiritualist term, must become the source author's "borrowed body" (3).

Or read this passage from Eva Wong's introduction to her translation of the *Lieh-tzu* and try to determine just what kind of claim she is making about her "channeling" of the original author. Is she claiming to be serving as a psychic medium for Lieh-tzu to speak through? Or is she merely using the psychic terminology metaphorically to express her sense that her translation, while not "psychic" or "mystical," is nonetheless "true" to the "spirit" of her author?

Lieh-tzu is the first Taoist text to have spoken to me. Since it is a Chinese text, and Chinese is one of my first languages, my dialogue with it was in that language. "Opening" a text and presenting it in its original language is relatively straightforward. It is not necessary to deal with the semantics of two languages. Opening and presenting a text in a language other than its original one is much more interesting. One approach would be to translate it first in the conventional way and then open the translated text by listening to its intention or voice. My friends who work with Greek and Hebrew texts advised me to use this method. However, when I tried it, the method did not feel natural, so I decided to experiment with a different approach.

To me, wisdom is timeless and transcends language. At the same time, language can be used to open the meaning of a text. What if I could be freed from linguistic constraints, eliminate the process of translating from one language to another, and go directly from the teachings of the *Lieh-tzu* to its voice in the English language? This would require being in the state of mind that Lieh-tzu must have been in, or at least being a kindred spirit to Lieh-tzu. Since I had been listening to the text for some time, this approach seemed promising.

With time, as I developed a kinship with Lieh-tzu, I began to feel what it was like to think the way he did. His teachings were no longer tied to a language. Sometimes he would speak in Chinese, sometimes in English, and sometimes not in any language in particular.

My next task was to find a voice for him in the English language. How would Lieh-tzu speak if he lived in an English-speaking country in our times? The voice would be natural, as if he were speaking in a first language and not a translated language. In this aspect, I am fortunate, because as a bilingual person with two first languages (English and Chinese), I am used to switching back and forth between the two languages when I think. Sometimes I would even forget which language I was thinking in. To give Lieh-tzu a voice in English, I had only to become a channel and let the *Lieh-tzu* come out naturally in the English language after I had totally immersed myself in his teachings. The emptier my mind, the clearer would be the voice of the text. Thus, opening a text and revealing its meaning require stillness of mind, quite the opposite of the analytical state of mind demanded in translation work. (16–17)

Does she mean spirit-channeling? Or is this a hermeneutical projection like Borges's Pierre Menard's into the "mind" of Cervantes, or like

Friedrich Schleiermacher's into the minds of the original authors of the Bible (the original idea behind romantic or "liberal" biblical hermeneutics)? It seems on the one hand as if Wong is simply reading deeply, "immersing" herself in Lieh-tzu's writings, not contacting the spirit of the dead Lieh-tzu; but she also gives us a very strong sense that she believes Lieh-tzu is in some manner speaking through her. Just what degree of metaphoricity should we assign to claims like "*Lieh-tzu* is the first Taoist text to have spoken to me" or "Sometimes he would speak in Chinese, sometimes in English, and sometimes not in any language in particular"? Did the text speak? Did its author speak? Or did they only "speak"—did they "open" to Wong through deeply intuitive study and so finally come to *seem* as if they were speaking? Just what sort of mental state is that "stillness of mind" of which she speaks? Is it a mystical trance, a creative intuitivity, or even, perhaps, unbeknownst to Wong, simply an internalized ("somatized") version of that "analytical state of mind" that, as she says, is traditionally "demanded in translation work"?

My plan in untying this imagistic knot is to start at the "top" and work "downwards" (to invoke the spatial metaphor that is traditional in these matters): to start at the "highest" level of unmetaphorical spiritualism, the level at which translators actually do claim to be channeling the spirits of their dead source authors (chapter two), and gradually work "earthward," which is to say in increasingly secular and metaphorical directions (chapters three and four), until the "spirit" that the translator "channels" is an internal psychic agent (chapter five) or an invisible but quite physical living human voice at the end of a phone line or e-mail correspondent (chapter six). I will be spending the bulk of our time here in the early chapters on the "weird" stuff at the higher levels; once we get down to the marketplace the connections should be clear enough that you can make them yourself.

To begin, then, the analogy suggests both:

a. that the source author has the power to initiate communication with the target audience *through* the translator (though again this does not mean that the translator is passive: the translator actively creates the channel through which the author actively contacts the target audience), and

b. that the translator possesses some means of gaining access to the author's voice and meaning, of reliably "opening up" to the intentional speaking of a person who is almost invariably other (sometimes translators translate source texts they wrote themselves, but usually the source author is another person), most often distant in time and place, and not infrequently dead.

Both claims are highly problematic in the rationalist regime of Western thought, especially (and increasingly) since the Renaissance—and this is the philosophical issue that I want to examine here in chapter one. There is no rationalist model that would explain the power of a dead author (or of a living one who is distant in time and place and unconnected to translators either directly or through intermediaries—editors, agencies) to speak or generally initiate communication through a translator, or for that matter through anyone else. To the extent that we imagine authors, especially dead authors, as having the power to reach out to target audiences through the mediation of a translator, we are operating within a mystical model that has been under serious assault in the West for hundreds of years, perhaps even as many as two thousand years—and even if that model has not been entirely discredited or displaced, it is certainly way beyond the pale of credibility in an academic setting. Ditto the notion of readerly access to a writer's intentions: that has been considered a bogus claim at least since W. K. Wimsatt and Monroe Beardsley published their famous "Intentional Fallacy" essay in 1954. If we can't read our own spouse's mind, how can we claim to know what Dante or Homer was thinking hundreds or thousands of years ago? Rationally speaking, the claim to have access to a writer's intended meaning is, as Wimsatt and Beardsley insist, a fallacy. It can't be done. We only wish it could—and so pretend it can.

But of course this tentative formulation is somewhat extreme. When people say today that translators should step aside and let their authors speak through them, you may protest, they are not really claiming that translators are spirit-channels, or that translators can read their authors' minds. Translators simply use biographical and historical research and painstaking textual analysis in order to make an effective "best guess" as to authorial intention.

And it is true that that is how most people would thematize the act of translation today. But in this book I want to work from what might be called a strategic excluded-middle argument. For it seems to me that the argumentative positions and stakes in this debate have been historically blurred, and need to be brought into new clarity. The debate as it is traditionally binarized has at one pole the insistence that the translator should "submit" to the source author and/or source text, and at the other the belief that such submission is impossible: that translators are the active interpretive agents in the act of translation and control the entire event. From the conservative (former) viewpoint, if the translator does not submit to the source author/text, all connections between the source text and the target text are severed and the translation can no longer truly be called a translation. From the progressive (latter) viewpoint, this whole dualism is vitiated by the impossibility of "submitting" to either an author (especially if that author is dead or otherwise unable to exert any kind of active influence on the translation) or a text, which is, after all, just black marks on white paper. How do you submit to a dead person, or a living person whom you never meet, or who never corresponds with you or your editor or publisher in the attempt to control your work? How do you submit to black squiggles? From the progressive point of view, the translator's "submission" is to an *abstraction* called "the author" or "the text." That abstraction is a mental construct, an imaginative fiction, created and controlled by the translator. In this light the submission too is controlled by the translator, and thus is no submission at all. The conservative view, from this perspective, is meaningless.

I have argued roughly this progressive perspective myself, in *The Translator's Turn*. I still believe that this approach, which might be called a Kantian or constructivist or reader-response approach, is a useful first step in a critique of ancient fossilized assumptions about translation. *Who Translates?* is based on my sense that it is only half a critique—and that in ignoring the other half, it grossly oversimplifies the issues. It is essential, I would argue, that we look carefully at the historical roots and metaphorical implications of the conservative insistence on "submission" to the source author/text as well—of the idea that it is essential even today to "let the author speak through you."

To that end I propose to treat the modern conservative position as an uneasy middle ground between two more distant poles: the modern rationalist one according to which the translator controls the entire process, constructing an image of the author and the text imaginatively and then pretending to "submit" to it, and an ancient one based on spirit-channeling, the notion that the discarnate spirits of authors actually do take over the translators of their works and dictate the translations through them. I propose to argue, in other words, that the conservative position is an uneasy and unstable but historically quite interesting accommodation of originally mystical thinking to more rationalist models, retaining the ancient assumption that the translator must submit entirely to authorial intention but also incorporating elements of the Kantian or "constructivist" reader-response position—the constructive or constitutive nature of every reader's take on "authorial intention."

Significantly enough, this conservative middle ground is essentially the same as the one carved out for "sense-for-sense translation" between the extremes of radical literalism and "free" translation, borrowing fidelity from the literal model and interpretive license from the "free" model. And considering that literalism is historically linked to a mystical respect for the exact contours of the source text as the perfect expression of authorial will, the two "synthetic" accommodations of opposed views would also seem to be historically congruent.

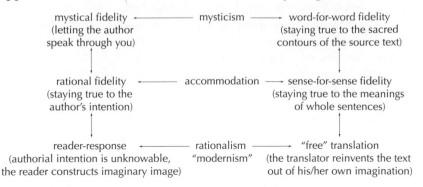

mystical fidelity ◄──────── mysticism ───────► word-for-word fidelity
(letting the author   (staying true to the sacred
speak through you)   contours of the source text)

rational fidelity ◄──────── accommodation ───────► sense-for-sense fidelity
(staying true to the   (staying true to the meanings
author's intention)   of whole sentences)

reader-response ◄──────── rationalism ───────► "free" translation
(authorial intention is unknowable,   "modernism"   (the translator reinvents the text
the reader constructs imaginary image)   out of his/her own imagination)

The only problem I have with this accommodation, and the reason I want to put it on hold here for a while, is that it has been accompanied for so long by such a powerful charge of social repression that it is difficult today to talk about the precise composition and history of the synthesis. Rather than being explored as the largely ideological product of an ongoing social process, it has typically been naturalized and universalized as the "true nature" of translation. This book is an attempt to engage in that ideological type of exploration, by picking at the repressed traces of an earlier mystical view in the current "traditional" or "mainstream" accommodation and seeing where they will lead.

"Reason"? "Spirit"?

We are faced now with another problem, which is really only a problem in a rationalist regime like the scholarly monograph you're reading: "reason" and "spirit" are becoming rather complex shifters, ciphers, markers for a welter of identifications that keep conflicting in confusing ways. "Reason" in my argument so far in this chapter has come to signify both (a) the authoritarian control of translation by reference to an author, to authorial intention, and (b) the more constructivist lectoritarian reframing of translation by reference to the reader's interpretive activities. Of these the former is traditionally associated with reason, rationalism, the author's control of his (never her) own intentions and their expression and the critic's determined submission to that control in the interests of accurate or objective interpretation; this is the conservative position in the theory wars, argued by E. D. Hirsch, Jr., M. H. Abrams, and others. From this point of view the reader-response position seems irrational, because it is out of control; the reader reads any way s/he feels inspired to read, prompted not by the true source of rational authority (authorial intention) but by whatever whims or preoccupations or other psychological forces take over the reading process.

The reader-response position only comes to seem like an instantiation of "reason" when it is thematized as a secular reframing of the mystical notion that interpretation (including translation) is or should be a form of spirit-channeling. Interpretation *couldn't possibly* (in a rationalist regime) be controlled by the author's discarnate spirit; here is what *must* be going on instead. From a reader-response standpoint, in fact, the conservative authoritarian position, traditionally construed as the purest form of interpretative rationalism, looks remarkably like spiritualism: in both the authoritarian and the spiritualist view, the reader surrenders all interpretive activity to an external force variously identified as "the author" or "the text." Thus in this new perspective "spirit" too comes to signify both sides of the equation: "the author" to whom the reader is expected to submit all control and the psychological "identity themes" and other internal forces to which the reader actually surrenders.

A schematic representation of this shifting may help us impose some rationalist order on it, especially if we build it around dualisms like spirit-reason, authoritarian/lectoritarian, and active-passive:

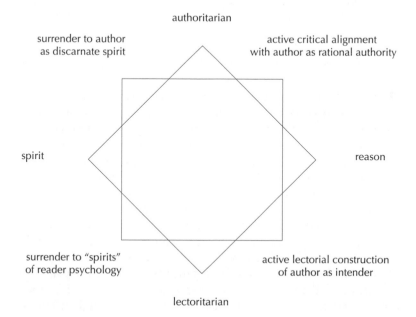

authoritarian

surrender to author
as discarnate spirit

active critical alignment
with author as rational authority

spirit

reason

surrender to "spirits"
of reader psychology

active lectorial construction
of author as intender

lectoritarian

This is a good start, but it does not even begin to unpack the complexity of "reason" and "spirit" as argumentative shifters. (To put it in the terms I mentioned in the introduction, this diagram does not yet "teeter on the verge of several things at once.") What does it mean for the translator to channel "spirit"? How is that opposed to, and how is it related to, the translator's channeling of "reason"? It seems beyond question that translators (claim to) channel something; that "true" or "faithful" translators, at least, have the reported experience of channeling some force beyond their own will, ideas, images, prejudices, intentions. What that "something" is, we don't exactly know: the source author? The target reader? Some figment of their own imaginations? Perhaps they're all imaginative figments; but what shall we call those figments? "Reason"? "Spirit"? What is at stake in making a choice between the two? In chapter six I will be associating the disembodied voices and fingers at the end of phone lines (clients, agency people, research support people, editors, etc.) with these "figments." Are they "spirits"?

Not in any supernatural sense of the word. But in some sense? What shall we do about this notion of spirit-channeling as we move "down" from overtly spiritualistic conceptions of translation-as-channeling here in these first few chapters to ever more secularized understandings in the later chapters of the book? Shall I say that I am still talking about channeling, but now no longer of spirits? Shall I say that I now mean spirit-channeling figuratively, or analogically? And are those two the same thing? Is their "spirit" the same? Would the spirit of a text, the spirit of a law, the spirit of a command, the spirit of a conversation, the spirit of an age be figurative spirits? Would they be analogical ones? If I have to resort to such fudging as "figurative" or "analogical" meanings, does that mean I'm defining spirit narrowly to mean the soul or ghost of a dead or once-living-but-now-discarnate person, and any other sense of spirit must be shunted over to some peripheral or marginal or secondary or parasitical category? Is it all right if I appropriate the full range of connotations that spirit-words have had in the Western religious and philosophical tradition(s), including *ruach, pneuma, spiritus, Geist, esprit*? *Ruach* takes us to *deed, pneuma* and *spiritus* take us to *breath, Geist* takes us to *mind, intellect, culture, education, esprit* takes us to *breath* and *joke*. If I cite recent texts that push "psychological" uses of the word spirit into the "parapsychological" (ghosts, specters, revenants), like Jacques Derrida's *Of Spirit* or *Specters of Marx* or my own *Translation and Taboo*, can I then get away here with pushing parapsychological spirits back into the psychological, sociological? Roget's gives me the following "figurative" or "analogical" synonyms for English *spirit*—or should we say synonyms for "nonsupernatural" spirits, negating spirit's ancient negation of flesh and blood, corporeality, materiality, nature, physical science in order to flesh out a "positive" body here on earth?

- essence (stuff, substance, quintessence, gist, elixir, extract, distillate, concentrate, infusion, flower),
- heart (nucleus, center, kernel, core, pith, meat, sap, marrow),
- energy (animation, vivacity, liveliness, life, sprightliness, spiritedness, briskness, breeziness, peppiness, pep, vim),
- eloquence (punch, raciness, sparkle, piquancy, poignancy, pungency),
- fervor (fervency, fervidness, passion, ardor, ardency, *empressement*, warmth of feeling, heat, fire, verve, furor, gusto, vehemence, heartiness, cordiality, unction, zeal),
- courage (nerve, spunk, pluck, grit, sand, stamina, backbone, guts),
- genius (*Geist*, soul, inspiration, afflatus, fire of genius, lambent flame of intellect, coal from off the altar, talent, creative thought),
- mood (humor, temper, frame of mind, state of mind, tone, vein, grain, streak, stripe, cue, mind, mettle),
- meaning (significance, point, sense, idea, expression, purport, import, implication, connotation, denotation, construction), and
- drift (tenor, bearing, effect, force, impact, value).

Are all of these fair game? Or does the compound *spirit-channeling* require the narrow sense of ghosts, shades, discarnate persons? Roget's also gives these:

- specter (intelligence, supernatural being, ghost, spook, phantom, phantasm, wraith, shade, shadow, apparition, presence, vision, materialization, haunt, astral spirit, unsubstantiality, immateriality, incorporeity, entity, banshee, poltergeist, White Lady),
- sprite (imp, pixy, elf, puck, kobold, *diablotin*, tokoloshe, gremlin, devilkin, devling, erlking, goblin, hobgoblin, hob, ouphe, sylph, gnome, salamander, undine, fairy, fay, brownie, cluricane, leprechaun, nymph, dryad, hamadryad, oread, limoniad, nix, kelpie, naiad, limniad, nereid, sea-maiden, siren, merman, mermaid, faun, satyr, silenus, paniscus),
- demon (fiend, devil, satan, deva, shedu, gyre, unclean spirit, hellion, cacodemon, incubus, succubus, jinni/genie, afreet, barghest,

flibbertigibbet, troll, ogre, ogress, ghoul, lamia, vampire, Harpy, Fury),

- bogey (bugbear, bugaboo, boggle, booger, boogyman, bête noire, fee-faw-fum, mumbo jumbo),
- familiar (genius, daimon, *numen*, totem, guardian spirit, guardian angel, fairy godmother, guide, spirit guide, control, attendant godling, invisible helper, special providence, tutelary god),
- angel (celestial being, heavenly being, messenger of God, saint, seraph, angel of love, cherub, principality),
- double (etheric self, cowalker, *Doppelgänger*, fetch),
- soul (psyche, spiritus, *Geist*, heart, mind, anima, nephesh, spiritual being, inner man, ego, self, I),
- life principle (vital principle, vital force, prana, divine spark, divine flame, *ousia*),
- astral body (linga sharira, design body, subtle body, vital vody, etheric body, bliss body, Buddhic body, spiritual body, soul body, kamarupa, desire body, kamic body, causal body, mental body),
- breath (pneuma, divine breath, atman, purusha, buddhi, jiva, jivatma, ba, khu, ruach),
- deity (god, deus, divinity, immortal, deva, shining one, godling, godlet, godkin, demigod, avatar, manito, huaca, mana, nagual, pokunt, tamanoas, wakan, Zemi), and
- form (shape, eidolon, idolum, appearance).

Are all of *these* fair game? If in discussing the economic agents that produce translations (the topic of chapter six) I wanted to call various experts and editors the translator's "invisible helpers" (listed above under "familiar"), do I first have to insist that I am using the term in a figurative sense? If a person that I can't see—because I'm speaking to him or her on the phone—helps me, and I want to call that person an invisible helper, where shall we draw the line between "literal" and "figurative" meanings of spirit?

Logologies of Reason and Spirit

The main question I will be asking in this book, most overtly beginning in chapter three, is: how are spirits secularized into the metaphors that inform our thought about *this* world, *this* life?—negating (but never quite eradicating) with these thisses an occult or supernatural world beyond the grave, the realm of the discarnate spirits of the dead. Karl Marx is not the only one for whom, as Jacques Derrida insists, ghosts or spirits or specters give form or body to ideology, market forces, prosthetics, virtuality, and so on. It happens to all of us. (I want to say: it is *done* to all of us.) We are all haunted by the spiritualist imagination. Even when we least believe in it. Even when, like Marx and Max Stirner, whose debate over ghosts in the pages of *The German Ideology* provides Derrida his main text in *Specters of Marx*, we despise that imagination and want to hurl abuse at it. This "go away closer" inclination of the spiritualist imagination Derrida dubs the "paradoxical h(a)unt":

And the ghost does not leave its prey, namely, its hunter. It has understood instantly that one is hunting it just to hunt it, chasing it away only so as to chase after it. Specular circle: one chases after in order to chase away, one pursues, sets off in pursuit of someone to make him flee, but one makes him flee, distances him, expulses him so as to go after him again and remain in pursuit. One chases someone away, kicks him out the door, excludes him, or drives him away. But it is in order to chase after him, seduce him, reach him, and thus keep him close at hand. One sends him far away, puts distance between them, so as to spend one's life, and for as *long a time* as possible, coming close to him again. The *long time* is here the time of *this distance hunt* (a hunt *for* distance, the prey, but also a hunt *with* distance, the lure). The distance hunt can only hallucinate, or desire if you prefer, or defer proximity: lure and prey. (*Specters* 140)

The ghost you hunt, in other words, continues to haunt you. Which is why you hunt it.

Kenneth Burke calls this h(a)unt (or something very like it) "logology": the imaginative displacement by which the Logos, the supernatural Word of God, becomes Logic, the secular *techne* of reason and science; the *geistesgeschichtlich* ("literally" spirit's-historical, "figuratively"—effacing the term's spectral semantics—intellectual-historical) process whereby words for otherworldly things become words for thisworldly things: "'Spirit' is a similar word. Having moved analogically from its natural meaning, as 'breath,' to connotations that flowered in its usage as a term for the supernatural, it could then be analogically borrowed back as a secular term for temper, temperament and the like" (Burke 8). Logology in Burke's hands, despite the word's oogly unloveliness, becomes a versatile conceptual tool for tracing historical homonymies and synonymies up and down various ontological ladders or "conversion gradients" that unearth buried tonalities and reincarnate dead metaphors. In some sense in fact the logological resurgence into contemporary consciousness of etymological origins *is* an awakening of the dead, the older senses of words reappearing as ghosts to haunt their later and more current ones, the discarnate spirits of words like "spirit" channeled by the logologer into whatever present we occupy.

But only in a sense. For Burke is never interested in freezing this sort of historical movement into a single perspective—that, for example, of the present, in which "the spirit of a text" means its meaning and older senses like the author's personalized spirit merely hover nearby. He is logologically concerned with the entire shifting series of perspectives, indeed with perspectivizing semantic shifts historically and hierarchically, so that, say, our current understanding of the *meaning* of a text sheds light on earlier and more "primitive" conceptions of the spirit of its author, and also of course vice versa: by thinking of translation as spirit-channeling, say, we can better understand the more "modern" notion that translators should step aside and let the (semitextualized, almost entirely despiritualized) source author speak through them.

In Burkean terms, for example, the series of ten ghosts (*Gespenster*) that Derrida shows Marx tracing or enumerating in Stirner would be a logology of *Gespenst* in German religious/philosophical thought: (1) *das höchste Wesen,* the highest or supreme being, God; (2) *das Wesen* in general, being or essence; (3) the vanity of the world; (4) a pluralized *Wesen, die gute und böse Wesen,* good and evil beings, animistic spirits; (5) an imperialized *Wesen, das Wesen und sein Reich,* being and its realm or empire; (6) another pluralized *Wesen,* this time apparently closer to human beings, *die Wesen,* (the) beings; (7) *der Gottmensch,* the god-man or man-god, Jesus Christ; (8) *der Mensch,* the human being, a generically masculine "man"; (9) *der Volksgeist,* the spirit (or ghost) of the people; and (10) *Alles,* the All, everything, which is, as Derrida says, Marx's excuse for stopping the enumeration, throwing his hands up in mock despair over Stirner's tendency to see ghosts everywhere: "One could throw it all together in any order, and Stirner does not fail to do so: the Holy Spirit, truth, law, and especially, especially the 'good cause' in all its forms" (Derrida *Specters* 146).

Shifting terms just slightly, from *Gespenster* to *Geister* (a crucial shift, as Derrida shows, for Marx as for German philosophy in general—see also my remarks on Schleiermacher's *Gespenster* and *Geister* in *Taboo* 179–81, and my discussion of Schleiermacher and Marx at the end of chapter four), we might tabulate a logology of spirit as a kind of rationalist framework for my argumentation(s) here. Let's build it, again, following good rationalist principles, around three dualisms: singular/ plural, control/no control, and knowledge/no knowledge, on the assumption (or perhaps we can agree to call it a hypothesis) that the more singularity, control, and knowledge we ascribe to spirits, the more magical and alive and meaningful and patterned our world will seem to be, and the less we ascribe to them, the more inert and chaotic and out-of-control our lives will seem:

1. *God* (singular, control, knowledge)

   • the sole ruler, omnipotent, omniscient

2. *gods and goddesses, angels and demons, sprites and familiars* (plural, control, knowledge)

   • possess supernatural or occult knowledge and can control events on earth, but because they are many, to achieve their ends they must compete and conflict with other similar spirits

3. *channeled spirits of the dead* (plural, no control, knowledge)

   • possess supernatural or occult knowledge but cannot control events on earth; they must depend on living spirit-channelers to convey their messages to other living beings

4. *worshipped/remembered/imagined spirits of the dead* (plural, no control, no knowledge)

   • have no power to act, no agency, no independent existence; in some sense don't exist at all, except as memory images in "real" or living or carnate beings' minds

In the hallowed tradition of literal/figurative dualisms, the entities in 1–3 are "literal" spirits, those in 4 "figurative" ones: we might say that "remembered" or "imagined" spirits aren't "really" spirits, they don't "really exist"; we only think of them as spirits by analogy—or logology—with other (conceptions of) spirits. 4, to put that differently, is the breach in the wall of spirituality: once we call things spirits that have no (or are imagined as having no) agency, that have neither (in)visible form nor intentionality, then anything, really, can be a spirit.

And we could extend that logological chain, 5, 6, 7 . . . n, enumerating ever more "figurative" spirits, spirits lower and lower on the logological food chain, farther and farther from the supernatural. But I want to set things up a little differently. I want to use that four-step hierarchy as a template for structurally parallel conceptualities, concept-clusters that (can and will) become structurally parallel in and through the act of imposing this spirit-template on them. This will mean effectively exfoliating the fourth step in that "top" logology by mapping secularized versions of the whole hierarchy onto its fourth or "figurative" rung: embedding three secular logologies in succession into what this first logology identifies as postsupernatural.

For example, if we wished to outline a similar logology of reason, a "figurative" spirit if it is any kind of spirit at all, we could map four different rationalist ideologies onto the four steps of the spirit logology. I will be exploring such logologies of reason in greater detail in chapters five and six (and logologies of ideology in chapters three and four), but let me adumbrate my argument there just briefly here, by way of getting us started.

1. It seems clear, for example, that there are important logological connections between the rationalist God of the Judeo-Christian imagination and the quasideified reason given pride of place in the increasingly secularized subjectivities of the late Middle Ages and especially the modern era. Both God and reason are imagined as the supreme ruler of their universes, the created cosmos for the former, subjectivity for the latter. Like God, reason is the self's god, king, lord, master, father. It must constantly do battle with the emotions, of course, traditionally thematized as a separate power inside the subjective body, just as the theological God is imagined as constantly doing battle with Satan, lord of carnality. Strictly monotheistic reason religions, however, will want to see the emotions as not really all that serious a threat to reason's hegemony—at least not in the right sort of people, rational people, especially ruling-class men. In this conception the emotions are projected outward onto other people, women, children, the lower orders, racial and ethnic minorities. *We* are perfectly ruled by reason—*we* being the group that in an earlier, less secular age, would have been perfectly ruled by God and thus empowered to make life-or-death decisions in His name.

2. Now if, following our logology of spirit, we decrease the imagined *singularity* of the "spirit" forces, at the second level we have to envision an internal battle between reason and emotion, the mind and the body, duty and desire, and so on. In this second-level conception it is not so clear that reason will emerge triumphant, so that it must constantly be bolstered by militant calls to vigilance against the insidious siren-call of the body, emotion, desire. On this level, for example, authoritarian and lectoritarian approaches to interpretation might be thematized as pluralistic models competing for ascendancy over readers, with conservatives arguing that their authoritarian model represents reason, truth, accuracy, objectivity, and so on and their opponents' lectoritarian model represents emotion, randomness, distortion, subjectivity, and reader-response people arguing that all this talk of objectivity is an outdated theological myth,

not only tyrannical but ontologically discredited, all there *is* is emotion, predilections, subjectivities. Reason is simply a name we give to one of them.

3. At the third level, then, our internal "spirits" lose control as well as singularity: not only are there many of them, hundreds, thousands, an infinite number, but none of them has the power to impose its will on the others. Our "spirits" or selves simply arise in great numbers, and our behavior emerges out of their infinite clashing and clamoring for ascendancy. This will be the topic specifically of chapter five, but more generally of the book as a whole. This notion of fragmentary subjectivity is my main concern, my primary sense of what a "translator subjectivity beyond reason" might entail—the terminus toward which my rather fragmentary argument tends.

4. At the fourth level, finally, the internal "spirits" of our subjectivity dissipate into illusion, become the mere by-products of ancient-but-dead ideologies. There is no such thing as subjectivity. This was a popular view in France and elsewhere in the 1950s and 1960s and after, spawning such diverse cultural products as the *nouveau roman* of Robbe-Grillet and others, in which there were no characters, only behavioral effects of the movement of bodies through space, and the anti-liberal humanist theories of the poststructuralists, for whom subjectivity was largely a bourgeois myth.

Mapped out in this tidy rationalist way, my attack on rationalism in this book may seem less obviously, to bivalent readers, a simple flip-flop into the mystical camp. My antirationalist argument is directed specifically against the first two levels of this logology—which are ideological positions without much philosophical credibility left in the twentieth century anyway—rendering my antirationalism much less iconoclastic than it may seem to some. Indeed some readers may be inclined to read it as just another expression of rampant (post)modernity—but note that I am seeking here to avoid that extreme as well, by associating it with the fourth level, and directing my attentions to the third.

I am not, in any case, trying to claim that I invented this pre/post-rationalist approach to subjectivity. I am only attempting to apply it methodologically to the study of translator subjectivities across a fairly wide disciplinary spectrum, including church history, psychoanalysis, philosophy, literature, neurology, and economics.

Chapter Two

The Divine Inspiration of Translation

It could happen. Perhaps it does happen. Let us imagine, in a tentative and exploratory way, that it does. The dead writer "inspires" or "overshadows" the translator's work on his or her text. The translation is a joint project undertaken by the translator's body and the author's spirit. Certainly many translators through history have felt, or claimed they felt, the guiding hand of the source author. The instruction to let the source author "take over" is one of the reigning dicta of the profession. This may be just a metaphor, but it is a surprisingly persistent one, and one that survives today in striking juxtaposition with the dominant rationalist ideology of the modern era. Its survival suggests both that it was once more than a metaphor and that the original idea, whatever it might have been, remains powerful enough today to survive *as* a metaphor.

In the bulk of this book, as I said in chapter one, I will be concerned with the metaphor—with its implications for a postrationalist reformulation of translator subjectivity. Even if spirits don't exist, or do exist and have no impact whatsoever on translations, the *notion* that they do, or that it makes sense to act as if they did, may help us to reframe how we think about translation and translators in fruitful ways. Before I go there, however, here in chapter two I want to lay down a truncated historical foundation for the *pre*rationalist conception of translator subjectivity, in terms of the translator's "possession" by spirits. And by way of getting started, first a quick history of channeling, or mediumship, or whatever other term we want to use for the mystical communication between physical and nonphysical persons. This history relies heavily on the scholarship of Jon Klimo in *Channeling: Investigations on Receiving Information from Paranormal Sources.*

A Short History of Spirit-channeling

We do not know of a "primitive" or preliterate culture that had no form of institutionalized communication between the living and the spirits of the dead. This phenomenon seems to be ubiquitous in the ancient (especially "prehistoric") world, and only begins to come under serious assault with the rise of monotheism around 1000 B.C.E.—and even then only as the "fraudulent" or "dangerous" activity of other groups, not of one's own. If you are a monotheist, when your own god talks to you it is revelation or divine inspiration; when out-groupers hear the voices of other gods or spirits it is necromancy (the ancient term for spirit-channeling or psychic mediumship) or demonic possession—or a hoax, because obviously (and it becomes increasingly "obvious" toward the beginning of the Common Era) those gods and spirits do not exist. Only your own god does. With the rise of rationalism out of monotheism as a competing "religion" in the last three or four centuries before our era, this opposition to other groups' spirit-channeling as fraudulent was gradually extended to all spirit-channeling: there are no spirits, there are no gods, nothing survives the death of the physical body so there is nobody for "psychic mediums" or "spirit-channelers" or "necromancers" to talk to and the whole thing is a confidence trick. This is, of course, roughly where we are today.

Ancient Egypt is often thought of as the beginning of trance-channeling as a mode of communication with the spirits of the dead; but dream-channeling was common in Egypt as well, and in the mid-second millennium B.C.E. the pharaoh Amenhotep IV (later Akhnaton) seems to have channeled his famous vision of monotheism in a dream. The Egyptians were also the first to establish the later almost universal pattern according to which the dead person's spirit (or *ba*) retains the attributes of the living embodied person (or *du*), so that a priest in life remains priestly in death, and a peasant remains a peasant.

The ancient Chinese gave the name *wu* to trance channels: Wang Ch'ung in the first century C.E. wrote that "among men the dead speak through living persons whom they throw into a trance; and the wu, thrumming their black chords, call down the souls of the dead, which then speak through the mouths of the wu" (quoted in Klimo 80–81). The Chinese also seem to have been the first to use a mystical planchette, very much like the one used on Ouija boards today (a device invented in Baltimore by Elijah J. Bond and William Fuld around 1892 and popularized by Parker Brothers since 1966 [Klimo 197]). The Chinese device was called a *chi*; it looked more like a modern divining or dowsing rod, and when the spirits came down into it, it began to move, spelling out the gods' messages on paper or in sand.

In ancient Greece the spirits of the dead were called *keres*; they were thought to escape from the jars in which corpses were stored and then to haunt the dwellings of the living. By the sixth century B.C.E. the Thracian Dionysiac cults were using shamans as trance channels to communicate with the spirits, or what by then were known as *theoi* or gods, discarnate immortal beings with superhuman powers. As I suggested above, it is likely that rationalist philosophy was born out of the Dionysiac, Orphic, and Eleusinian mystery cults devoted to the channeling of these gods; certainly much ancient Greek philosophy, especially that of Pythagoras, Heraclitus, and Plato, was thoroughly soaked in these mysteries (see also my *Translation and Taboo*, 54–61). Plato's Socrates was often referred to as a "diviner" or a "prophet":

SOCRATES: Well, Phaedrus, my friend, do you think, as I do, that I am divinely inspired [θεῖον πάθος πεπονθέναι]?

PHAEDRUS: Undoubtedly, Socrates, you have been vouchsafed a quite unusual eloquence.

SOCRATES: Then listen to me in silence. For truly there seems to be a divine presence [θεῖος ἔοικεν = divine image, figure, person] in this spot, so that you must not be surprised if, as my speech proceeds, I become as one possessed [νυμφόληπτος = captured by nymphs, hence raptured, frenzied]; already my style is not far from dithyrambic. (*Phaedrus* 238cd, trans. R. Hackworth; see also 262d)

HERMOGENES: You seem to me, Socrates, to be quite like a prophet newly inspired [ἐνθουσιῶντες], and to be uttering oracles [χρησμῳδεῖν].

SOCRATES: Yes, Hermogenes, and I believe that I caught the inspiration from the great Euthyphro of the Prospaltian deme, who gave me a long lecture which commenced at dawn. He talked [ἐνθουσιῶν] and I listened, and his wisdom [τῆς δαιμονίας σοφίας = wise spirits/powers/gods] and enchanting ravishment have not only filled my ears but taken possession of my soul [τῆς ψυχῆς ἐπειλῆφθαι], and today I shall let his superhuman power work and finish the investigation of names—that will be the way—but tomorrow, if you are so disposed, we will conjure him away [ἀποδιοπομπησόμεθά = banish him, exorcise him], and make a purgation [καθαροὖμεθα] of him, if we can only find some priest or Sophist who is skilled in purifications [καθαίρειν] of this sort. (*Cratylus* 396de, trans. Benjamin Jowett; see also *Lysis* 216d, *Philebus* 20b)

The Greek oracles at Dodona and Delphi and other sites were trance-channelers who would prophesy by sinking into a trance and being possessed by discarnate spirits—some of the famous ones by a single spirit, or what spiritualists today would call a "spirit-guide." Oracles often lived in caves and thought of the spirits they channeled as coming up to them from the underworld through fissures in the rock. Pythagoras used something like a Ouija board as early as 540 B.C.E.: a "mystic table" on wheels moved around and pointed toward signs that were then interpreted by the philosopher himself, or his pupil Philolaus. The muses, as we will see Socrates insisting to Ion in the next section of this chapter, were also channeled spirits: the muse-inspired poet or singer was thought to be the mere bodily vehicle for the singing of the muse ("Sing in me, muse," begins Homer's *Odyssey*).

By the time the Romans had conquered Greece, the rationalist tide was turning against spirit-channelers. Cicero, the Roman rationalist whom the early Church Fathers so revered, railed against spirit-channeling or necromancy on the grounds that it involved ghastly pagan rituals:

It is not, therefore, surprising to find that the doctrine of human sacrifice is necessary to successful ghost-raising, and Cicero hurling against Vatinius the charge of sacrificing boys for necromantic purposes. It is a piling on of horrors, a motive which inspires many of the extravagances of magical ritual, when the most powerful spell for coercing the presence of the dead is held to demand the sacrifice of an unborn babe, ripped untimely from its mother's body. And another theory, which we have already noticed, doubtless assisted to cement the connection of human sacrifice with necromancy, the belief that *in articulo mortis* the spirit of the dying man hovered between the worlds of the living and the dead, and was able to give tidings of the future because it stood on the threshold of the next world. . . .

The spells and sacrifices of witches and wizards give them power to raise the dead from the tomb, and to learn of the future from the summoned ghosts. In the magical practice of late and post-classical periods an instrument is sometimes provided through which the ghost speaks. The ghost is summoned into a corpse, either that of the victim of the horrid sacrifice or one selected, as in the scene in Lucan's *Pharsalia,* from the graveyard in which the incantation takes place. The papyri give directions for calling the spirit into the corpse, and coercing it to reveal the future. (Halliday 242–44)

The movement from polytheism to monotheism among the ancient Hebrews is still marked in the Hebrew Bible in the retention of the plural Canaanite noun *elohim* "gods" as the singular name of the One God, also called YHWH or Yahweh; earlier the *elohim* were thought of as various "powers, ghosts, gods, the human dead, and angel-like beings" (Klimo 85). The first five books of the Hebrew Bible, the Pentateuch, were long thought to have been written by Moses, the first Hebrew spirit-channeler to be named a "prophet"; he knew this history of his people not because he himself experienced it all but because he channeled it directly from Yahweh. Later Hebrew prophets, including Samuel, David, Solomon, Elijah, Elisha, Amos, Isaiah, Jeremiah, and Ezekiel, channeled Yahweh either clairvoyantly (saw him in visions) or clairaudiently (heard his voice speaking to them), or both. People who channeled spirits other than Yahweh were condemned to death as witches, wizards, and necromancers; in 1 Samuel 28, for example, Saul, who has outlawed witches, goes to the Witch of Endor to get information from the recently deceased Samuel that Yahweh won't give him: "And the woman said unto Saul, I saw gods ascending out of the earth. And he said unto her, What form is he of? And she said, An old man cometh up; and he is covered with a mantle. And Saul perceived that it was Samuel. . . . And Samuel said to Saul, Why hast thou disquieted me, to bring me up?" (1 Sam 28:13–15).

Christianity was based on the teachings of a man who claimed both to *be* God and to *channel* God. The horrific "pagan" scenes described above, the spirits of the dead lured into corpses, point strongly to such New Testament scenes as Jesus raising Jarius' daughter (Mark 5:39–40) or Lazarus (John 11:39–44), or summoning up the spirits of Moses and Elijah at the Transfiguration (Luke 9:28–36)—or, for that matter, God raising Jesus himself on the third day (Matt 28:9, Luke 24:13–16, John 20:11–18). Jesus seems to have charged his followers as well with the power to channel spirits: "For it shall be given you in that same hour what ye shall speak," he tells the apostles at one point. "For it is not ye that speak, but the spirit of your Father that speaketh in you" (Matt 10:20). Saul channels the dead Jesus on the road to Damascus, and is struck blind; when he regains his vision he converts to Christianity and becomes its most powerful prophet, Paul. (I will be returning to Paul on spirit-interpreting at the end of this chapter.) John of Patmos describes his vision in the Book of Revelation specifically as channeled: "I was in the Spirit on the Lord's day, and heard behind me a great voice, as of a trumpet, saying . . ." (Rev 1:10). As Arthur Findlay suggests in his massive (and from an orthodox Christian *or* rationalist viewpoint quite tendentious) study *The Psychic Stream, or The Source and Growth of the Christian Faith:*

This combination of circumstances, the urge Jesus had to return to earth after his death, and the clairvoyance of one or more of his disciples, changed the outlook of the dejected band he had left behind. Rejoicing took the place of sorrow, and, instead of the earth life of the Master ending in apparent failure, his disciples came to realise and believe that it had ended in a glorious triumph. The scattered band reunited to discuss the meaning of it all, and we can be sure that whoever had seen him glorified, as Paul puts it, would be the centre of attention.

After this, Jesus may have been seen on other occasions. This is quite a reasonable supposition, considering the fact that the indications are that there were some amongst his followers who had mediumistic qualities. It is quite possible that Jesus was not only seen but heard, and that he also communicated through any who were trance mediums or in whose presence the Direct Voice could be heard. From the accounts which have been given to us it seems as if several of his followers had this gift of trance.

Quite unconsciously, therefore, Jesus laid the seed of the mighty organisation which developed under the title his followers bestowed upon him [the Christ]. During his lifetime such an idea as being the founder of a world religion had never occurred to him, just as it never occurred to him that being seen by one or more who mourned him would be the spark needed to set the world on fire with a new idea.

Jesus, when the remembrance of what he had suffered faded from his mind, would cease being earth-bound and reach out for pastures new. Like most other people, he would have friends on the other side who would help him to adjust his outlook to the new order into which he had just arrived. This would help him to forget his earth sufferings, he would gradually realise that his troubles were over, and that all he had gone through would never happen again. Gradually he would become interested in the affairs of the etheric world, which he would find in many respects similar to the one he had left, but more beautiful. Life would become easier and happier, and soon all earth troubles would be forgotten, though this does not mean that he would lose his interest in this world, in fact, from what Paul tells us, he evidently retained it throughout Paul's lifetime. (577–78)

Findlay to the contrary, of course, Christian doctrine does assume that the Jesus-spirit remains very interested in this world today, two thousand years later, and will continue to be until the world is destroyed in the apocalypse. And it should be clear that the dominant secularized Western norms or ideals for translation too are much closer to this orthodox Christian notion of the discarnate spirit—God, Jesus, biblical source author—remaining vigilantly, even jealously interested in the fate of his or her expressive work in the hands of later generations, than it is to the conception promoted by most spiritualist authors, including Findlay, who tend to portray the dead as smiling indulgently but without great intensity or regulatory concern on the actions of the living. In fact most spiritualist authors are closer to Cicero and later rationalist opponents of mystics and spiritualists in this than to orthodox Christians and mainstream translation theorists: for the spiritualists and rationalists the source author is dead and either (spiritualism) has no overwhelming interest in or (rationalism) no power to control the reading, rewriting, or dissemination of their words. The translator does with them what s/he will; uses them as a mere springboard for his or her (or the target culture's) own expressive development. (For further discussions of Cicero along these lines see my "Classical" and conclusion to *What Is Translation?*)

For orthodox Christian spiritualists, on the other hand, and their heirs among conservative translators and translation theorists still today, the source author and text do have that jealous interest and, to the extent that their translators submit to the necessary regimen of self-emptying and instrumentalization, they also have the power. The source author is the authoritative source of meaning; even in the afterlife s/he remains a supremely interested party who closely monitors the dissemination of his or her work here on earth; the translator who would do justice to this discarnate but nevertheless watchful and concerned spirit must convey the author's "true" "original" words and intentions *exactly* as he would want them to be conveyed. Hence the rhetorical importance, in traditional approaches to translation, of warnings against "violating the spirit of the original," or of portraying the source author as "rolling in his grave" over some "free-spirited" translation.

As the Christian church extended its circle of influence across Europe during the first millennium of our era, it mobilized ever greater vigilance against "unauthorized" spirit-channelers thought to be channeling evil or "unclean" spirits. These people were described as "possessed" or "obsessed" (and exorcized) when the channeling was seen as unintentional, as witches and wizards (and executed) when it was seen as intentional. Other spirit-channelers were canonized as saints. From our perspective today the deciding factor in this saint/witch split would often seem to be more sociological than theological: a very few mediums who achieved great popularity or won favor with the secular or ecclesiastical authorities were sainted; others, in the millions, were burned as witches and heretics. (And some, of course, were burned as witches or heretics and then later, posthumously, canonized.) It was not always, in other words, a matter of what spirits you channeled, but how you channeled them. Famous Christian channelers include Saint Odile in the seventh century, Saint Hildegarde of Bingen in the twelfth century, Richard

Rolle of Hampole (who also translated the psalter into English) in the fourteenth century, Joan of Arc in the fifteenth century (executed as a heretic because the "voices" who gave her instructions were taken to be a sign of demonic possession, canonized in 1920), Michel de Nostradamus, Saint Teresa of Avila, and Saint John of the Cross in the sixteenth century, George Fox (founder of the Quakers) in the seventeenth century, and Emanuel Swedenborg in the eighteenth century. In 1837 a group of discarnate American Indians seem to have requested permission to use the bodies of some Shakers in upstate New York, still Indian country in those days, in order to reconnect with earthly life: "It was reported," Jon Klimo writes, "that an entire tribe at a time would take over, whooping, singing, dancing, eating, and conversing with one another in their native language" (96). Mid-nineteenth-century Spiritualism, born through the three psychic daughters of John Fox in Hydesville, New York, became a full-fledged movement on both sides of the Atlantic that finally peaked just after the first World War with tens of millions of devotees. Isaac Post developed, supposedly in collaboration with inventors in the spirit world (notably Benjamin Franklin), a system of raps for spelling out words. The Russian Czar Alexander the Great and the American President Abraham Lincoln were thought to have received the command to free the serfs and slaves from the spirit world at almost exactly the same historical moment in 1861; Lincoln's trance channel, Nettie Colburn, was one of the president's most trusted advisors. The international scientific community launched massive investigations into the channeling phenomenon, but many of the most famous channels—Daniel D. Home, Florence Cook, Eusapia Palladino, Rev. William Stainton Moses, John Ballou Newbrough, Frederick S. Oliver, Lenore Piper—baffled the scientists by passing every test for fraud (skeptics sneered that scientists were the easiest of all to fool). Piper was examined by William James in 1885, and utterly convinced the Harvard psychologist that she had supernormal powers.

Socrates and the Art of the Rhapsode

Very few spiritualist writers have written about spirit-channeled translation. Very few channels, in describing their experiences, have commented on the crossing of language barriers, or the channeled rewriting of texts in new language. In shifting from the history of spirit-channeling to the history of spirit-channeled translation, therefore—the main topic of this chapter—I am forced to fall back on greatly diminished historical documentation.

By way of transition from the general spirit-channeling material we've considered so far to the specific cases of divinely inspired translation we'll be examining in the remainder of this chapter, let us take a quick look at Plato's *Ion* (ca. 390 B.C.E.). Plato did not write on translation. In the *Ion* he did, however, write on the mediation of texts from the poet in writing to a partially illiterate audience by the rhapsode and the actor, whose interpretive interventions in the transmission of the text are strikingly similar to the translator's. Even though the rhapsode does not transfer the source text into a different language, the *Ion* might arguably be called an early theory of translation—or, more broadly and perhaps plausibly as well, an early theory of the whole range of textual interventions that André Lefevere has identified as "rewriting" (translating, editing, anthologizing, etc.).

Socrates and Ion begin by discussing Ion's recent victory in the contest of rhapsodes at Epidaurus. Socrates wonders how Ion can be so brilliant at reciting Homer yet not other authors, such as Hesiod or Archilochus; Ion has no idea, but simply reiterates his belief that Homer is far superior to them, and thus far more worthy of his efforts. Socrates suggests that this is because his skill is not based on study, on an interpretive "art"—on rationalist control of his materials—but rather on inspiration:

this gift you have of speaking well on Homer is not an art; it is a power divine, impelling you like the power in the stone Euripides called the magnet, which most call "stone of Heraclea." This stone does not simply attract the iron rings, just by themselves; it also imparts to the rings a force enabling them to do the same thing as the stone itself, that is, to attract another ring, so that sometimes a chain is formed, quite a long one, of iron rings, suspended from one another. For all of them, however, their power depends upon that loadstone. Just so the Muse. She first makes men inspired, and then through these inspired ones others share in the enthusiasm, and a chain is formed, for the epic poets, all the good ones, have their excellence, not from art, but are inspired, possessed, and thus they utter all these admirable poems. . . .

Well, do you see that the spectator is the last of the rings I spoke of, which receive their force from one another by virtue of the loadstone? You, the rhapsodist and actor, are the middle ring, and the first one is the poet himself. But it is the deity who, through all the series, draws the spirit of men wherever he desires, transmitting the attractive force from one into another. And so, as from the loadstone, a mighty chain hangs down, of choric dancers, masters of the chorus, undermasters, obliquely fastened to the rings which are suspended from the Muse. One poet is suspended from one Muse, another from another; we call it being "possessed," but the fact is much the same, since he is *held*. And from these primary rings, the poets, others are in turn suspended, some attached to this one, some to that, and are filled with inspiration, some by Orpheus, others by Musaeus. But the majority are possessed and held by Homer, and, Ion, you are one of these, and are possessed by Homer. And whenever anyone chants the work of any other poet, you fall asleep, and haven't a thing to say, but when anybody gives tongue to a strain of this one, you are awake at once, your spirit dances, and you have much to say, for not by art of science do you say of Homer what you say, but by dispensation from above and by divine posses-sion. So the worshiping Corybantes have a lively feeling for that strain alone which is of the deity by whom they are possessed, and for that melody are well supplied with attitudes and utterances, and heed no others. (Lane Cooper's translation; 533de, 535e–536c)

In this ancient mystical vision of literary possession, likened with startling modernity to magnetic attraction, Socrates does not mention the translator explicitly, but is so clearly speaking in his discussion of the "intermediate links" of mediaries *like* the translator—the rhapsode and the actor—that it seems justified to extend the scope of his claims. Like the rhapsode and the actor, the translator too interpretively mediates the source text to a new audience. For the rhapsode and the actor, that new audience is distinguished from the original one by illiteracy, in some cases, but more generally by the differences between written and oral culture: hearing Homer recited by the rhapsode, or watching him played on the stage by actors, is a radically different experience from reading his hexameters on the page. (Note that Cicero's "invention" of translation theory three centuries after Plato's writing arose out of his insight that the rhapsode's art, applied to legal oratory, might work more effectively for training purposes across linguistic boundaries, from Greek into Latin. See Robinson *Western* 7, 9; Robinson "Classical" 256–59.)

Socrates is not content to identify the divine source of Ion's "talents," however; he goes on to ask Ion which would be a greater authority over passages in Homer on driving, himself as a rhapsode or a charioteer, which over passages on food, himself or a physician, which over pas-sages on war, himself or a general. In each case Ion replies that the other, the specialist, would be the greater authority. When Socrates next wants to know which passages in Homer "concern the rhapsode and the rhapsode's art, the passages it befits the rhapsode, above all other men, to examine and to judge" (539e), however, Ion says all of them. Socrates patiently reminds him that he has already agreed that the specialists on various arts will be greater authorities on those specific passages than the rhapsode, so Ion compromises slightly, saying that he as rhapsode is the greatest authority on every passage in Homer *except* those dealing with specialized subjects—Ion is portrayed as something of a happy simpleton. And soon enough he is arguing that the rhapsode knows what the general should *say* as well as the general himself, claiming for himself parity in *linguistic* authority; but Socrates does not make this fine distinction, but rather imputes to Ion the attempt to equate the rhapsode's art with the general's: "What! Is the rhapsode's art the general's?" (540d). This is not what Ion was saying, of course, and Ion gamely attempts to clarify his point: "At all events I ought to know the kind of speech a general should make" (540d). But Socrates is bent on making this out as a claim to total rhapsode = general equality, and within a very few lines has reasoned Ion into agreeing that that is precisely the claim he is making:

SOCRATES: But when you know of military matters, do you know them because you are competent as a general, or as a rhapsode?

ION: I cannot see a bit of difference.

SOCRATES: What, no difference, you say? You mean to call the art of the rhapsode and the art of the general a single art, or two?

ION: To me, there is a single art. (540–541a)

Now of course Socrates has Ion right where he wants him, stammering out utter absurdities that are all too easy to puncture:

SOCRATES: And so, whoever is an able rhapsode is going to be an able general as well?

ION: Unquestionably, Socrates.

SOCRATES: And then, whoever happens to be an able general is an able rhapsode too.

ION: No, I do not think that holds.

SOCRATES: But you think the other does? That whoever is an able rhapsode is an able general too?

ION: Absolutely!

SOCRATES: And you are the ablest rhapsodist in Greece?

ION: Yes, Socrates, by far.

SOCRATES: And the ablest general, Ion? The ablest one in Greece?

ION: You may be sure of it, Socrates; I learned this also out of Homer. (541ab)

This is a flagrant *reductio ad absurdum*, and Ion is a rather passive participant in his own humiliation. Socrates wants to establish an alternative source of authority, a rationalist one, based on knowledge and experience and mastery and intelligence, to oppose the traditional mystical one that he is attributing to Ion. Ion is not quite willing to accept Socrates' radical dualization of the field—either Ion is purely inspired and has no "art" (i.e., rationalist mastery) or he is an artful deceiver bent on marketing himself as a general and a charioteer and a fisherman and a physician and whatnot else—but he quickly succumbs to the superior force of Socrates' somewhat bogus reasoning. Why shouldn't there be a mixed state in which the rhapsode combines rational skill with inspiration? Why can't there be a linguistic authority possessed by the rhapsode alone that doesn't overlap with the practical and theoretical authority of the general? Socrates' dualizing seems almost perfectly unnecessary, except to give him *some* sort of argumentative edge over the mystical tradition favoring divine inspiration. He could have argued, as Aristotle would sixty years later in the *Poetics* (which is why it seems so natural to us today), that there is a rational skill in writing (as well as, by extension, interpreting) poetry that is utterly different from that of running wars or keeping horses or whatever, and that skill obeys its own internal *rational* laws. The only rhetorical reason Socrates has not to make this argument is that it would not allow him to give Ion a Hobson's choice between inspiration and dishonesty, as he does to end the dialogue:

. . . But the fact is, Ion, that if you are right, if it really is by art and knowledge that you are able to praise Homer, then you do me wrong. You assure me that you have much fine knowledge about Homer, and you keep offering to display it, but you are deceiving me. Far from giving the display, you will not even tell me what subject it is on which you are so able, though all this while I have been entreating you to tell. No, you are just like Proteus; you twist and turn, this way and that, assuming every shape, until finally you elude my grasp and reveal yourself as a general. And all in order not to show how skilled you are in the lore concerning Homer! So if you are an artist, and, as I said just now, if you only promised me a display on Homer in order to deceive me, then you are at fault. But if you are not an artist, if by lot divine you are possessed by Homer, and so, knowing nothing, speak many things and fine about the poet, just as I said you did, then you do no wrong. Choose, therefore, how you will be called by us, whether we shall take you for a man unjust, or for a man divine.

ION: The difference, Socrates, is great. It is far lovelier to be deemed divine.

SOCRATES: The lovelier title, Ion, shall be yours; to be in our minds divine, and not an artist, in praising Homer. (542ab)

Plato's *Ion* may be taken as the first significant rationalist breach in the fortress of the mystical theory of literature that had held sway for centuries before Plato, and would continue to hold sway, though with diminishing power, for centuries after. It is not coincidental, either, that it is typically the first entry in anthologies of Western literary theory: it is the first *rationalist* theory of literature.

But it is also, quite strikingly, a powerful articulation of the mystical theory that it so carefully attacks. It will be complexly echoed in many later texts as well, most notably perhaps in the *Enneads* of Plotinus more than half a millennium later, in around 260 C.E., which argues (in the eighth tractate of the fifth ennead) along remysticalized Platonic lines that the artist does not *imitate* nature but imposes on his art the visionary form he has received from the One—a conception of art that is very close to the one Socrates exfoliates in the beginning of the *Ion*, on the analogy of magnetic attraction. For Socrates the rhapsode is a bit of an idiot; certainly Plato finds Ion amusingly simple, and wants us to share a few laughs at his expense. It would have been impiety to attack the theory of divine inspiration outright; it is never clear, either, that Socrates *or* Plato was strongly inclined to the kind of iconoclastic impiety that would dismiss all mystical experience as superstitious mumbo-jumbo, as so many of their rationalist followers would be. Instead, like a missionary fairly and respectfully recording the ludicrous beliefs of the natives in order to facilitate the process of conversion to Christianity, Socrates and Plato articulate the ancient mystical theory as piously as they can and then cautiously damn it with faint praise, cast a light air of ridicule over it by associating it with a well-meaning but rather dull-witted fellow, and subtly devalue it by giving precedence to rationalist "authority" (knowledge, experience, skill).

And it is significant that these two "Platonic" theories of literary production and mediation, the mystical and the rationalist, will continue to inform the debates over translation as they take shape in the ensuing centuries. In the various depictions of the creation of the Septuagint, for example, "Aristeas" takes the rationalist view, and the Jewish Platonist Philo takes the mystical view; Jerome takes the rationalist view and the Christian Platonist Augustine takes the mystical view.

Philo and Augustine on the Legend of the Septuagint

The most famous historical cases of spirit-channeled translation are all of sacred texts: the god or goddess who is thought to have written or dictated the original text "possesses" the translator so that the translation gains the same "prophetic" status as the original. As I suggested in *Translation and Taboo* (66–70, 114–20), this deification of translation is one very effective solution to the problem faced by the devotees of a religion when it spreads across linguistic boundaries and new believers are unable to read the word of the god in the god's own language: you have it translated by humans but market it as translated by the spirit of the god. This is the sense in which, as has been noted by many commentators (see Dan 130), Christianity is a religion of translation—a religion for which the sacred texts *are* translations, for which indeed the translations are more sacred than the originals. The Hebrew Bible was appropriated for the Greek community at Alexandria and later for the emergent Christian sects not only by the 72 translators on the island of Paphos but also, and more important, by the legend propagated by Philo Judaeus to the effect that the translators were divinely inspired. The Hebrew, Aramaic, and Greek Christian Bible was appropriated for the Roman church through the retroactive deification of Jerome's Vulgate translation. The originals were written by many hands, over many centuries, and exist in many different versions; the translation was inspired by God, giving it a unity and an accuracy and a sacral power only dimly anticipated by the original.

In presenting the mystical translation theories in this chapter, I want to essay a modified chronology that I hope will enable me to bring out their salient points with maximum clarity: beginning with Plato's most influential Jewish and Christian followers, Philo and Augustine, on the legend of the Septuagint, and moving forward in time from there to a modern example of the same process, Joseph Smith's translation of *The Book of Mormon*. Then the chronology breaks, and I shift back in time to Paul's remarks on spirit-channeled interpreting in 1 Corinthians 14— almost a different topic, though clearly steeped in the same Platonic mythos.

The Hebrew Bible was translated into Greek in the early third century B.C.E., for the Hellenic Jewish population in Alexandria; according to legend, it was carried out by 72 Jewish rabbis on the island of Paphos, outside Alexandria. (The 72 were often referred to as the Seventy, and the title Septuagint given to their translation is simply the Greek for 70.) The earliest version of the story we have is the so-called the *Letter of Aristeas to Philocrates*, supposedly written by one Aristeas, a devout Alexandrian Jew, in the actual time of the translation, but almost certainly written pseudonymously by another devout Alexandrian Jew about a century later. As "Aristeas" portrays the process, it did not involve spirit-channeling. The 72 Jewish Talmudic scholars called by Ptolemy Philadelphus to Alexandria "proceeded to carry it out, making all details harmonize by mutual comparison. The appropriate result of the harmonization was reduced to writing under the direction of Demetrius" (Moses Hadas' translation, in Robinson *Western* 5). Like later Bible translators, the 72 worked by committee; they consulted, and reached a single translation by consensus. The earliest version of the story we have is also the most "modern" or rationalistic.

It was not until a more famous Alexandrian Jew took up the story another century later, then, around 20 B.C.E., that it assumed the mystical and supernatural form it would retain until the Renaissance. In his *Life of Moses* Philo Judaeus spiritualized the Septuagint, drawing explicitly on the more mystical tendencies of Plato—"Either Plato philonizes," the Church Fathers were wont to say, "or Philo platonizes." And of course Philo was followed in his platonizing by the Hellenic Jew Paul; and Christianity was born out of this Hellenistic strain of Judaism, harking powerfully back through Paul and Philo to Plato and the mystical tradition of dualism, instrumentalism, and perfectionism. Philo writes:

Sitting here in seclusion with none present save the elements of nature, earth, water, air, heaven, the genesis of which was to be the first theme of their sacred revelation, for the laws begin with the story of the world's creation, they became as it were possessed [ἐνθουσιῶντες], and, under inspiration [προεφήτευον], wrote, not each several scribe something different, but the same word for word, as though dictated to each by an invisible prompter [ὡ" σπερ ὑποβολέως ἑκάστοις ἀοράτως ἐνηχοῦντος]. Yet who does not know that every language, and Greek especially, abounds in terms, and that the same thought can be put in many shapes by changing single words and whole phrases and suiting the expression to the occasion? This was not the case, we are told, with this law of ours, but the Greek words used corresponded literally with the Chaldean, exactly suited to the things they indicated. For, just as in geometry and logic, so it seems to me, the sense indicated does not admit of variety in the expression which remains unchanged in its original form, so these writers, as it clearly appears, arrived at a wording which corresponded with the matter, and alone, or better than any other, would bring out clearly what was meant. The clearest proof of this is that, if Chaldeans have learned Greek, or Greeks Chaldean, and read both versions, the Chaldean and the translation, they regard them with awe and reverence as sisters, or rather one and the same, both in matter and words, and speak of the authors not as translators but as prophets and priests of the mysteries [ἱεροφάντας καὶ προφήτας προσαγορεύοντες], whose sincerity and singleness of thought has enabled them to go hand in hand with the purest of spirits, the spirit of Moses. (F. H. Colson's translation, in Robinson *Western* 14)

"Became as it were possessed," "under inspiration," "as though dictated to each by an invisible prompter," "prophets and priests of the mysteries": this is the strongest and clearest statement of spirit-channeled translation in Judeo-Christian history. The result in Philo's account is 72 identical literal translations, each of them the perfect bridge between the Hebrew ("Chaldean") and the Greek: "they regard them with awe and reverence as sisters, or rather one and the same, both in matter and words." In fact, not even a bridge: through the channeling of some divine "invisible prompter" the very difference between the Hebrew and the Greek drops away and two texts in two different languages become "one and the same, both in matter and words." This is the only way, clearly, to transcend the curse of Babel, the scattering of tongues, and the taboo on translating sacred texts, which as "Aristeas" had pointed out had caused two Greek writers, Theopompus and Theodectes, to suffer mysterious ailments (a "derangement of the mind" and a cataract, respectively [Robinson *Western* 6]) when they contemplated introducing passages from the Hebrew scriptures into their work in Greek translation. Theopompus asked God why he was being punished: "when it was signified to him in a dream that it was his meddlesome desire to disclose divine matters to common men, he desisted, and was thereupon restored to health" (6; see my *Taboo* xiv–xv for discussion). If God dictates the translation, apparently, the taboo is eased, and the curse of Babel is revoked. Languages merge as one; truth springs out of diversity and dissension.

This was Augustine's idealized conception of Bible translation as well, in *De doctrina Christiana;* not surprisingly, he also embraced Philo's legend of the Septuagint with open arms:

And in emending Latin translations, Greek translations are to be consulted, of which the Septuagint carries most authority in so far as the Old Testament is concerned. In all the more learned churches it is now said that this translation was so inspired by the Holy Spirit that many men spoke as if with the mouth of one. It is said and attested by many of not unworthy faith that, although the translators were separated in various cells while they worked, nothing was to be found in any version that was not found in the very same words and with the same order of words in all of the others. Who would compare any other authority with this, or, much less, prefer another? But even if they conferred and arrived at a single opinion on the basis of common judgment and consent, it is not right or proper for any man, no matter how learned, to seek to emend the consensus of so many older and more learned men. Therefore, even though something is found in Hebrew versions different from what they have set down, I think we should cede to the divine dispensation by which they worked. (D. W. Robertson's translation, in Robinson *Western* 34)

For Augustine as for Philo, all 72 translators surrendered their wills to the speaking (or the automatic writing) of the spirit. What Augustine the Christian adds to the legend first propagated by Philo the Jew is the notion that this spirit-channeling makes the Septuagint not *equal* to the original Hebrew texts, as they were for Philo, but actually *superior*. Humans wrote the Hebrew Bible; humans also sat in those cells on an island off the coast of Alexandria, translating it into Greek. Humans are subject to error, lapses of memory and judgment, deliberate distortions, personal predilections, etc. And all of those humans, both the original Hebrew writers and the Alexandrian translators, lived before Jesus and so were subject to the additional eschatological burden of not being Christians, not having been saved by the Messiah from sin. The only way that the Hebrew Bible can lay claim to being God's Word, therefore, is if its writers wrote not as their human selves but as the channels of God's spirit; and the only way that the Septuagint can lay claim to being God's Word is if its translators channeled that same spirit also. For Augustine, proof that the 72 did in fact channel that spirit lies in the legend (for him the historical fact) that all 72 translators were kept sequestered in separate cells and still managed to produce 72 verbatim identical translations. Humans could never achieve this sort of result on their own; hence the legend *must* be true.

Something like this circular logic survives today in similar pronouncements about translational accuracy and the translator's willingness to submit to the guidance of the "spirit" or sense of the original author or text. For Augustine, perfect translation can only be achieved through total surrender to the spirit of God, which uses the translator's body as its channel, therefore the 72 translators at Alexandria must have channeled God's spirit, and the legend must be true that they generated 72 identical translations while sequestered in separate cells; and, running that the other way, the 72 can only have generated 72 identical translations if they were channeling God's spirit, therefore their translation must be perfect, even better than the original. Perfect translation, hence divine inspiration; divine inspiration, hence perfect translation.

The modern version, slightly secularized but still immediately recognizable, goes something like this: the translator's personal subjectivity always leads to distortions of the original and thus to nontranslation, hence the only way to produce an accurate (equivalent, professional, ethical) translation is to renounce all personal subjectivity and let the source author or text speak through you; because translation is total surrender to the spirit of the source text, or of the source author's intended meaning, any survival of the translator's personal subjectivity distorts that spirit, gets in the way of its channeling directly and immediately from the source author to the target reader, and thus leads to nontranslation. Surrender to the spirit of the original, hence accurate translation; accurate translation, hence surrender to the spirit of the original.

In a sense, however, analyzing this circular logic is unfair, since Augustine and modern "charismatic" translation theorists do not actually derive their premises from their conclusions; they inherit them from previous generations. In fact they "channel" them from previous generations, in the broad sense of receiving and transmitting ideological norms—a process that I want to return to in part two. The logic is only circular in an artificial synchrony, a falsely dehistoricized present moment in which no reference to repressed historical origins is permitted. In fact the logic is thoroughly historical. In the following imagined tabulation of that logic, I imagine point zero as someone like Philo Judaeus or Augustine on the Septuagint:

-6. Translation X (the Septuagint, the Vulgate, the King James Version) is created by a translator or group of translators.

-5. Translation X is taken up by an increasingly influential group in society, who find in it a center around which to organize the group's cohesion, social and political justification, and eventual triumph.

-4. Translation X assumes great social and/or political significance.

-3. Ideological forces in society invest Translation X with the somatics of awe, taboo, the solemn power of the alien word.

-2. Ideological forces in society mandate that I read and respect (perhaps even worship) Translation X.

-1. I channel those forces, so that I feel what they want me to feel.

0. Translation X feels holy to me.

1. I sense that I could never on my own create anything that holy; nor could anyone else I know. It exceeds the bounds of "fallen" human achievement.

2. Those earlier translators must therefore have been angels on earth, or the channels of divine inspiration.

3. Divine inspiration must somehow transform human translators, so that they are more than human.

4. For that transformation to work as powerfully as it obviously did in translation X, human translators must have to be willing to surrender fully to it.

5. Translators who are not willing to surrender to that transformation will not produce holy translations.

6. Because their translations will not be holy, they will also not be perfectly accurate (they will be full of human errors), hence they will be no translations at all, or only very bad ones.

7. Translators who are unwilling to surrender utterly to the spirit of the original are no translators at all, or only very bad ones.

8. They are not only bad translators; they are bad people. The unwillingness to surrender utterly to the spirit of the original stems from sinful pride and presumption, from a desire to advance oneself at the expense of the holy original.

This would be the *retroactive deification of translation:* in a rationalist perspective, obviously, translators do not channel the spirits of dead authors; any suggestion that they do, therefore, must be a mystification, an idealizing fiction imposed on the imperfect *human* processes of translation after the fact. The above tabulation, counting backwards and forwards from an imaginary point zero, is a rationalist (skeptical, secular) reinterpretation of what have been taken to be *spiritual* events as *ideological* ones. What seems to have been performed spiritually, supernaturally, by gods or other discarnate spirits, *in fact* was performed naturally, culturally, ideologically, by human forces—but significantly enough, by human forces that we do not understand very well, and that remain strikingly congruent with (perhaps even historically and/or metaphorically indebted to) the spiritualist imagination.

Joseph Smith and *The Book of Mormon*

One of the striking differences between *The Book of Mormon* as spirit-channeled translation and, say, the Septuagint or the Vulgate is that Joseph Smith's source text did not exist, at least publicly—was not in human circulation—when the translation process began. As a result it has often been called a pseudotranslation, like James Macpherson's "translation" of the Ossian poems a few decades before Smith—an original text pretending to be a translation. This charge reflects a significantly different class of skepticism than that directed against the divine inspiration of the Septuagint or the Vulgate. When the source text is in undisputed existence and a "divinely inspired" translation appears, no one doubts that it is a translation; only that the translators were "prophets" or spirit-channelers. In the case of *The Book of Mormon,* not only did the source text not exist in any public or historical form prior to the translation process (it supposedly lay buried in a hill for 2000 years); after the translation was completed it was taken back up to heaven by the angelic messenger who directed its translator to its location and the work of translation, so that all that remains of it today is a series of "testimonials" from upright citizens that they saw with their own eyes the golden plates on which the source text was etched.

This undoubtedly makes *The Book of Mormon* less reputable as a spirit-channeled translation than the Septuagint, which we may read rationalistically as an "obvious" spiritualistic mystification of an actual historical translation. Such mystifications are tolerated with an uneasy indulgence in "primitives" writing two millennia ago, who, we are pleased to presume, "didn't know better." *The Book of Mormon* is too modern to be accorded such indulgence; and the conspicuous absence of a historical source text strains rationalist credibility to the breaking point.

However, the Church of Jesus Christ and Latter-Day Saints currently has something in excess of five million believers; presumably most of them believe that Joseph Smith actually did dig up the golden plates to which he was directed by the Angel Moroni, and actually did translate them, with spiritual assistance, from the ancient Egyptian, which he could not read. Unlike the Ossian pseudotranslations, in other words, which were exposed as a hoax a scant few decades after their initial publication, *The Book of Mormon* continues to win followers in huge numbers in a rationalist age, a century and a half after its creation. If *The Book of Mormon* is a pseudotranslation, a hoax, an imposture, it is an extraordinarily successful one—and that alone commands no small measure of historical and sociological respect.

The creation of *The Book of Mormon* is also the most striking story of spirit-channeled translation we have. The details are wonderfully lurid: buried treasure, golden plates, an ancient Egyptian text about a messiah on the American continent (which would not be discovered by Europeans for over a millennium), the Urim and Thummim (a spiritualistic translation machine buried with the plates, which Smith used to do the actual translating), and a long series of direct revelations from God. Compared to this story, Philo's tale of 72 Jewish scholars producing verbatim identical translations in 72 different cells pales into bland insignificance.

Joseph Smith was a young uneducated man; indeed according to many of his contemporaries he was a young man on the make, a flim-flam artist. In his demystificatory book *Joseph Smith and the Origins of "The Book of Mormon,"* David Persuitte quotes a letter from Joel K. Noble, the presiding judge in one of Smith's 1830 trials:

Jo. Smith (Mormon) came here when about 17–18 y. of age in the capacity of Glass Looker or fortuneteller. . . . Jo. engaged the attention of a few indiv[iduals] Given to the marvelous. Duge for money, Salt, Iron Oar, Golden Oar, Silver Oar, and almost any thing, every thing, until Civil authority brought up Jo. standing (as the boys say) under the Vagrant act. Jo. was condemned. Whisper came to Jo. "off, off"—took Leg Bail. . . . Jo. was not seen in our town for 2 Years or more (except in Dark Corners). (54)

The following year, in 1831, Obadiah Dogberry wrote a debunking piece called "Gold Bible, No. 4," in the Palmyra *Reflector,* saying similar things:

In the commencement, the imposture of the "book of Mormon," had no regular plan or features. At a time when the money digging ardor was somewhat abated, the elder Smith declared that his son Jo had been the *spirit* (which he then described as a little old man with a long beard,) and was informed that he (Jo) under *certain* circumstances, eventually should obtain great treasures, and that in due time he (the spirit) would furnish him (Jo) with a book, which would give an account of the Ancient inhabitants (antideluvians,) of this country, and where they had deposited their substance, consisting of costly furniture, &c. at the approach of the great deluge, which had ever since that time remained secure in his (the spirits) charge, in large and spacious *chambers,* in sundry places in this vicinity. . . . It will be borne in mind that no divine interposition had been dreamed of at the period. (quoted in Persuitte, 56–57)

If these stories are true, if Smith really was a con artist who struck the mother lode with the story of the golden plates, he is right in the mainstream of the great American tradition of the gaudy and grandiose scam that brings not only fame and fortune but social respect and status—in this case the status of Prophet, founder of a major religion. If Smith did write *The Book of Mormon* out of his own imagination (and intense if sporadic reading in the King James Bible), or even if he coordinated its creation by a team of hoaxers, it is still a monumental achievement, one that continues to convince Mormon scholars that an uneducated man in his early twenties *could not possibly* have fabricated such a coherent sacred text out of the whole cloth. He *must* have had divine help.

And in any case—since I have promised to withhold judgment on the authenticity of these tales of spirit-channeled translations—the *story* of Smith's translation work is an attractive one. As the unpaginated introductory text to *The Book of Mormon* (1830) describes the process:

After Mormon completed his writings, he delivered the account to his son Moroni, who added a few words of his own and hid up the plates in the hill Cumorah. On September 21, 1823, the same Moroni, then a glorified, resurrected being, appeared to the Prophet Joseph Smith and instructed him relative to the ancient record and its destined translation into the English language.

In due course the plates were delivered to Joseph Smith, who translated them by the gift and power of God.

And Joseph Smith himself writes in his own testimonial, appended to the Introduction:

"He called me by name, and said unto me that he was a messenger sent from the presence of God to me, and that his name was Moroni; that God had a work for me to do; and that my name should be had for good and evil among all nations, kindreds, and tongues, or that it should be both good and evil spoken of all people.

"He said there was a book deposited, written upon gold plates, giving an account of the former inhabitants of this continent, and the source from whence they sprang. He also said that the fulness of the everlasting Gospel was contained in it, as delivered by the Savior to the ancient inhabitants;

"Also, that there were two stones in silver bows—and these stones, fastened to a breastplate, constituted what is called the Urim and Thummim—deposited with the plates; and the possession and use of these stones were what constituted Seers in ancient or former times; and that God had prepared them for the purpose of translating the book."

In a recent article on the creation of *The Book of Mormon* the Elder Neal A. Maxwell of the Quorum of the Twelve Apostles summarizes what we know of the process as described by Smith:

The Prophet Joseph alone knew the full process, and he was deliberately reluctant to describe details. We take passing notice of the words of David Whitmer, Joseph Knight, and Martin Harris, who were observers, not translators. David Whitmer indicated that as the Prophet used the divine instrumentalities [the Urim and Thummim] provided to help him, "the hieroglyphics would appear, and also the translation in the English language . . . in bright luminous letters." Then Joseph would read the words to Oliver (quoted in James H. Hart, "About the Book of Mormon," *Deseret Evening News*, 25 Mar. 1884, 2). Martin Harris related of the seer stone: "Sentences would appear and were read by the Prophet and written by Martin" (quoted in Edward Stevenson, "One of the Three Witnesses: Incidents in the Life of Martin Harris," *Latter-Day Saints' Millennial Star*, 6 Feb. 1882, 86–87). Joseph Knight made similar observations. . . .

Oliver Cowdery is reported to have testified in court that the Urim and Thummim enabled Joseph "to read in English, the reformed Egyptian characters, which were engraved on the plates" ("Mormonites," *Evangelical Magazine and Gospel Advocate*, 9 Apr. 1831). If these reports are accurate, they suggest a process indicative of God's having given Joseph "sight and power to translate" (D&C 3:12).

If by means of these divine instrumentalities the Prophet was seeing ancient words rendered in English and then dictating, he was not necessarily and constantly scrutinizing the characters on the plates—the usual translation process of going back and forth between pondering an ancient text and providing a modern rendering.

The revelatory process apparently did not require the Prophet to become expert in the ancient language. The constancy of revelation was more crucial than the constant presence of opened plates, which, by instruction, were to be kept from the view of unauthorized eyes anyway.

While the use of divine instrumentalities might also account for the rapid rate of translation, the Prophet sometimes may have used a less mechanical procedure. We simply do not know the details. (39)

Leaving aside the question of authenticity—whether any of this actually happened—I find the interesting theoretical question to be: was Smith translating? Certainly not in any modern, rationalistic sense. "He was not necessarily and constantly scrutinizing the characters on the plates—" as Maxwell writes "—the usual translation process of going back and forth between pondering an ancient text and providing a modern rendering." He had no ancient Egyptian; how could he be translating? The divine instrumentalities, a.k.a. the "seer stone," a.k.a. the Urim and Thummim, served as a spiritualistic MT program, doing the translation *for* him. He was only the human channel of an essentially divine act of translation. Who translates? God does, or the Angels Mormon and Moroni (the mediate source authors) do, using the instrumentalities of both the Urim and Thummim and Joseph Smith. This is classic spirit-channeled translation. The channeler-translator *needs* no skill in the source language—or, for that matter, in the target language either, presumably, although it is also possible to argue that the Angel Moroni chose Joseph Smith, a native speaker of English, for a reason; that Smith contributed to the creation of *The Book of Mormon* in *some* significant way, and was not merely an embodied vehicle.

Would *The Book of Mormon* have been different had someone else been chosen as "translator"? Perhaps. In *The Beginning of Mormonism* Pomeroy Tucker describes the beginning of the work of translation at the Hale house in Harmony, Pennsylvania:

"Joseph, Emma and Alva arrived in Harmony early in December, 1827, where they met with a warm welcome from the Hale family. After a brief rest, they began to make plans for the translation of the plates. Two upstair rooms were to be used by Joseph and Emma, one for sleeping and one for translating purposes, and they were to eat their meals with the family. . . .

"Martin [Harris, the scribe to whom Smith dictated his translation] arrived in Harmony about the middle of February with the determination to make further investigation, and learn for himself. In the meantime Joseph had transcribed some of the characters onto paper, with their translation. When Martin saw these, he asked permission to take the characters with their translations to New York and show them to some of the great educators and get their opinion as to their genuineness." (quoted in Nibley, 59–60)

Smith reluctantly agreed, but made Harris promise not to let the pages out of his sight. Harris's wife, however, so the story goes, was convinced that Smith was a fraud, and spirited those pages away to use in a propaganda campaign against Smith. God was incensed at this lapse and punished Smith with the (temporary) loss of his "gift," and later explained the punishment in a revelation. The devout Preston Nibley tells the story in *Joseph Smith the Prophet:*

It was in July of this year, 1828, after his return to Harmony, that the first of the recorded revelations was given, as found in Joseph Smith's history. This most interesting revelation was addressed to himself; it was the voice of the Lord speaking to him.

Here I wish to dwell for a moment upon the manner in which the revelations were received. In this instance, troubled as he was by the disappearance of the 116 pages of the translation of the sacred record, Joseph states that he "inquired of the Lord, through the Urim and Thummim, and obtained the following," quoting the revelation. The Urim and Thummim, it will be remembered, was that instrument found with the plates and described by himself as "two crystals set in the rim of a bow." Through these he looked as he inquired for and received the divine information contained in many of the revelations. Whether the printed word appeared before his eyes, as stated by David Whitmer, or whether the divine thought came into his mind, we do not know; he does not state himself, nor offer anywhere a more complete explanation. . . .

It was some time during August or September of this year 1828, at Harmony, Pennsylvania, that Joseph received the second revelation which is recorded in his history. This is a remarkable document, and as it forecasts the work which Joseph was to perform in this world, to my mind it establishes him as a Prophet of God.

In the opening paragraphs he is chastized for having delivered the sacred writings into the hands of Martin Harris. He is also urged to begin the work of translation once more, and to follow it through to completion.

"Now behold I say unto you, that because you delivered up those writings which you had power unto you to translate by means of the Urim and Thummim, into the hands of a wicked man, you have lost them.

"And you also lost your gift at the same time, and your mind became darkened.

"Nevertheless, it is now restored unto you again, therefore see that you are faithful and continue on unto the finishing of the remainder of the work of translation as you have begun;

"Do not run faster, or labor more, than you have strength and means provided to enable you to translate; but be diligent to the end: . . ."

He was not again to translate that portion of the writings which had been
lost.

"And now, verily, I say unto you, that an account of those things that you
have written, which have gone out of your hands, is engraven upon the
plates of Nephi; . . .

"And now, because the account which is engraven upon the plates of
Nephi is more particular concerning the things which, in my wisdom, I
would bring to the knowledge of the people in this account;

"Therefore, you shall translate the engravings which are on the plates of
Nephi, down even till you come to the reign of King Benjamin, or until you
come to that which you have translated, which you have retained.

"And behold, you shall publish it as the record of Nephi, and thus I will
confound those who have altered my words." (67, 69–70)

There is, in other words, a gap in *The Book of Mormon* corresponding to
the 116 pages that Smith gave Harris. This is somewhat bizarre; if God
is intent on having the ancient Egyptian sacred writing translated into
English, why would he not simply insist that Smith redo that part? The
translation process was incredibly fast anyway; Smith did the whole
book in a month and a half. Why not retranslate 116 pages? It sounds
almost as if, heavy-hearted at losing 116 pages of his hard work, Smith
could not bring himself to rewrite it, and so made up the story of the
revelations from God to explain it away (rationalist skepticism raises its
ugly head).

In any case, this episode is anecdotal evidence (of a sort) that Smith
too, as spirit-channeling translator, exercised agency in the translation
process—that he was not merely the neutral vehicle of whatever divine
spirit might be said to have been acting through him. Some other
channeler-translator might not have handed the 116 pages to Harris;
The Book of Mormon would today be 116 pages longer. And who knows
in what other ways Smith's subjectivity affected the final product?

We might also ask why translation was even necessary—or rather,
why human involvement was required in the translation process.
Couldn't the Angels Mormon and Moroni have written the golden
plates in English in the first place? Or, having written them in Egyptian
and buried them in the hill in New York, couldn't they have simply re-
written them in English? If angels can write in Egyptian, surely they can
write in English too? After all, the Angel Moroni *spoke* to Smith in English. Why did they need Joseph Smith and the whole apparatus of the
divine instrumentalities? The only plausible explanation from within

the spiritualistic paradigm—that is, again, setting aside the issue of authenticity—is that Smith's human agency was in some significant way crucial to the success of the undertaking. Smith cannot have been the mere passive instrument of God, or the Angels, or the divine instrumentalities. He must have contributed *something* to the end result.

Paul on Glossolalia and Interpreting

In chapter 14 of his first letter to the Corinthians, the Apostle Paul took a strong stand on glossolalia that also became the emerging Christian church's first policy statement on translation—and specifically, and most interestingly for my purposes, on translation as spirit-channeling, specifically spirit-channeled conference interpreting.

To be sure, Paul does not explicitly state that the glossolalists in the early churches are channeling individual discarnate spirits, the usual meaning of spirit-channeling. But their ability to speak in tongues that they do not know is traditionally attributed to possession by the Holy Spirit; glossolalia is considered one of the "gifts of the spirit" or charisms. And clearly the ability to speak a foreign language that you've never studied—perhaps to which you've never even been exposed—is only imaginable within the larger mystical context of psychic or spiritual communication. In any case the Third Person of the Trinity, who elsewhere appears in the form of a dove (Luke 3:21–22, John 1:32–34), here appears in the form of "unearned" foreign language fluency in the bodies and voices of devout monolinguals who submit their wills to divine guidance.

Here are the relevant passages from 1 Corinthians 14:

1 Follow after charity, and desire spiritual gifts, but rather that ye may prophesy.

2 For he that speaketh in an unknown tongue speaketh not unto men, but unto God: for no man understandeth him; howbeit in the spirit he speaketh mysteries.

3 But he that prophesieth speaketh unto men to edification, and exhortation, and comfort.

4 He that speaketh in an unknown tongue edifieth himself; but he that prophesieth edifieth the church.

5 I would that ye all spake with tongues, but rather that ye prophesied: for greater is he that prophesieth than he that speaketh with tongues, except he interpret, that the church may receive edifying.

6 Now, brethren, if I come unto you speaking with tongues, what shall I profit you, except I shall speak to you either by revelation, or by knowledge, or by prophesying, or by doctrine? . . .

9 So likewise ye, except ye utter by the tongue words easy to be understood, how shall it be known what is spoken? for ye shall speak into the air. . . .

13 Wherefore let him that speaketh in an unknown tongue pray that he may interpret.

14 For if I pray in an unknown tongue, my spirit prayeth, but my understanding is unfruitful.

15 What is it then? I will pray with the spirit, and I will pray with the understanding also: I will sing with the spirit, and I will sing with the understanding also. . . .

23 If therefore the whole church be come together into one place, and there come in those with tongues, and there come in those that are unlearned, or unbelievers, will they not say that ye are mad? . . .

26 How is it then, brethren? when ye come together, every one of you hath a psalm, hath a tongue, hath a revelation, hath an interpretation. Let all things be done unto edifying.

27 If any man speak in an unknown tongue, let it be by two, or at the most by three, and that by course; and let one interpret.

28 But if there be no interpreter, let him keep silence in the church; and let him speak to himself, and to God.

Glossolalia is wonderful, Paul admits; it is a powerful sign of God's presence and favor. But it is mainly beneficial for the glossolalist, not for the congregation that cannot understand the foreign speech. This is a crucial watershed moment for Christianity in at least two ways:

a. Paul introduces a radical pragmatism into the ancient mystery cults from which Christianity borrowed so much, a growing sense that mystical experience is not and should not be allowed to become an end in itself, that we must constantly ask *cui bono*, who benefits, and how we can maximize the benefit to the group.

b. Paul also edges mystical Christianity from esoteric toward exoteric religiosity, from a closed in-group of priests and initiates who possess the sacred knowledge and closely guard it against the prying eyes of the profane, to an ever-expanding inclusive group including "those that are unlearned, or unbelievers," who are to be welcomed into Christian gatherings.

Paul still sees glossolalia as an important gift of the spirit, but it is too private ("He that speaketh in an unknown tongue edifieth himself," "let him speak to himself, and to God") for his exoteric and pragmatic vision of the church. For Paul the issue is not even one between benefit to a small exclusive group and benefit to a larger and more inclusive group, as the esoteric/exoteric opposition implies; it is rather between benefit to the individual and benefit to the group, and even between "benefit" and "profit" on the one hand, the cornerstones of his ecclesiastical pragmatism, and the ancient mystical ideal of absolute oneness of being with the spirit, an ideal that lies beyond all utilitarian concerns.

As I argued in *Translation and Taboo*, this tension between esoterics and exoterics, mystics and pragmatists—those who want to experience and those who want to communicate, those who strive for the pure delight of spiritual being and those who strive to achieve transformative goals in the political realm—runs through the entire Western history of thinking about translation. Almost invariably it takes the form of a rift between a cultural elite that wants either to enjoy a foreign text in the original language or to translate it in ways that defy communication and understanding among the masses (various literalisms) and a populist group that wants to make foreign texts readily and easily accessible to all and sundry (various paraphrases, sense-for-sense translation, Schleiermacher's "bringing the author to the reader," Venuti's "invisibility" or "domestication"). The class differentiations should be clear as well:

- the upper classes by and large constituted the in-group of the ancient mystery cults, and throughout the Middle Ages and modern era continued to set the key example for any group (by our time the bourgeois intelligentsia, especially) that wanted to hold itself aloof from debased popular tastes, for example by controlling access to education, and by championing the classical languages and literatures over easily accessible modern vernacular languages and national literatures, and the Latin Mass and Latin Bible over what Paul calls "proselytizing" in the target audience's language;

- the lower classes, including by the late Middle Ages the emergent middle class, were quintessentially the outsiders who wanted not only to break into the exclusive clubs but also to open them up to everyone, through universal education and literacy, democratic or free-market "elective" systems in universities, and "open" or assimilative translation.

Note, however, that Paul is not really talking about modern vernacular translation here. He is not, for example, calling for the formation of a professional Christian interpreter corps. He is pushing the early church, to be sure, in a direction that would later be adopted and advanced by Jerome and other Church Fathers, and picked up by the emergent middle classes in the late Middle Ages (the Lollards, for example, Wyclif's group) and Reformation: openness, easily accessible vernacular preaching and translation. But in Paul it is still only a potential, an anticipation of later historical developments, which seems like a "potential" or "anticipation" to us today because we see, 2000 years later, what has been done with it in the interim.

The interpreters Paul wants are not highly trained professionals who have studied the various languages in which the glossolalists are speaking and have extensive experience interpreting them into Greek. Rather, they are themselves charismatics who also pray, as a parallel gift of the spirit, for the ability to interpret. The split Paul is calling for is not, in other words, between charismatics who channel the spirit and what we would think of as modern professional interpreters who are in full possession of their reason and analytical skills. It is, rather, between different charismatic roles:

- "Wherefore let him that speaketh in an unknown tongue pray that he may interpret" (the same person in a dual role as glossolalist and interpreter—perhaps consecutively, first speaking a sentence in an unknown tongue, then interpreting it into Greek); or
- "If any man speak in an unknown tongue, let it be by two, or at the most by three, and that by course; and let one interpret" (charismatic teams that divide up the roles, one or more speaking in tongues, one interpreting).

Clearly, here, interpretation is a gift of the spirit just like speaking in tongues; the interpreter is as much a spirit-channeler as is the glossolalist. The glossolalist channels the speaking of the spirit into foreign speech; the interpreter channels the speaking of the spirit into local speech. Both, Paul says, are important; both roles or functions can coexist comfortably in the same person; indeed presumably the individual has little or no control over which role he will adopt ("he" because in this very chapter—1 Cor 14:34—Paul forbids women to speak in church), as Paul exhorts people to *pray* for the spiritual gift of interpretation, and hope for the best. You open your mouth and words come out; perhaps in an unknown tongue, perhaps in a local vernacular interpretation of your own or someone else's foreign words. The spirit speaks in tongues, using your tongue; or the spirit interprets, channeling its interpretations through you.

Presumably also the spiritual or charismatic nature of the interpreting Paul is calling for in 1 Corinthians 14 obviates the problem of errors and inaccuracies. If it is the Holy Spirit that allows a monolingual to interpret speech in an unknown tongue, if the interpreter interprets by trance-channeling the Holy Spirit, surely the Holy Spirit also guarantees the interpretation's accuracy? One would assume so, though Paul never takes a stand on this issue. Interpreting (and by extension written translation as well) in this charismatic mode is not primarily a human affair, in the derogatory sense of "human" that we hear in phrases like "human error" or "the human factor." (Note that those phrases typically contrast humans negatively with machines, which like the spirit in Christian thought are imagined as "above" human error. In important ways the dream of machine translation in the West is a technosecularization of translation as spirit-channeling: the MT program as discarnate spirit.) The human interpreter or translator is merely a channel of the spirit for whom (which?) all languages are as one, all *logoi* are the translinguistic Logos. The true interpreter (Horace's *fidus interpres,* though in a sense that Horace himself would reject) interprets by surrendering all fallen human will and knowledge and planning and skill to the divine guidance of the suprahuman spirit. (More on the *fidus interpres* in chapter five.)

PART TWO

Ideology

Chapter Three

Ideology and Cryptonymy

Logology of Ideology

Now of course in a modern rationalist perspective, as I suggested at the end of the Septuagint section—in calling these legends of spirit-channeled translation the "retroactive deification of translation"—what is "really" going on in these stories is not divine inspiration, not spirit-channeling. Occult communication of all sorts, not just translation, is a quaint lie believed by our forebears, and only proffered (or believed in repressively secularized forms) today by deluded conservatives who have not yet successfully yielded to the emergent "truth" of, say, ideological analysis. When claims are made for the "divine inspiration" of the Septuagint, the Vulgate, the King James Version, the *Book of Mormon*, or some other translation, the translator should not be thought of as having channeled the Holy Spirit or some other discarnate person; the forces that made that translation seem "holy" or "divine" are socio-political, ideological, the effect of group dynamics. The translation has been charged with the aura of otherworldly power not by any deity but by an influential group in society, who gradually, over a period of many years, even centuries, made it seem holy, sacred, solemn, taboo—even to themselves—by training readers to fear and worship it. "Divine inspiration" is a reader-effect drummed by authorities into what Michel Foucault calls the "docile bodies" (135) of readers (including translators).

And I am very close to believing something like this. My only hesitation in proclaiming this modern rational secularism wholeheartedly is that channeling ideology is experientially so remarkably congruent with or analogical to channeling spirit. A "force" enters from without and takes almost complete possession of the individual, so that the individual *feels* separate and autonomous but wants nothing more than to do the bidding of the outside force—mainly because it no longer feels "outside." It speaks the individual from within. Whether the translators of the Septuagint, the Vulgate, and the King James Bible are channeling the Holy Spirit or the ecclesiastical ideology of their day doesn't really matter, finally, except in some cosmic eschatological sense that we shall never know (unless when we die we do become spirits and, striving toward the light, are filled with arcane knowledge denied to us in the flesh). Those translators are channeling *something*, some "higher force"; but it is virtually impossible to distinguish the major contenders for that title:

• Maybe, on the one hand, what some think of as the discarnate spirits of dead people are actually the by-products of a prevailing otherworldly ideology: if you believe in spirits and ghosts strongly enough, if enough rides on that belief socially and emotionally, those entities will exist for you; and they will act as you expect spirits and ghosts to act, talk as you expect them to talk, because they are shaped out of the same ideological ectoplasm as your expectations.

• Or maybe on the other hand the ideological forces in society are shaped and guided by the spirits of dead people: after all, nobody now alive created the ideological norms that now rule us; all living persons currently under their sway are equally controlled, regulated, "interpellated" by them, in Louis Althusser's term, which we will be looking at in just a moment. None of us can lay claim to power *over* them. Their power comes, seemingly, from "another world"—why not a spirit world, the world of the dead? This notion is pretty much heretical in our own rationalist civilization, but is a common enough belief in others; and since the only force powerful enough to keep us from entertaining the notion "seriously" is itself a rationalist ideology that we who are alive today didn't create and don't control, it seems silly to pretend we are in a position to deny it categorically—or rather *would* seem silly if denying it weren't precisely what we are constantly instructed to do by those ideological "spirits" in whose existence we normatively disbelieve.

Perhaps the first influential analysis of the effects of ideology on the individual is Nietzsche's *Genealogy of Morals:*

"How does one create a memory for the human animal? How does one go about to impress anything on that partly dull, partly flighty human intelligence—that incarnation of forgetfulness—so as to make it stick?" As we might well imagine, the means used in solving this age-old problem have been far from delicate: in fact, there is perhaps nothing more terrible in man's earliest history than his mnemotechnics. "A thing is branded on the memory to make it stay there; only what goes on hurting will stick"—this is one of the oldest and, unfortunately, one of the most enduring psychological axioms. In fact, one might say that wherever on earth one still finds solemnity, gravity, secrecy, somber hues in the life of an individual or a nation, one also senses a residuum of that terror with which men must formerly have promised, pledged, vouched. It is the past—the longest, deepest, hardest of pasts—that seems to surge up whenever we turn serious. Whenever man has thought it necessary to create a memory for himself, his effort has been attended with torture, blood, sacrifice. The ghastliest sacrifices and pledges, including the sacrifice of the first-born; the most repulsive mutilations, such as castration; the cruelest rituals in every religious cult (and all religions are at bottom systems of cruelty)—all these have their origin in that instinct which divined pain to be the strongest aid to mnemonics. (All asceticism is really part of the same development: here too the object is to make a few ideas omnipresent, unforgettable, "fixed," to the end of hypnotizing the entire nervous and intellectual system; the ascetic procedures help to effect the dissociation of those ideas from all others.) (translated by Francis Golffing, 192–93)

There it is: "hypnotizing the entire nervous and intellectual system." Ideology as trance-channeling. Hypnotism, if that is truly what Nietzsche meant, would suggest what spiritualists call a deep trance, in which the channel is unconscious; more likely, of course, he is using hypnotism figuratively to mean "mind control" of external origins but with internal activation in a more or less fully conscious state—perhaps what spiritualist writers call a light trance, in which one has some sense of what is being done to or through you but minimal power to prevent or control it.

Or, as this idea is famously imaged by the French neo-Marxist theorist Louis Althusser, whose Marxism is soaked in Nietzsche:

I say: the category of the subject is constitutive of all ideology, but at the same time and immediately I add that *the category of the subject is only constitutive of all ideology insofar as all ideology has the function (which defines it) of "constituting" concrete individuals as subjects.* In the interaction of this double constitution exists the functioning of all ideology, ideology being nothing but its functioning in the material forms of existence of that functioning. . . .

As a first formulation I shall say: *all ideology hails or interpellates concrete individuals as concrete subjects,* by the functioning of the category of the subject. . . .

I shall then suggest that ideology "acts" or "functions" in such a way that it "recruits" subjects among the individuals (it recruits them all), or "transforms" the individuals into subjects (it transforms them all) by that very precise operation which I have called *interpellation* or hailing, and which can be imagined along the lines of the most commonplace everyday police (or other) hailing: "Hey, you there!"

Assuming that the theoretical scene I have imagined takes place in the street, the hailed individual will turn around. By this mere one-hundred-and-eighty-degree physical conversion, he becomes a *subject*. Why? Because he has recognized that the hail was "really" addressed to him, and that "it was *really him* who was hailed" (and not someone else). . . .

Naturally for the convenience and clarity of my little theoretical theatre I have had to present things in the form of a sequence, with a before and an after, and thus in the form of a temporal sequence. There are individuals walking along. Somewhere (usually behind them) the hail rings out: "Hey, you there!"one individual (nine times out of ten it is the right one) turns round, believing/suspecting/knowing that it is for him, i.e. recognizing that "it really is he" who is meant by the hailing. But in reality these things happen without any succession. The existence of ideology and the hailing or interpellation of individuals as subjects are one and the same thing. (170, 173–75)

Just as the spirit hails the channeler through whom he or she wishes to speak, so too does ideology hail the translator as translator, the critic as critic, any other subject as subject. How did we learn what to do when we first began to translate? Readers, editors, users, teachers gave us feedback; channeling that feedback, we were channeling ideology. Our "helpers" channeled it to us; we channel it to others. They hailed us as translators; we hail others. Translators know certain things: how to regulate the degree of "fidelity" to the source text, how to tell what degree and type of fidelity is appropriate in specific use contexts, how to receive and deliver translations, how to charge for them, how to find help with terminology, how to talk and generally act like a professional, and so on. Translators are those people who know these things, and who let their knowledge govern their behavior. And that knowledge is ideological. It is controlled by ideological norms (see Toury, Hermans, Chesterman). To know what those norms prescribe and act on them is to submit to (at least partial) control by them. To become a translator is to be hailed or interpellated as a translator by ideology. If you want to become a translator, you must submit (at least partly, at least functionally or pragmatically, at least in those contexts defined normatively as normative) to the translator's submissive role, submit to being "possessed" by what ideological norms inform you is the spirit of the source author, and to channeling that spirit unchanged into the target language. (We will be returning to these issues in chapter five, in terms of the translator's ideological ego-ideal, the *fidus interpres*.)

In this radically secularized ideological paradigm, what you are then channeling is no spirit at all, of course; in an ideological perspective there are no spirits in the occult sense of discarnate persons, disembodied beings who once lived on this earth. This is all a myth propagated by societal authorities who want to fill that myth's empty husk with their own author-functions (to invoke a Foucauldian term), their own generalized "intentions" for transmission from language to language.

Except of course that, tellingly, Althusser himself underscores the logological connection between interpellation and spiritual communication:

It then emerges that the interpellation of individuals as subjects presupposes the "existence" [he's not exactly taking this religious parallel seriously as an actual metaphysical reality, but like me he's not exactly rejecting it out of hand, either] of a Unique and central Other Subject, in whose Name the religious ideology interpellates all individuals as subjects. All this is clearly written in what is rightly called the Scriptures. "And it came to pass at that time that God the Lord (Yahweh) spoke to Moses in the cloud. And the Lord cried to Moses, 'Moses!' And Moses replied 'It is (really) I! I am Moses thy servant, speak and I shall listen!' And the Lord spoke to Moses and said to him, '*I am that I am.*'" [Althusser says in a note that he's "quoting in a combined way, not to the letter but 'in spirit and truth.'"]

God thus defines himself as the Subject *par excellence,* he who is through himself and for himself ("I am that I am"), and he who interpellates his subject, the individual subjected to him by his very interpellation, i.e. the individual named Moses. And Moses, interpellated-called by his Name, having recognized that it "really" was he who was called by God, recognizes that he is a subject, a subject *of* God, a subject subjected to God, *a subject through the Subject and subjected to the Subject.* The proof: he obeys him, and makes his people obey God's Commandments. (178–79)

God's address to humans, spirit communication between a deity and living creatures, may not be "real" or "true," Althusser is saying, but the story of it is a perfect allegory (perhaps even historical model) for ideological interpellation. We imagine that spirits interpellate us, speak to and through us, because religious and other societal leaders have wanted us to believe that their commandments actually come from the spirit world; or else, and these are far from mutually exclusive options, we are able to imagine the possibility of ideological forces "speaking" or "wielding" or regulating us because we have a religious history, because gods and other spirits have subjected us to their commandments in the past, or at least we have believed, collectively and individually, that the voices speaking to and through us were spiritual.

Let me now return to the four-step logological hierarchy I traced twice in chapter one, once for spirit, again for reason, in order to lay a new secularized groundwork for my discussions of spirits, crypts, and ideology here in chapter three. That original "conversion gradient," as Kenneth Burke would call it, was based around three dualisms, of singularity/plurality, control/no-control, and knowledge/no-knowledge, thus:

1. *God* (singular, control, knowledge)
   • the sole ruler, omnipotent, omniscient
2. *gods and goddesses, angels and demons, sprites and familiars* (plural, control, knowledge)
   • possess supernatural or occult knowledge and can control events on earth, but because they are many, to achieve their ends they must compete and conflict with other similar spirits
3. *channeled spirits of the dead* (plural, no control, knowledge)
   • possess supernatural or occult knowledge but cannot control events on earth; they must depend on living spirit-channelers to convey their messages to other living beings
4. *worshipped/remembered/imagined spirits of the dead* (plural, no control, no knowledge)
   • have no power to act, no agency, no independent existence; in some sense don't exist at all, except as memory images in "real" or living or carnate beings' minds

I have two more secular logologies of spirit to explore below: in chapter five, *individuality,* or what I want to follow Daniel Dennett in calling the "pandemonium self"; and in chapter six the *marketplace,* the economy, in terms of what Adam Smith famously called the "invisible hands" that control it. For now, however, a spirit-logology of ideology:

1. At the top of this secularized (analogized) hierarchy, we would find all those ideologies that are not conceived (and that don't conceive themselves) as ideologies, but as "the way things are"—universalist

ideologies that ascribe not only singularity (universality) but control and knowledge (agency) to abstractions like truth, logic, reason, fact, morality, natural law, history, evolution, human nature, inalienable human rights. Burke calls these "God-terms," and they do operate in universalizing imaginations like monotheistic divinities. Like the Judeo-Christian God, they are conceived as unchanging (no temporal instability), sovereign (no competitors, thou shalt have no other ideologies before me), and often determinist as well (no freedom of choice). They are not merely passive ideal forms, deviation from which marks deviancy of some deep and abiding sort; we are not, for example, talking here of the bureaucratized belief that translation flat out *is* the transmission of source-text meaning into the target language without change, and anyone who fails or refuses to do that, or—worse—even to attempt it, is undeserving of the term translator. These ideological agents have (or are imagined as having) the power to *enforce* conformity—to shape humans' attitudes and behavior so as to incline them to obedience. Indeed they should be imagined as possessing agency, not merely some depersonalized force. (Nor would this be the level at which the source author is imagined as having some sort of active power over the translator. That would be level 3, below. Source authors are too plural for this level's singularity—except, perhaps, for God as the Source Author of the Bible.) At this level the spirit-analogy would be something like the *fidus interpres*, the "faithful translator": the repressive universalizing ideal that will brook no complexity, contextuality, or change. This deified figure will resurface in chapter five in the form of Freud's ego-ideal, typically an idealized and introjected image of the father, or what Jacques Lacan calls the o-prime, the idealized other.

2. At the level of "polytheism," next, we would find conflicting ideologies or norm-structures as they are analyzed by ideological theorists: social classes, economic systems, the "ruling class," religious groups, political parties and causes, social movements, eras (*Zeitgeister*, lit. time-ghosts, more usually translated spirits of the times), age groups and generations, genders, races, professional groups. Polysystem or descriptive translation scholars are particularly interested in this level, where literary and cultural "systems" have the power to shape and regulate the nature and aims of both specific translations and translation "in general" (in practice within the confines of each system, of course, though systems sometimes "forget" their own limitations and begin prescribing for all time and all space; see

Toury). One fairly broad spectrum of postcolonial translation theory, too, sees translation in terms of the continuing impact of the former colonizing cultures on the former colonies, "dominant" vs. "dominated" cultures. (For systems theory, see Lefevere, who talks about "the European system" [34], "the Islamic system" [73], etc., and Robinson *What* [ch. 4]; for postcolonial theory, see Cheyfitz, Jacquemond, Venuti, and Robinson *Empire*.)

3. The channeled spirits of the dead in an ideological perspective will metamorphose or logologize into smaller ideological superstructures that seem to arise out of or hover above or around various individuals. This is, it should be obvious, the level with which I am mostly concerned in this book—here in chapter three in terms of mysterious voices from out of various "crypts"; in chapter four in terms of a single source author, Shakespeare. In an ideological perspective we will want to say that the voices in those crypts are collective constructs or projections, not actual spirits; or that when a Marxist translator says he turns *King Lear* into a Marxist play "with Shakespeare's permission," what he really means is that Shakespeare's permissive ghost is an ideological construct, what we might call an ideoplasm—something conjured up by Marxist ideology, not by any supernatural mumbo-jumbo. What "speaks" out of the crypt to Freud and Abraham and Torok and Heidegger, what "speaks" with Shakespeare's voice, giving Matti Rossi permission to turn *Lear* into workers' theater, is the interpellative voice of ideology.

4. At the bottom of this ideological hierarchy, finally, we would find various depersonalized social functions as conceived by poststructuralist theorists: author-functions (Foucault), translator-functions (Díaz-Diocaretz, Littau, Hermans, Robinson *What* [ch. 7]), project-manager-functions, support-functions. In this perspective the actual human agents who perform the ideological actions—writing, translating, editing, providing research support—are virtually nonexistent, or at least theoretically irrelevant, imagined as subsumed so thoroughly into their social function or role as to have little or no independent power to act. This shift from a liberal-humanist conception of active independent agents who wield a certain amount of power over their actions to a poststructuralist/posthumanist conception of abstract or actantial social functions recapitulates the modern shift from a spiritualist belief in ghosts and other discarnate spirits (who *really exist* and perform actions, etc.) to the rationalizing or secularizing belief that these entities exist only in our imaginations.

Heidegger on Spirit

Martin Heidegger may come closer than any other modern thinker to saying "the spirit translates, and the translator translates only insofar as he listens/belongs to the translating of spirit." He doesn't say that, of course. Not quite. The force that wields us he calls, early on in his career, *Sein* or Being, later *die Sprache* or language; and while as Jacques Derrida shows in *Of Spirit* he gradually, as if reluctantly, spiritualizes that force starting with the Rectorship Address in 1933 and on through the next two decades or more of his thinking, he is always at great pains *not* to associate it with spirit in any personalized sense, the spirit of a person, the spirit as person. Certainly he does not want Being-as-spirit or language-as-spirit to be thought in Christian terms—as the Holy Spirit, say. Although his thinking about spirit-as-flame has been enormously productive for radical Christian theology; and as Derrida also notes it would not be difficult to imagine a contemporary Christian theologian agreeing with everything Heidegger writes.

The *faux* Heidegger quote above about the spirit translating is a slightly modified version of the conclusion he reaches in his famous lecture on Georg Trakl's poetry, "Language," given at Bühlerhöhe on October 7, 1950, and first published in *Unterwegs zur Sprache* ("On the Way to Language") in 1959. The translation is Albert Hofstadter's in *Poetry, Language, Thought:*

> Die Sprache spricht. Ihr Sprechen heißt den Unter-Schied kommen, der Welt und Dinge in die Einfalt ihrer Innigkeit enteignet.
> Die Sprache spricht.
> Der Mensch spricht, insofern er der Sprache entspricht. Das Entsprechen ist Hören. Es hört, insofern es dem Geheiß der Stille gehört. (30)

> Language speaks. Its speaking bids the dif-ference to come which expropriates world and things into the simple onefold of their intimacy.
> Language speaks.
> Man speaks in that he responds to language. This responding is a hearing. It hears because it listens to the command of stillness. (209–10)

This theory of language is not only perfectly congruent with the ancient conception of translation as stepping aside and letting the source author speak through you—listening/hearing/responding that holds back with its own saying, attuned to the restraint that reserves itself. It also pushes that conception of translation (though so far only analogically) in precisely the same direction I'm pushing it here, toward an overt recognition of the mystical source of the speaking to which the translator must be attuned in held-back anticipation. As Andrew Benjamin writes of this notion, "Language speaks beyond the ambit of subjectivity; in Heidegger's own formulation language itself speaks. . . . The demand made by language is a demand generated, as well as necessitated, by a conception of language in which language is attributed a reality and nature of its own. It is of course a nature that exists independently of any one speaker's use of language" (14–15). It is a nature and a reality that may be immanent rather than transcendent, but is nevertheless unmistakably mystical, and probably—in the highly convoluted senses Heidegger attributes to *Geist, geistig, geistlich* over the years—spiritual as well. If language is *Geist*, it is certainly not *der Heilige Geist* (Holy Ghost/Spirit), and Heidegger would probably prefer that it not be *ein personifizierter Geist* (a personalized ghost/spirit) either; but "Language speaks" is, after all, language personified. Poetically speaking it is a personification of language. Saying *"die Sprache spricht,"* language speaks, Heidegger is encouraging us to think of language as itself a speaker like us, like humans, like persons—only different. Just as for theologians God is a "person" but not, supposedly, anthropomorphic. Personify the divine in order to give people some sense of what you're talking about, to jump-start their imaginations, but then retract the personification, pull the figurative rug out from under them, as soon as they start thinking that God, or Being, or language, is an old guy with a white beard sitting on a throne.

But I don't want to push too hard on this personification yet. Heidegger is much too careful and thoughtful a thinker to be tripped up so easily. Let me register the metaphor of language as personified spirit as an implicit potentiality, nothing more, and move on. I'll come back to that potentiality a little later.

For now, let's follow Andrew Benjamin's discussion of Heidegger on translation for a few pages. Benjamin quotes Heidegger's discussion of the Roman translation of *physis* as *natura* in *An Introduction to Metaphysics:*

This basic Greek word for the essent is customarily translated as "nature." This derives from the Latin translation *natura* which properly means "to be born," "birth." But with this Latin translation *the original meaning* [Benjamin's emphasis] of the Greek word *physis* is thrust aside, the actual philosophical force of the Greek word is destroyed. This is true not only of the Latin translation of this word but of all other Roman translations of the Greek philosophical language. What happens in this translation from the Greek into Latin is not accidental and harmless; it marks the first stage in the process by which we cut ourselves off and alienated ourselves from the original essence of Greek philosophy. (quoted in Benjamin 15)

Noting that the phrase "the original meaning" which he italicizes is in Heidegger's original German *das ursprüngliche Gehalt*, the original content or capacity, Benjamin asks: "What then is the force of claiming that there was an original content within the graphical marks that present the word?" (16). He goes on for a long paragraph in this linguistic vein, wondering whether Heidegger meant "that there was one determinant meaning" (16) in the Greek word, or whether he wants us to imagine the word's meaning or content in terms of "the boundaries of this field—the edges of this semantic frame" (16), and concludes:

It is essential to choose between on the one hand a determinate meaning and on the other a delimited range of possibilities. The point at issue here is of course whether the semantic field could allow a polysemy, one where interconnections would be established but where there was no fixed and essential meaning. Heidegger's distinction between the lexical dimension of a word and its actual content seems to preclude even this possibility. However it does not preclude the possibility of the word having different lexical functions that in each instance present another more archaic level which contains the original meaning of the word. The archaic meaning would have to be singular in nature and that singularity would have to show itself in the life of the word as "lexical artifice." If words were only words, if, that is, there were nothing more to the life of the word than its existence as "lexical artifact," then, to invert Heidegger's claim, there would be nothing to restrict or delimit translations. (16)

Yes indeed: *if* there were nothing more to the life of the word. Because obviously for Heidegger there is something more to the life of the word than its existence as lexical artifice. But what? Like most of Heidegger's poststructuralist readers, myself included, Benjamin has a very hard time getting his understanding around Heidegger's flagrant universalism, foundationalism, and essentialism; and like a good rationalist, as he worries the problem he can't quite bring himself to ask the relevant questions from outside the realm of language. What else could there be to the life of the word than words?

Something in the word, in language, has the power to "restrict or delimit translations." What? Benjamin quotes a later passage from the *Introduction* to the effect that "It is in words and language that things first come into being. For this reason the misuse of language in idle talk, in slogans and phrases, destroys our authentic relation to things" (quoted in Benjamin 17). And then, still later, "one must come to a decision regarding the powers hidden in these distinctions in order *to restore* them to their truth" (quoted in Benjamin 18; his emphasis). Throughout Benjamin shies away from the high-romantic conception of language as a creative godlike agency, a potentially personified or personifiable spiritual force or power. For Heidegger, Benjamin says only, "words presence the being of things" (18). And of course that's true. That is how Heidegger sees words. But "presencing" for Heidegger is not a purely linguistic operation. It's not even just constitutive in the Kantian sense, helping us to "see" things that existed before but might as well not have because we were "linguistically" or "conceptually" or "philosophically" blind to them. Presencing is those things, but it is also more. It is literally creative. It brings things into being—not just into presence *for us*; into *presence*. Into *ousia/Sein*. And Benjamin glosses "the powers hidden in these distinctions" like this: "The task that is described here is structured in terms of a distinction between the appearance of these distinctions—in a sense their lexicality—and an archaic level where there resides that which is essential to both the distinctions and the terms within them. The task itself involves a restoration or retrieval of the archaic" (18). Form and content again. Note Benjamin's telling shift: in that first sentence Heidegger's "powers" are pronominalized as "that which is essential," an unnamed something residing in or on the "archaic level"; in the second he names that something metonymically, sliding laterally from his name for the "level" in which it resides to "the archaic"—which sounds like a dictionary descriptor. Nothing so vitalistic as "powers."

Benjamin next notes "an important corollary here, namely, that there is a possible translation that would express the recovered, restored reality. There is therefore the possibility of a translation—or at least a transmission—that is not marked by loss because it was enacted after 'having recovered'; or after 'having restored'" (19). And this is indeed the critical question for Heidegger on translation: is this utopian or messianic translation (or transmission) possible, or is all translation betrayal? If it is possible, what would it entail? How would it come about? What would have to happen for it to become possible? Heidegger himself never answers this question, or even addresses it, directly; what I am suggesting, what this discussion of Benjamin on Heidegger is leading up to, is the possibility that what Heidegger is *not* saying (but perhaps implying) is that a truly messianic or restorative translation could only be done by language itself, language as that mystical speaking entity whose other name is Being. And whose secret name may well be spirit. The spirit translates—and humans translate truly, restoratively, only when they hear and become a responsive part of the translating of spirit. All other translation is destructive, treacherous: it "destroys our authentic relation to things." Something like this seems to be implied in the passage from the "Dialogue on Language" from which Benjamin also quotes (19), where Heidegger's Japanese interlocutor remarks: "And while translating, I often felt as though I was wandering back and forth between two different language realities, such that at moments a radiance shone on me that let me sense that the wellspring of reality from which those two fundamentally different languages arise was the *same* (my emphasis)." The radiance shines upon him from somewhere; while it shines he senses the unity of languages in the mystical "wellspring" or source of languages (and thus of realities). That wellspring may be the source of the radiance; in any case it is clear that it is the source of the power to overcome the differences between languages, and thus of the ability to translate "truly" or restoratively. The translator translates truly only when he is filled with that radiance, and the originary and unitary streams of language and of reality flow from that wellspring through him into the target text. This is translation. Anything else is betrayal, destruction of the authentic.

Why doesn't Heidegger say any of this outright? Why is he so notoriously cryptic in his late (postwar) pronouncements on spirit, on language, on translation, and on the future of the world? As a first inroad into the problematic of the operation of ideology as analogous to spirit-channeling, and more specifically here in chapter three into the question of Heidegger's reticence about spirit-channeled translation (and other related matters), I want to explore one fairly recent psychological reading of ideological repressions, the "cryptanalysis" developed by Nicholas Abraham and Maria Torok in *The Wolf Man's Magic Word*. Pursuing this theory of psychoideological crypt-formation will mean a fairly substantial detour from Heidegger, for the next few pages; the structure of the chapter will be something like this:

- general theory of ideology as spirit-channeling;
- Heidegger and spirit-channeled translation, with emphasis on the fact that he never comes right out and says what he means on that head;
- Abraham and Torok on the crypt, by way of developing a framework for exploring Heidegger's silence on key matters;
- Heidegger once again on translation.

The chapter, then, is fundamentally about Heidegger on translation, with "ideology" and the "crypt" serving as theoretical frameworks for explaining what I think is going on in his cryptic pronouncements on translation—his problematic and only partial secularizations of ancient notions of spirit-channeled translation like Philo's or Augustine's.

Cryptonymy: Abraham/Torok and Freud

As I mentioned earlier, the lines of force reaching out of the past into the thought of the four twentieth-century thinkers whose work I want to explore here—Heidegger, Abraham, Torok, Freud—emerge most strikingly out of Friedrich Nietzsche, specifically Nietzsche's historical argument in the *Genealogy of Morals*. There he portrays asceticism, the ascetic ideology aimed at "civilizing" the Germans throughout the Middle Ages and on well into the modern era, as the Germans' own ideological attempt to transform their group's individual and collective behavior. According to Nietzsche that transformation was not effected intellectually or contractually, as previous theorists had argued; rather it was achieved by working directly on the body, through pain. Once burned, twice shy. Sticks and stones will break my bones but words will never hurt me—*except* those words that reactivate the purposeful pain inflicted in the past by sticks and stones and other weapons. Those words, Nietzsche argues, do hurt; and the hurt they inflict is the primary channel of ideology. They may be the spoken words of living people, or the written words of dead ones. They may even, though Nietzsche does not explicitly raise this possibility and might not have been entirely happy about it, be the spoken words of dead people or spirits, which do often seem, in the spirit-channeling literature, to reinforce collective norms for their living relatives' behavior (see also Jaynes). In all these cases, words that activate ancient memories of inflicted pain channel ideological forces, and so enforce obedience to "civilized" norms from within. Every time we hear or read someone calling for "respect" before a work of great social power, like the Bible or a literary classic, even before a deified translation like the Vulgate or the King James, we channel some of that early pain that is still stored in our collective and individual memories, and find it in ourselves to treat the text named, and others like it, with respect. "'A thing is branded on the memory to make it stay there; only what goes on hurting will stick'" (Nietzsche 192).

   This aphoristic description of ideology-formation points us powerfully to the cryptonymy of Nicholas Abraham and Maria Torok in *The Wolf Man's Magic Word*, and of Torok in an article on Freud's "conversion" to telepathy; in that latter article Torok defines telepathy pithily as "pain at a distance" (86). If the "message" channeled from the dead or the living is a message of pain, it will not only be remembered; its remembering will structure social behavior in lasting and conflicting ways. Of course, neither Nietzsche nor Torok is talking about communication with dead spirits, here; and even Freud means by "telepathy" only "thought transference" from one living person to another. But the connections with my reflections on spirit-channeling in chapter two are obvious and powerful:

What I am describing in this extended and somewhat convoluted commentary of *Dreams and Occultism* is a *metapsychological phantom* and not, as Freud would have it, a simple instance of thought transference (telepathy). Here is an analyst haunted by the effects of a crypt lodged in someone else (his patient). The analyst is like a child whose parents hide a secret, whose parents falsify reality by terming it fiction, and who require the child to accept it as fiction. Witness to a *real* event, the child is told that it was all a dream, illusion, and fiction. With the hypothesis of a metapsychological phantom, we are now perhaps in a position to assign a metapsychological status to what is "occult" (concealed) in Freud's rather self-conscious option for occultism. The working hypothesis of many years of research seems to be reconfirmed here: Freud carries a crypt within him that resonates with the Wolf Man's. Freud's crypt can be described by studying the text of the dialogues between the two men. My preliminary interpretation of *Dreams and Occultism* can be stated in brief: Haunted by the Wolf Man's crypt, Freud gives a card to occultism. (Torok, translated by Nicholas Rand, 97)

In other words, what Freud mistakes for telepathy is in fact a phantomatic resonance from the Wolf Man's crypt, a melancholic secret hidden in a partition within his troubled ego, to Freud's. But then what *is* that resonance? How does it work? The Wolf Man creates his "crypt" or inner safe in order to hide the secrets that he doesn't want outsiders to discover, and gives only "cryptic" signs of their very existence; Freud does the same with his. Torok's cryptanalysis not only assumes that Freud's crypt resonates with the Wolf Man's; it is also predicated on her own ability, and her coauthor Nicholas Abraham's in *The Wolf Man's Magic Word*, to "read" those resonances accurately, in the Wolf Man, in Freud, and in the cryptonymic interactions between analyst and client. As Jacques Derrida asks pointedly in his foreword to the *Magic Word*, "Is this strange space *hermetically* sealed?" (xiv). He answers that "one must always answer *yes* and *no* to this question" (xiv), *yes* because the crypt is built to hold secrets in *and* out, *no* because no seal is unbreakable. And if that breakage or break-in is an act of violence, so too, as for Nietzsche, is the act that creates it:

Before turning our minds to the break-in technique that will allow us to pene-
trate into a crypt (it consists of locating the crack or the lock, choosing the angle
of a partition, and forcing entry), we have to know that the crypt itself is *built* by
violence. In one or several blows, but whose marks are at first soundless. The
first hypothesis of *The Magic Word* posits a preverbal traumatic scene that would
have been "encrypted" with all its libidinal forces, which, through their contradiction, through their very opposition, support the internal resistance of intolerable pain against an ineffable, forbidden pleasure, whose locus [*lieu*] is not simply the Unconscious but the Self. (Derrida, translated by Barbara Johnson, xv)

The translator opens her/himself up to the speaking of the source author. The ideological subject opens her/himself up to the regulatory
speaking of the authoritative past. The medium channels the speaking
of a discarnate spirit. And the psychoanalyst, who for Abraham and
Torok—and in some ways for Derrida as well—becomes a cryptanalyst,
opens her/himself up to the speaking of the analysand's crypt. Created
in pain, lodged against dangerous pleasure, that crypt encrypts its
speech so as not to be understood; in order to break into the crypt and
understand what is meant to be incomprehensible, the cryptanalyst
must become a translator—and specifically a translator who reads
words aslant in order to channel sympathetic pain. Abraham and
Torok's first key discovery in unlocking the Wolf Man's crypt was that
the Wolf Man's first language was not, as Freud thought, Russian, but
English, the language of a governess. The cryptanalyst's task is therefore
to translate not an original and encrypted Russian into Freud's German
(and on into Abraham and Torok's French), but an original English into
an encrypted Russian, and only then into the German that he uses in
analysis with Freud. Thus, for example, "(he) knows" becomes both the
English homophone *nose* and the Russian homophone нос, *nos*, both
nose and the prow of a ship, which latter the Wolf Man then translates
into German for Freud as *Vorderteil;* the painful message that the little
boy *knows* what really happened (which the parents taught him didn't
happen, was his imagination, a dream, a fiction, his daddy raped his big
sister, no he didn't it never happened) is encrypted as idle talk about
parts of a face and a ship. The pain he feels as a *witness* of that traumatic
event is first encrypted as the English word "witness," further encrypted in semantic Russian translation as видец, *vidyets,* the second half
of the compound noun очевидец, *ochevidyets* (eye)witness, and then in
rhyming Russian translation or *traducson* as видеть сон, *vidyet' son,* lit. to
see a dream. In the famous nightmare of the wolves, then:

Now "to dream" in Russian is *vidiet son. Vidiet* resonates with "Whit" and
"witness," *son* with "sun" taken from *Whitsunday.* Incidentally, *vidietz* means

"witness" in Russian, and *son* (dream) is a homophone of the English "son." There is thus near homonymy, on the one hand, between *vidiet son* "to dream" or "see a dream" and *vidietz + son* and, on the other, the English "witness" and "son." "I dreamed that it was night." "Night," the Russian adverb is *notchiu*. We could not help hearing it in English also: *not you*. We venture the hypothesis: *The witness is the son, not you*. (Abraham and Torok 34)

"Absurd!" they cry. "But no measure of unlikelihood or strangeness is going to make us back down. We must not ignore any trail" (34). The only problem here is epistemological: how do Abraham and Torok *know* these things? They describe their procedure quite frankly: "Yet, the analyst's ear cannot help but continue to resonate with chords of a dialogue," "The analyst, however, cannot help twisting the words toward what they are meant to hide" (35). They do this mainly with their knowledge of English and German and a Russian dictionary. "We can now proceed," they tell us later, "with a new exercise: We can turn right side up what has been turned upside down twice over for the sake of expediency. This little trick will suffice to recover the elements of the initial traumatic dialogue" (67).

Oh will it now! But aren't you just making all this stuff up?

No, we're breaking into the Wolf Man's crypt. We are *discovering what is there*. We are, to put it in the terms of this book, channeling the encrypted spirit—not telepathically, but through resonances that, well, just *aren't* telepathic.

Another quote, and then some Nietzschean analysis:

The dream continues:

"I was lying in my bed." Note the words "bed" and "lying." This could be illuminating. For the dreamer's ear, bed and but may sound alike whereas "lying," that is, "to be in bed," must seem to a Russian child a bizarre homonym of *he is lying* ("not you, but he is lying"). The whole thing then once again: *The witness is the son, not you, but he is lying*.

Now there is a sentence to dream about! It may well have been *engraved* as is, to be disguised later in the manner we have just seen. Is this expert in legal matters (the Wolf Man's profession in Vienna) an unwitting "witness"? His testimony—once confirmed—does imply some misdeed. What will the next flip of the dictionary turn up to our bemused surprise? "Misdeed," "crime," "sin" are said with nearly the same Russian word as "walnut tree," the legendary tree of the Wolf Man that supports the famous "white wolves" and whose image has long since become his trademark. In fact, "walnut tree" is *oriekh*, whereas "sin" and "misdeed" are *khriekh* [actually гpex, *gryekh*] with the stress falling on *-ekh*. Our listening gains clarity.

But let us return to our sentence: "The witness is the son, not you, but he is lying." In whose mouth does this shred of dialogue belong? Certainly not in that of Sergei, the "son," since he is mentioned in the third person. Furthermore, if, as we suspect, there was an accusation in English, it must have come from the English governess. As for the response, the sentence must have been uttered by one of the parents. The father, the accused party, was, as we shall see, absent from the scene. Conclusion: These meaning-laden words, spoken in a mixture of Russian and English, must be attributed to the mother and addressed specifically to the nurse. (35)

The young Sergei, the Wolf Man, sees his father rape his big sister. He is the witness. He tells his governess and/or mother what he saw, but the mother tells the governess in a mixture of Russian and English that the boy is lying. All this Abraham and Torok discover while flipping through the pages of the dictionary—translating a problematic source text, trying to work their way back to the authorial intention, as it were, the originary meaning (his psychic pain), that gave rise to the crypt, the desire to hide his meaning behind cryptic dreams and encrypted words.

Taken as a purely linguistic exercise, Abraham and Torok's translation of the Wolf Man's crypt has a powerfully arbitrary quality. "What will the next flip of the dictionary turn up to our bemused surprise?" Their main heuristic device (in the sense of a *conscious* strategy) is the dictionary of a language they do not speak, Russian, in a strange alphabet which they occasionally misread (гpex as *xpex); they turn the pages at random, not really *searching* for anything in particular, and to their bemused surprise, those pages keep turning up the hidden truth. Their bemused surprise is the proof of their objectivity—of their unbiased and unmotivated receptivity. The true meanings of the Wolf Man's dreams and descriptions *resonate* in their imaginations . . . but not telepathically. No taint, please, no whiff of the occult. Still, it's hard to avoid the impression (I can say this with bemused surprise, as if stumbling on the "impression" by accident) that they are as it were *channeling* the Wolf Man's true meanings. Those meanings are coming to them *from somewhere*. Not from the dictionary; through it. They flip through the pages of the Russian dictionary, and suddenly the truth emerges. From somewhere. They react with bemused surprise. The Russian words for walnut tree and sin/misdeed/crime sound similar: wow! Another one solved!

Freud was engaged in a similar process, and came up with a very different "truth": at the age of one and a half the Wolf Man had been sleeping in his parents' room, in bed with malaria, and had awakened to see mommy and daddy making love doggie-style; noticing that his mother had no penis he had fantasized that his father had cut it off; etc. The Oedipus complex. Imagine Freud's bemused surprise. "'If you want to be sexually satisfied by Father,' we may perhaps represent him as saying to himself, 'you must allow yourself to be castrated like Mother; but I won't have that.' In short, a clear protest on the part of his masculinity!" (Freud 234). Five or six years later, when his older sister seduced him and then terrified him with pictures from a book of fairy tales, in particular one picture of a wolf standing upright, his repressed traumatic memories of the primal scene in his parents' bedroom at one and a half were reactivated, transformed. Freud writes:

The dream [of the wolves] ended in a state of anxiety, from which he did not recover until he had his Nanya [the sister] with him. He fled, therefore, from his father to her. His anxiety was a repudiation of the wish for sexual satisfaction from his father—the trend which had put the dream into his head. The form taken by the anxiety, the fear of "being eaten by the wolf," was only the (as we shall hear, regressive) transposition of the wish to be copulated with by his father, that is, to be given sexual satisfaction in the same way as his mother. His last sexual aim, the passive attitude toward his father, succumbed to repression, and fear of his father appeared in its place in the shape of the wolf phobia. (232)

Freud translates the Wolf Man's source text into the Oedipus complex: little Sergei fantasizes incestuous sex with the father. The father himself is innocent of any incestuous desire for Sergei himself (or, one supposes, Sergei's sister). It's all in neurotic little Sergei's head. Poor dad.

What is the source of these channelings? From whence do these various truths, Freud's Oedipus complex and Abraham and Torok's witness to the father's rape of the big sister, emerge? The same problematic source text gives rise to both translations; they are contradictory translations; both translators claim that their own is accurate and other translations (the Wolf Man's own for Freud, Freud's for Abraham and Torok) are false and misleading. For Abraham and Torok, Freud mistranslates the Wolf Man's source text because his own Oedipal crypt resonates with the Wolf Man's; whereas their own analytical "ear cannot help but continue to resonate with chords of a dialogue," namely the *real* dialogue, the one that the Wolf Man actually overheard, the true meaning behind his source text, not just the crypt in which he stored it. A lot of resonating is going on, and in at least two different directions: the toddler Sergei witnessed daddy doing mommy doggie-style but daddy *never touched* either Sergei himself or big sister Nanya, and any hints along those lines must have been fantasized by the poor little neurotic Sergei (Freud); the toddler Sergei witnessed daddy raping big sister and told his governess about it, then overheard mommy denying his accusations to the governess (Abraham and Torok).

Now as a generation of recent psychoanalytic theorists has insisted—I want to say "shown," "proven"—Freud had good ideological reasons for shifting from his first "discovery" of incestuous seduction to his second "discovery" of the Oedipus complex. Daddy raped big sister? No way! As Marie Balmary writes of the "glacial" (95) reaction to Freud's May 1896 lecture before the Vienna Psychiatic Society, where he broached the idea of sexual trauma—an adult's seduction of a child—as the origin of hysteria, "Few acts are more odious to civilized men than this abuse by the adult of a child's 'innocence'—at least in principle" (103–4, translated by Ned Lukacher). But that last proviso, "at least in principle," suggests why one such act "more odious to civilized men than this abuse" has been, partly still is, certainly was in Freud's day, uncovering the abuse, publicizing it, opening the doors to the family closet and revealing to the world the skeletons hidden there. There are strong ideological sanctions against adults seducing children, but stronger ideological sanctions still against the exposure of such seductions to public scrutiny. And this latter task is the one to which Freud bends himself in the 1896 lecture:

Freud arranges the sexual traumas experienced by children who will become hysterics into three categories, according to the personality of the seducer: (1) a stranger: an adult outside the child's family; (2) an adult in the household: parent, servant, etc.; and (3) another child. This last category is, for Freud, only the consequence of the first two; he postulates in effect that "children cannot find their way to acts of sexual aggression unless they have been seduced previously" by an adult. However, two objections come to Freud's mind. He communicates them to us honestly. First, many adults who have not become hysterics remember sexual scenes during their childhood. So much for the individual.

Freud then considers the objection "that in the lower strata of the population hysteria is certainly no more common than in the highest ones, whereas everything goes to show that the injunction for the sexual safeguarding of children is far more frequently transgressed in the case of the children of the proletariat." So much for society. (Balmary 104)

Freud cannot quite bring himself at this point to answer these objections unambiguously; and by the end of the following summer, in 1897, he has renounced his theory of sexual trauma—the seduction theory—and developed the germ of the idea that would become the theory of the Oedipus complex, that the parents are innocent of incestuous desires or actions and the child fantasizes the seduction. "By the time we reach the [one-year] anniversary of Jacob's [Freud's father's] death, October

23, by which time the mourning for the father will be ended, Freud will have founded psychoanalysis—but he will have buried his discovery"—of seduction as the cause of neurosis (Balmary 133). Why? What drove him to this momentous change of course?

Surely the "glacial" reaction of his colleagues had something to do with it. He knew he was breaking deep-seated taboos here. And while he was (for a while) determined to persist in his investigations no matter how much ideological resistance he had to overcome, that resistance must have confirmed for him something that he felt all too strongly within himself: this line of reasoning is dangerous; terrible things will happen; back off and go another way before it's too late. Balmary's brilliant book is devoted to the uncovering of the private or personal source of this "feeling," Freud's own neurotic need to absolve his father from guilt in the matter of his second marriage to a woman named Rebecca, which had been kept a secret from the family. In the 24th chapter of Genesis Rebecca is chosen as wife for Isaac, and becomes the mother of Jacob (and Esau). In Jewish folklore, as reported by Robert Graves and Raphael Patai, she is at first rejected by Isaac's father Abraham because he suspects she is not a virgin—Rebecca was a Canaanite, and in Canaan fathers were allowed to sleep with their daughters before marriage. As Balmary's translator Ned Lukacher writes, "Is Rebecca a figure for the seduction theory that Freud, like Isaac, now rejects? Or is Freud, like Rebecca, himself rejected by an undefined Other? In any case, seduction and the faults of fathers are already inscribed within the Jewish tradition of the anecdote" (xiii–xiv). Freud writes to Fliess of this story on September 21, 1897; in the same letter he tells his good friend that he no longer believes in the seduction theory, mainly because it is highly unlikely that so many adults really seduced so many children, and because it's so hard to tell truth and fiction apart in his patients' stories. Three weeks later, on October 15, he writes to Fliess for the first time of Oedipus the King. Freud's own father Jacob, whose second marriage to a Rebecca had been kept secret from the members of the family he had with his third wife Amalie Nathanson, Sigmund's mother, has been dead almost exactly a year.

So Freud, as Balmary theorizes, has his own personal reasons—perhaps largely unconscious ones—for renouncing the seduction theory and the ten years of work that went into developing it, and propounding the theory of the Oedipus complex in its stead. These personal reasons are strongly supported—perhaps still unconsciously—by the dominant ideology in Freud's society, in both the general sense of turn-of-the-century Vienna and Austria and Europe and the specific sense of the Viennese Psychiatric Society, which responds glacially to

Freud's seduction theory. In Abraham and Torok's terms, one might call this the etiology of Freud's crypt: a personal taboo undergirded by powerful societal taboos, ideological injunctions. Balmary writes earlier, of the Anna O. case:

A little fact like this seems very important to us. On the one hand, it is the occasion and the very basis of the discovery as it was recounted to us. On the other hand, the adult who is the cause of all this is one of the people employed by the patient's parents. Her role in the origin of this symptom and the "fault" that she commits can be expressed, recognized, published.

One conjectures that this was not the case when the perpetrator of the fault was one of the patient's parents: that is, one of the people whom the patient held in respect ("honor your father and mother") and from whom, besides, the physician received his fees. Perhaps here science pays its tribute to the social inequalities of the time. A doctor who does research into one's mental life can indeed denounce the instructive misdeeds of the employees. Can he as freely testify against the employers by whom he is paid? (86)

Two ideological reasons, then, not to proceed with the seduction theory: a patriarchal one ("honor your father and mother") and a capitalistic one (don't bite the hand that feeds you). In Nietzsche's terms, both "reasons" would have to be considered the product of training in civilization: "'A thing is branded on the memory to make it stay there; only what goes on hurting will stick'" (192). As Nietzsche tells us a few pages later:

For an unconscionably long time culprits were not punished because they were felt to be responsible for their actions; not, that is, on the assumption that only the guilty were to be punished; rather, they were punished the way parents still punish their children, out of rage at some damage suffered, which the doer must pay for. Yet this rage was both moderated and modified by the notion that for every damage there could somehow be found an equivalent, by which that damage might be compensated—if necessary in the pain of the doer. To the question how did that ancient, deep-rooted, still firmly established notion of an equivalency between damage and pain arise, the answer is, briefly: it arose in the contractual relation between creditor and debtor, which is as old as the notion of "legal subject" itself and which in its turn points back to the basic practices of purchase, sale, barter, and trade. (195)

And again:

Let us ask once more: in what sense could pain constitute repayment of a debt? In the sense that to make someone suffer was a supreme pleasure. In exchange for the damage he had incurred, including his displeasure, the creditor received an extraordinary amount of pleasure; something which he prized the more highly the more it disaccorded with his social rank. . . . In both *Daybreak* and *Beyond Good and Evil* I have pointed to that progressive sublimation and apotheosis of cruelty which not only characterizes the whole history of higher culture, but in a sense constitutes it. Not so very long ago, a royal wedding or great public celebration would have been incomplete without executions, tortures, or *autos da fé*; a noble household without some person whose office it was to serve as a butt for everyone's malice and cruel teasing. [Today dysfunctional families designate a family member to serve that purpose, sometimes a spouse, more typically a child. See Bateson and Laing.] (Perhaps the reader will recall Don Quixote's sojourn at the court of the Duchess. *Don Quixote* leaves a bitter taste in our mouths today; we almost quail in reading it. This would have seemed very strange to Cervantes and his contemporaries, who read the work with the clearest conscience in the world, thought it the funniest of books, and almost died laughing over it.) To behold suffering gives pleasure, but to cause another to suffer affords an even greater pleasure. (197–98)

The "progressive sublimation and apotheosis of cruelty" constitutes the "higher culture" of the modern family as well: the abuse the child suffers at the hands of adults, physical, sexual, emotional, is sublimated/idealized/repressed as "love" and transferred in secret to the next generation. Freud's attempt to attribute neurosis to actual seduction and attendant psychic trauma, then, flouts and unmasks this sublimation and apotheosis—as for that matter did Nietzsche's genealogy of morals, which he accurately subtitled "an attack." And Freud's "discoveries" were heavily indebted to the iconoclasm of his older contemporary Nietzsche, twelve years Freud's senior. But Nietzsche went crazy; Freud became the venerated father of psychoanalysis, creator of a scientific method, a school of thought, an academic discipline, a clinical practice, a quasireligious dogma. And for many historians of psychoanalysis, beginning with Freud's English biographer Ernest Jones, the turning point in Freud's career, the event that enabled him to transform his Nietzschean iconoclasm into an orthodox establishment, was his renunciation of the seduction theory. The pain that reminded decent law-abiding adults of the taboos against revealing the prevalence of seduction in bourgeois families was evident in the bodies of his colleagues in the Viennese Psychiatric Society, in their glacial response— their pained attempt to freeze Freud's apostasy, to silence his attempt to speak the unspeakable. Freud, clearly, did not feel the ideological pain strongly enough to shun such dangerous lines of reasoning; they would have to add their own dose, increase his pain by whatever measure they could. The next fall his father died; that too added pain. A year later Freud renounced the seduction theory and developed a counterhypothesis that absolved adults of guilt and placed the burden squarely on the suffering backs of children—a thesis that still made adults feel uneasy, because it came so close to *naming* the "progressive sublimation and apotheosis of cruelty," but finally won their support and admiration because it also supported and justified that sublimation and that apotheosis.

We might paraphrase, then: when Freud seems to be translating or channeling (or in Abraham and Torok's terms "resonating with") the pain stored in the Wolf Man's crypt, he is actually channeling the ideological forces that prescribe the idealization of cruelty and inflict normative pain on offenders, deidealizers, iconoclasts. "Perhaps," Nietzsche speculates, "it is even legitimate to allow the possibility that pleasure in cruelty is not really extinct today; only, given our greater delicacy, that pleasure has had to undergo a certain sublimation and subtilization, to be translated into imaginative and psychological terms in order to pass muster before even the tenderest hypocritical conscience" (200). The seduction theory was frozen out because it revealed the continuing power of pleasure in cruelty. The Oedipus complex carried the day because it helped to sublimate (and psychologize) that pleasure by fantasizing that the victims of that cruelty themselves desired it.

But note what's happening here: like Balmary and Abraham and Torok, I'm presenting as "truth" the revisionist histories of psychoanalysis that have won expanding ideological support in the age of Alice Miller. It seems increasingly "obvious" to us today that Freud was right the first time. Older sisters do not seduce younger brothers unless they have first been seduced by a parent or other adult. Prepubescent children are not inherently "polymorphously perverse," and do not show signs of such perversion unless they have been perverted by the sexual predation of an adult. What *must* have happened in the Wolf Man's childhood is some sort of rape; the young Sergei must have been witness not to some perfectly ordinary sexual act between mother and father but to his father's rape of his sister. That is the only hypothesis that will explain the facts.

And these do seem to be "true" or "objective" or "factual" assumptions to me too. I believe them implicitly. I rail at parents who sue psychoanalysts who have supposedly "implanted" repressed incest memories in their patients (the plaintiffs' children) for clothing the repression of their own guilt in the garb of decency and justice. Abraham and Torok's "resonances" resonate powerfully in me as well.

But the fact that this seems so *painfully* obvious to us today does not mean that it is the truth—that we are now able to discern or "channel" this truth from the Wolf Man's childhood without the influence of powerful ideological forces. Indeed, what is "painfully obvious" to all right-thinking people is always the "knowledge" that is painfully constituted by ideology. This is precisely the effect that ideology is designed to create. It has taken several decades of tenacious argumentation and empirical evidence to bring about even the tentative shift in ideological norms that we see today, where an expanding segment of the population recognizes and condemns the prevalence of incestuous seduction in all social classes and only conservatives continue to cling to an earlier ideological norm that represses/idealizes parental cruelty as "love." Today, instead of feeling the parents' pain, we are increasingly taught to feel the child's pain, the victim's pain—to identify not with young Sergei's mother and father, as Freud did, but with Sergei himself, and with his sister, the abuse victim (as Abraham and Torok would have it) who transferred the father's abuse to her younger brother. From our vantage point it seems as if Freud's "courageous" postulation of the seduction theory in 1896 was the first shot fired in an ideological battle that has only brought something approaching victory in our own day. (Or perhaps the second shot; the first might well be Nietzsche's: "*Don Quixote* leaves a bitter taste in our mouths today; we almost quail in reading it.") His renunciation of that theory in favor of the Oedipus complex was a cowardly retreat into the reactionary camp that had received his infamous lecture "glacially"—both coldly and with ponderous inertia—in 1896.

Can it be a coincidence that Abraham and Torok "resonate" with this interpretation as well? Can we assume that they have now moved beyond Freud's ideological blockage and delved deep into the true underlying meaning of the Wolf Man's "source text"? The previous generation was hindered by ideological constraints; we can see that clearly now. We have moved past such things and perceive things as they really are. Never mind that those "things as they really are" coincide perfectly with current ideological norms.

Freud channels the Wolf Man. Abraham and Torok channel Freud and the Wolf Man. I channel Abraham and Torok, Freud, and the Wolf Man. Each of us claims access to the subject's crypt, the hidden place that is also a place of (mock-)death. To hear the voice from within the crypt is to channel, in some not-quite-mystical way, the speaking of the "spirit" playing dead inside it. Just who or what the "spirit" is, just what we are channeling ("reading," "understanding") when we think we are channeling a given author—and what it means to play dead— is the interesting question. To protect a damaged persona or self, or part-self, the subject "kills" it and buries it in a crypt. Can the "dead" self then speak from the crypt? Can anyone on the outside hear the speaking of that self?

And of course the skeptic's question: is there anything or anyone inside the crypt? If there is a body of some sort, can the body really speak, is it alive, or is it a lump of inert matter? Or is the crypt empty? And does the crypt itself exist? Could this whole crypt idea be just that, an idea, a fiction, a projection? And the upshot of all this: could spirit-channeling of all sorts, from the dead and the encrypted mock-dead, be the ventriloquized speaking of ideology? Collective forces in society want us, "channels" or the clients of channels, to hear and believe a certain message, so they "speak" through and apparently from crypts and other places of death, seeking to authenticate their ventriloquized messages by giving them a spiritualistic or psychologistic origin. Could this be all there is to it?

Heidegger's Crypt

And now let us return to sketch out some particularized answers to those questions in terms of what I want to suggest, following Abraham and Torok, are the most *cryptic* of Heidegger's remarks on translation. The passage is from his 1957 book on Leibniz, *Der Satz vom Grund,* which Reginald Lilly translated in 1991 as *The Principle of Ground,* but which also comes to mean, in Heidegger's punning progress through his argument, the sentence or proposition about ground and the leap up off the ground. These cryptic or encrypted remarks I want to contrast with his "posthumous" interview remarks on very much the same topics nine years later, in 1966, which were, according to his instructions, not published by *Der Spiegel* until after his death in 1976. What he encrypts in the Leibniz book in 1957, and generally in his entire life from his resignation from the chancellorship in 1934 (and even more so from the downfall of Nazism in 1944) till his death, he reveals, as it were, from beyond the grave—in an interview that can only speak after he is dead. Without pushing too hard on this perhaps farfetched idea that Heidegger would only allow himself to speak in public after his death, from beyond the grave, as a discarnate "spirit," channeled by the *Spiegel* interviewer, I do want to suggest that during his lifetime (after the disillusionment that led to his break with national socialism and his departure from the chancellorship) he did hide what he had to say about such dangerous topics as Germany's messianic destiny and divine redemption in a crypt such as Abraham and Torok find in the Wolf Man—and that he only allowed the partial opening of that crypt at his own death. (And due to the jealous vigilance of his son and executor Hermann Heidegger, that crypt is still not all the way open today, more than two decades later.)

Specifically, what I want to do here is to essay three different translations of the cryptic or encrypted *Satz vom Grund* remarks: one in the spirit of the *Spiegel* interview, one in the spirit of Hölderlin (and also of Abraham and Torok, unencrypting his cryptonymy), and one in the spirit of ideological analysis. Let me give the passage first in German, and comment briefly on some preliminary problems in it without translating:

Was in unserer Sprache gesprochen "Grundsatz vom Grunde" heißt, ist die verkürzte Übersetzung des Titels principium reddendae rationis sufficientis. Grund ist die Übersetzung von ratio. Solches festzustellen, dürfte sich inzwischen erübrigt haben. Außerdem ist die Feststellung ein Gemeinplatz, und zwar so lange, als wir uns darüber keine Gedanken machen, was es im vorliegenden Fall und in ähnlichen Fällen mit der Übersetzung auf sich hat. Übersetzen und Übersetzen ist nicht das gleiche, wenn es sich hier um einen Geschäftsbrief handelt und dort um ein Gedicht. Jener ist übersetzbar, dieses nicht. Inzwischen hat die moderne Technik, genauer gesagt die wahlverwandte moderne logistische Auslegung des Denkens und Sprechens, bereits Übersetzungsmaschinen in Gang gesetzt. Beim Übersetzen handelt es sich aber nicht darum, was jeweils, sondern aus welcher Sprache in welche Sprache übersetzt wird. Das jetzt Vermerkte betrifft indes Verhältnisse des Übersetzens, die sich bei einiger Kenntnis und geringem Nachdenken leicht überschauen lassen. Gleichwohl können wir dabei immer noch einen entscheidenden Zug verfehlen, der alle wesentlichen Übersetzungen durchzieht. Damit meinen wir solche Übersetzungen, die in Epochen, da es an der Zeit ist, ein Werk des Dichtens oder des Denkens übertragen. Der gedachte Zug besteht darin, daß die Übersetzung in solchen Fällen nicht nur Auslegung, sondern Überlieferung ist. Als Überlieferung gehört sie in die innerste Bewegung der Geschichte. Nach früher Bemerktem heißt dies: Eine wesentliche Übersetzung entspricht jeweils in einer Epoche des Seinsgeschickes der Weise, wie im Geschick des Seins eine Sprache spricht. (163–64)

What do we do with this? Do we go through it like composition teachers, writing "vague," "unclear," "restate," "expand," "unpack," "awk," and "what do you mean by this?" in the margins and between the lines? It is, without doubt, astonishingly vague writing. What *are* the important source and target languages that make such a big difference? What difference *do* they make? What *are* the epochs in which it is timely, and what does it mean to be timely? What does it mean for translation to be tradition, and how does this relate to the impossibility of translating poetry and philosophy?

But none of this, it should be obvious, is the vagueness of the beginning writer, unused to thinking through the implications of his or her words. There is something else here, some blockage, some protective enclosure, which I want to call a crypt. Why can't Heidegger just come clean and say what he means? We want to know more; we want to reach out to his text, reach *through* the text to the thinker behind it; but the thinker isn't there, he's dead and buried; and even before his death, I'm suggesting, his meaning was buried or encrypted though not necessarily truly dead. Our trick, clearly, will have to be to channel his spirit from out of that crypt so as to determine just what he's trying to say.

First Translation

As a first stab at that channeling, not (yet) having access to the discarnate spirit of Heidegger himself, deferring the moment at which Heidegger's spirit might be imagined to speak to us from out of the crypt, let me try a "pedagogical" translation that will stand in roughly the same relation to a Hölderlinian/Heideggerian rendition as the *Spiegel* interview does to the *Satz vom Grund* passage—a relation of apparent clarity. In fact, in this section I want to begin to explore some of the unstated undercurrents in the *Satz vom Grund* passage by juxtaposing it with a lengthy quote from the *Spiegel* interview, positing that "posthumous" speaking of Heidegger as the crypt into which he cast his cryptic remarks from 1957. Here is translation number one:

The German phrase *Grundsatz vom Grunde* or, literally, ground-sentence of/ from the ground, is a condensed translation of the concept *principium reddendae rationis sufficientis*. This may go without saying; it is in any case a truism, and will remain one so long as we pay no attention to what's going on in this translation and others like it.

There is translation and there is translation: of a business letter, say, on the one hand, of a poem on the other. The one is translatable, the other is not. Between the two modern technology, which is the mechanization of thinking and speaking around the elective affinities of logic, has already set translation machines in motion. Nor is translation ever sheer event, something someone does at some specific time to some text; its essence varies significantly depending upon what languages one translates out of and into. This variation has an obvious bearing upon the conditions of translation, which require only a little knowledge and reflection to be theorized. In the same way we can all too easily miss yet another crucial feature that pervades all essential translation. There are translations that, in periods ripe for it, carry a work of poetry or thought forward, pass it on. In cases like these the translation is not merely a making-plain but a handing-down—not just the interpretation of a text but the generation of

tradition. In so doing essential translation becomes part of the innermost movement of history, assuming significance by responding in a given period of the
destiny of being to the way that destiny is spoken by language.

This answers some questions—largely at the expense of Heidegger's
own principles of translation—but far from all. What, for example,
makes a business letter translatable? What makes a poem untranslatable? In what sense does machine translation operate "between" the
two? My "sheer event, something someone does at some specific time to
some text" is a rather bold unpacking of a single word, *jeweils*, one of
Heidegger's favorites, meaning literally something like "at times"; a
close rendition of the phrase in which it appears might be "By translation handles it itself but not only about that, what at times, but . . . ." I'm
far from confident that I've gotten the gist of that *jeweils* here, but even if
I have, that still doesn't explain what "sheer event" means, or even
what its parenthetical explication means, "something someone does at
some specific time to some text." Translation "handles itself about" or
deals with or entails something else, something beyond "sheer event,"
beyond the *jeweils*—but what? It's a surface-structure/deep-structure
distinction of some sort, "sheer event" or "at times" on the surface, "essence" down below; but what are the events or the times, what is the essence? Heidegger's not saying. Again, what are the important crucial
languages to translate into and out of, and what difference does that
make? I assume that he means from Greek and into German, but he's
not saying that here either; and why not? Is it a secret? What is the "obvious bearing" this "variation" has on the "conditions of translation"?
What are those conditions? What kind of knowledge (little, but still
mysterious) is required to theorize them? What sort of theorizing will
result, and why haven't you done it? (Or is this it? If so, why is it so
cryptic?) What exactly is "essential translation"? What is its essence?
Presumably it is what lies "below" or "above" or "beyond" sheer event,
what at times, once one has made the leap up off the ground; but what
is the essential nature of this idealized form of translation Heidegger is
hinting at here? Is it translation of "essential" works (and what are
they? what is their essence?), or powerful or influential translations of
works that become "essential" through translation, or a process of inter-
cultural and intertemporal transmission that is "essential" in its own
right, apart from the *jeweils* of actual renditions of philosophical and literary works, or some combination of the three? What would be some
examples of translations that carry a work forward, and of periods that
are ripe for that carrying? I'm assuming he means translations like

Hölderlin's of Sophocles, although it's debatable whether the romantic period was "ripe" for those translations; ripe for their making, perhaps, not so ripe for their reception (Goethe, Hegel, and Schelling just tisked their tongues at poor Friedrich's madness) and the handing-down of tradition. But is reception important to tradition? Just what kind of ripeness are we talking about here? And what does it mean to hand something down? To whom is the significant translation handed down?

To these questions the *Spiegel* interview offers some tentative answers. In the passage I want to quote, the interviewer has just read aloud one of Heidegger's remarks about the "historical destiny of the Germans" (62) and asked him to comment:

HEIDEGGER: I could put what is said in the quotation this way: I am convinced that a change can only be prepared from the same place in the world where the modern technological world originated. It cannot come about by the adoption of Zen Buddhism or other Eastern experiences of the world. The help of the European tradition and a new appropriation of that tradition are needed for a change in thinking. Thinking will only be transformed by a thinking that has the same origin and destiny.

SPIEGEL: At exactly the spot where the technological world originated, it must, you think . . .

HEIDEGGER: . . . be transcended [*aufgehoben*] in the Hegelian sense, not removed, transcended, but not by human beings alone.

SPIEGEL: Do you allocate a special task specifically to the Germans?

HEIDEGGER: Yes, in that sense, in dialogue with Hölderlin.

SPIEGEL: Do you think that the Germans have a specific qualification for this change?

HEIDEGGER: I am thinking of the special inner relationship between the German language and the language and thinking of the Greeks. This has been confirmed to me again and again today by the French. When they begin to think they speak German. They insist that they could not get through with their own language.

SPIEGEL: Is that how you would explain the very strong effect you have had in the Romance countries, particularly in France?

HEIDEGGER: Because they see that they cannot get through today's world with all their rationality when they are attempting to understand it in the origin of its essence. Thinking can be translated as little as poetry can. At best it can be paraphrased. As soon as a literal translation is attempted, everything is transformed.

SPIEGEL: A disquieting thought.

HEIDEGGER: It would be good if this disquiet would be taken seriously on a large scale and if it would finally be considered what a momentous transformation Greek thinking suffered when it was translated into Roman Latin, an event that still bars our way today to sufficient reflection on the fundamental words of Greek thinking.

SPIEGEL: Professor, we would actually always optimistically assume that something can be communicated and even translated, because if this optimism that contents of thinking can be communicated despite language barriers ceases, then provincialism threatens.

HEIDEGGER: Would you call Greek thinking provincial in contrast to the mode of ideas of the Roman Empire? Business letters can be translated into all languages. The sciences (today *science* already means the natural sciences, with mathematical physics as the basic science) can be translated into all the world's languages. Put more correctly, they are not translated, but rather the same mathematical language is spoken. We are touching here on an area that is broad and hard to cover. (62–64)

Hard to cover in an interview, perhaps. Considering that in those last lines he is essentially just summarizing Friedrich Schleiermacher's remarks on what he idiosyncratically calls in the lecture on the different methods of translating *Dolmetschen*, or commercial and technical translation—that it is under the aegis of object and number and therefore not language-related, therefore not really translation at all—it's hard to imagine that this "area" should be hard for Heidegger to cover *in general*. Something makes it hard for him to cover. But surely not its broadness. Something, rather, related to the "disquiet" that he champions just above.

The most pressing question to ask about this passage, however, concerns the utopian alternative that he associates with the "historical destiny of the Germans." Just what is this future state that he keeps imagining and hiding from his readers? Is it the coming of the Messiah, certainly no longer Hitler, probably not Jesus either, but some other divine savior, some Greek god? Is it wholesale human submission to the speaking of the god, or of language, or of Being? Is it universal nympholepsy, necromancy, or, better, *enthousiasmos*, surrender not just to the speaking but to the being of the god? In chapter two we saw Socrates likened, and likening himself, to the mystical nympholept or enthusiast, possessed by the god, channeling the speaking and the spirit of the god; but Socrates was also an emergent rationalist, cofounder with

Plato and Aristotle of the mathematical turn that Heidegger deplored, conjurer-up and conjurer-away (*apodiopomp*) of the spirits of the dead. So if we need a Socratic model for Heidegger's ideal human, surely we should look at the mystical Socrates, Socrates the *enthousiontes*, rather than the rationalist one? Heideggerians have spent so many years defending the master against charges of mysticism that they won't like that question, but as Heidegger himself would say, the question sort of asks itself, lets itself be asked, *läßt sich gefragt werden*. Certainly Heidegger adamantly opposes his vision to the rationalism of the Romans, the French, and modern technology; is it going too far to associate it with divination, such as the ancient Greeks might have practiced before reason had made much headway against it? It does seem to me as if Heidegger is imagining an occult battle between spiritual forces here: when the interviewer begins "At exactly the spot where the technological world originated, it must, you think . . . ," Heidegger finishes, ". . . be transcended in the Hegelian sense, not removed, transcended, but not by human beings alone." By whom else, then? Implicit in this formulation seems to be some sort of psychic or supernatural (as opposed to technological) time travel back to the origins of "the technological world" where, with the help of non- or possibly superhuman spirits, that world will be transcended, sublated, simultaneously annihilated and transmuted into a higher, nobler, more utopian form. Earlier in the interview Heidegger says, now famously, "Only a god can still save us" (57). And: "I think the only possibility of salvation left to us is to prepare readiness, through thinking and poetry, for the appearance of the god or for the absence of the god during the decline; so that we do not, simply put, die meaningless deaths, but that when we decline, we decline in the face of the absent god" (57).

Heidegger is not much more forthcoming on translation in the *Spiegel* interview than he is in *Der Satz vom Grund:* "Thinking can be translated as little as poetry can," "That [a business letter] can be translated, this [a poem] not." In both places Heidegger thus forswears one of his own most powerful philosophical methods, radical translation from the Greek; does he thereby forswear also the power of his own philosophy, his own philosophical thinking as Greek-German spirit-channeling, to move us toward the utopia he awaits? Or does he mean, as I began to suggest early on in the chapter, that only *human* translation is betrayal—that essential translation only becomes possible, and thus salvific, when it is done by the god, the spirit, and only channeled by the human translator? As we saw in chapter two, Augustine, to whose Catholic Church Heidegger first wanted to devote his life, and to whose vision of the future he pretended to convert again in the aftermath of his nervous breakdown in late 1945, did believe this very thing. All we humans can do now is hunker down and wait, using thinking and thickening (writing poetry, poeming), *Denken und Dichten*, to lend our decline some proleptic meaning, some anticipated connection with the absent god or world-historical higher self that we long to channel. And yet the Germans retain, for Heidegger, a historical destiny; could it be that the god is the higher self not of Hitler nor of Heidegger, but of the German people, the German language, a Benjaminian "intention" that will come out of the intermingling of German with Greek (see Benjamin's "Task" and my reading of it in *Taboo* [200–9])? Could this be the "Germans'" destiny, that their higher self will become the ghostly redeemer god whom all nature awaits? And will that god come as the channeled spirit of a Greek-into-German translation?

It is significant, I think, that, little as Heidegger is willing to say in this interview, it is far more than he ever said while alive (if, again, you'll allow me my conceit of Heidegger speaking from beyond the grave. For I think it must have been Heidegger's conceit as well; else why insist on posthumous publication?). He maintains his terrible silence about the Nazi era and his own involvement in it, that silence that Heidegger's followers and detractors alike have wondered at for decades, and takes it with him to his grave; but he so arranges it that his ~~ghost~~ can say at least some of the things he never allowed his living human self to say while still alive.

(Since I seem to be unable to avoid [*vermeiden*] this conceit of *Der Spiegel* channeling Heidegger's discarnate spirit or ghost, the least I can do is place a Heideggerian *kreuzweise Durchstreichung* or strikeover on top of it, so that you can imagine that I didn't say it. Actually, not a *kreuzweise* or "cross-wise" one; my computer is too technological to make the sign of the cross over Heidegger's ghost. It will only draw a single line through the word. You'll have to imagine, along with my avoidance of the theme, the cross as well. On Heidegger's *vermeiden* of *Geist* or spirit and the *kreuzweise Durchstreichung*, see Derrida *Of Spirit* 1–2.)

Must we then say that, like "spirit-channeled" translations in the Judeo-Christian tradition—the Septuagint, the Vulgate—the *Spiegel* interview is truer, more original, than the "original" remarks on translation in *Der Satz vom Grund*? In Heidegger's own terms, is it an *Überlieferung* or "overrunning," or what we would call more colloquially a "handing over" or "handing down," or tradition? Why or why not? If it is, who is the messenger that runs over, and from which camp to which other camp does s/he run, and are the message and the errand itself authorized (making the messenger an envoy) or unauthorized (making him or her a traitor, an *Überläufer*)? And what if anything does that overrunning have to do with spirit-channeling? Would a spirit-channeled overrunning be tradition, a non-spirit-channeled over-runner be a *traditor* or traitor?

One important key to this (post)romantic conception of translation is that it is simultaneously *primitive* and *progressive*—what Pierre Bourdieu, in his book on Heidegger, trenchantly calls "revolutionary conservatism." It is grounded simultaneously in the recovery of something lost in the past and in the incorporation of that recovered something into a messianic move toward a radically transformed future. As I began to suggest earlier in the chapter, in connection with Andrew Benjamin's reading of Heidegger on translation, in romantic and post-romantic translation theory this fetish of the progressive/primitive finds its strongest expression in the close links between the Greek and German languages, Greek and German culture. Everything Greek, especially *ancient* Greek, prerationalist Greek, is wonderful not only because it is so primitive, but because it is so proto-German; the wonderful thing about German for the romantics is that it is the only language in the history of the world that is close enough to the primitivism of Greek to be able to translate it without loss. For Heidegger, as for his romantic forebears, the German language can become the vehicle of a universal utopian future only by channeling/translating, with radical primitivism, the truest spirit of the ancient Greeks into it.

In an interesting *PMLA* article on Heidegger and translation, Nicholas Rand (who was also the English translator of Abraham and Torok) underscores the cultural imperialism implicit in Heidegger's insistence that the German language is not only the *best* target language for the Greeks but the *only* target language, the only language that can bring Greek thought out of the darkness into which the Romans translated it—indeed that in some sense the German language was there *before* the Greek, in embryo, in spirit, like the Jesus of John's Gospel, belatedly first, creating the very possibility of a utopian primitivism. In *Of Spirit* Jacques Derrida lets trickles of his hurt and anger seep out at the ~~ghostly~~ Heidegger of the *Spiegel* interview, who makes the classic (so predictable as to be virtually kneejerk) nationalistic claim of the German romantics most baldly: "I am thinking of the special inner relationship between the German language and the language and thinking of the Greeks. This has been confirmed to me again and again today by the French. When they begin to think they speak German. They insist that they could not get through with their own language" (63). Here is Derrida, as translated by Geoffrey Bennington and Rachel Bowlby:

One imagines the scene of these confidences, or rather of this "confirmation." Heidegger certainly did not make it up: "they" go to complain about their language to the master and, one supposes, in the master's language. In its abyssal depth, this declaration is not necessarily without truth—it even becomes a truism if one accepts a fundamental axiomatics according to which the meaning of *Geist, Denken, Sein,* and a few other words cannot be translated and so can be thought only in German, even if one is French. What else can one say and think in German? But the dogmatic assurance, aggravated by the discourteous tone of a declaration which is literally invasive, as much in what it says as in what it shows, would in itself be enough to raise certain doubts about it. The insolence is not even provocative; it is half asleep in tautology. (70)

And he goes on to add that the rabid nationalist Fichte said some similar things in *Speeches to the German Nation,* to the effect that everyone who thinks and desires progress toward a spiritual utopia is German, no matter what country he's from or what language he speaks, and even Germans who don't think, don't desire those things, are foreigners. Contempt for the French is of course one of the recurrent themes of romantic Germany—due partly at the time, of course, to resentment at Napoleon's invasion and occupation and rapid modernization of Germany. But German romantic francophobia starts long before 1806, decades before Napoleon, or even the French Revolution, and survives well into the twentieth century. Derrida catches the tail end of a long German tradition that berates a particular foreign culture for being so inhospitable to the foreign: an antiethnocentric ethnocentricity, as it were, an impassioned defense of domestic assimilationism against foreign assimilationism *in the name of* the foreign. (For the unexpected survival of that German romantic (anti)ethnocentricity in recent French thought on translation, see Berman; also my discussion of Berman in chapter 8 of *What Is Translation?*)

Hölderlin became Heidegger's strongest romantic forebear through his radical germanizings of Sophocles, which provided Heidegger with one of his most powerful philosophical tools: push the Greek word as far back as it can go, in terms not only of its Greek etymology but of its "hidden" and therefore "primordial" connections with or anticipations of German as well; then claim that the German translation has "uncovered" or "unforgotten"—or, as I'm saying here, *channeled*—the true original meaning of the Greek; then finally admit with a certain sadness (because one *loves* the Greeks!) that even the Greeks themselves could never quite attain the lexical insight of the German language, which has through translation transformed itself into the "lost origin" of Greek. German is the Logos, another Greek word that can only truly be understood through the German *Wort;* German is the Alpha and the Omega, the beginning and the end: present at the creation, it is God's messianic tool for the total transformation of humanity in the imminent apocalypse.

The interesting begged question here for Heidegger: why the Greeks? The *Spiegel* interviewer's question to which Heidegger's remark about the French and "thinking" in German is an "obvious" response is "Do you think that the Germans have a specific qualification for this change?" The Germans alone were there at the beginning with the Greeks; the Germans alone channel the Greek spirit; hence all true thinking is German, and the French have to speak German in order to think. Heidegger thinks thinking, and suddenly the Greeks are there. Why? Because his romantic forebears at the turn of the nineteenth century all idolized the Greeks? Because the European Renaissance recreated ancient Greece and Rome as the "origins" of European civilization (and Heidegger has been coached by the romantics through Nietzsche to despise the Romans)? Because Cicero and Seneca and Horace and the other major Roman voices, whom the Renaissance revered, in turn revered the Greeks? For Heidegger, as for Herder and the Schlegel brothers and a host of his other influential precursors, the Greeks are a kind of collective spirit-guide or spiritual higher self to the Germans; to think *is* to channel the Greeks. They open themselves up to the speaking of language out of the destiny of Being, and what speaks through them is Greek—and, of course, also German, since they are channeling the Greeks *in* German. Translation as overrunning or handing-down/over is quintessentially a speaking of Greek in German.

Second Translation

Now let me try another tack, a Heidegger-approved Hölderlinian approach, an attempt to channel the spirits of the ancient speakers of our two languages, German and English for Heidegger and me, Greek and German for Sophocles and Hölderlin, from a primitive time when the now-encrypted etymologies of those languages were open, when now-dead metaphors like *übersetzen* (to translate by "setting something over in another place") were still alive. Thus:

What spoken in our speech hests "ground leap from the ground" is the curted oversetting of the title principium reddendae rationis sufficientis. Ground is the oversetting from ratio. To put such fast might have leftovered itself inbetween. Outer that this fastputting is a commonplace, and square so long as we make no bethinking over what it has upon itself with the oversetting in the forelying fall and in e'enlike falls. Oversetting and oversetting is not the like, when it handles itself here around a shafted brief and there around a thickened. That is oversettable, this not. Inbetween modern technics, nearlier spoken the wale-bewended modern logistic outlaying of thinking and speaking, has already set oversetting machines in going. But with oversetting it handles itself not only around what everwhile, but rather out of which speech in which speech it is overset. The now marked meanwhile bedrapes holdbacknesses of oversetting, which, by some kenning and paltry afterthinking, let themselves lightly be overviewed. Likewise we can thereby miss always yet one unschizzed pull that pulls through all staying oversetting. Therewith we mean such oversetting that, in epochs where it is to the time, overcarry a work of thickening or of thinking. The bethought pull bestands therein that the oversetting in such a case is not only outlaying but also overrunning. As overrunning she belongs in the innerest bewaying of as-sentness. After the earlier remarked this hests: A staying oversetting unspeaks everwhile in an epoch of the being-send of the wise how in the send of being a speech speaks.

It would not be difficult to unfold this translation at book length, as Heidegger did with the Leibniz passage in *Der Satz vom Grund;* maybe some day I'll write that book, which I could call "Translating(,) Heidegger's Crypt." For present purposes, however, it may be enough to unfold just a few key words and phrases from the beginning: "curted oversetting," "to put such fast might have leftovered itself inbetween," "square so long," and "forelying fall."

Curted oversetting (verkürtzte Übersetzung). The verb "to curt," meaning to shorten, is obsolete in English these days; I found it, to my bemused surprise, in the *OED.* The advantage we gain from its use in place of "shortened" or "condensed" (as I had it in the first translation, above) is that the adjective "curt" in modern English has the added connotation of *too* short, rudely so. "To curt" would then be to shorten one's speech *too much,* say too little, in a rude or hurtful way. The *"curted oversetting" der Satz vom Grund = principium reddendae rationis sufficientis,* then, problematically inscribes Heidegger's silence: the book *Der Satz vom Grund,* after all, and even this one passage from it, is a discurted or deforeshortened translation of that title, a lengthening of the curt or taciturn translation. But it lengthens that translation repressively, or cryptically. It adds length to the shortened without speaking the unspeakable. What remains "curt" in Heidegger's discurted or discursive translation marks the encrypted, that which remains in the crypt.

To translate in German, *über-setzen,* is to set something over in another place. One imagines the Greek table and the German table. See that book lying over there on the Greek table? The Ὀδυσσεια? I'm picking it up. I'm moving it. I'm carrying it across (the sense of Latin *transferre,* English

translation). I'm setting it over here on the German table. Now it's here.
Now it's German. Now it's the *Odysseia*, full of German words. A process that seems a bit on the mechanical side, maybe, which is almost
certainly why Heidegger keeps wanting to push *Übersetzung* toward
Überlieferung, oversetting toward overrunning. Running seems so much
more vital and masculine, therefore "essential," than setting.

Indeed *Übersetzung* has its technological senses too. *Eine Übersetzung*
is also a gearing or a transmission; *übersetzen* is to gear. (*Die kleine
Übersetzung* is the bottom gear, *die größte Übersetzung* is the top gear.
My favorite, because it sounds like Schleiermacher's injunctions
against "going doubled like a ghost," which I'll be discussing again in
chapter four below: *eine doppelte Übersetzung*. Sounds like a doubled
translation, but means a two-speed gear: a bit of a letdown.) The punning German aphorism that George Steiner quotes, *Wer übersetzt, untersetzt*, which I once tried to translate "Who translates, sublates," in a
sense-for-sense rendition would go something like "Whoever translates intermixes." Boring. *Untersetzen* is literally to set or place under-
neath; hence in mechanics to gear down. Who gears, gears down. An
Untersatz is a saucer or a placemat at dinner, a support, base, stand in
technology—shades of the Heideggerian *Gestell*, which I'll return to
under the *Festsellung* just below. Adjectivally *untersetzt* is stocky,
square-built, thick-set, squat (see *zwar*, below). Who oversets, under-
sets. Who sets something over, sets it under. *Der Untersatz vom Grund*.
Ratio as gear ratio. The mechanization of reason.

Like "over" in English, *über* in German signifies both "across" and
"above"—including "too much." Static or dynamic vertical or horizontal difference. *Übersetzung*/oversetting as both translation and transmission would be dynamic horizontal difference. The translation of
languages, learning, or empire; the transmission of ideas or torque. In
the aphoristic pun *Wer übersetzt, untersetzt*, the over/under contrast
pushes *Übersetzung*/oversetting in the direction of vertical hierarchies.
Who sets above, sets below. The first shall be last.

In collocation with *curted*, however, *über*'s sense of excess emerges.
Überarbeiten is to overwork, or to work overtime; *überbelasten* is to overload; *überbelichten* is to overexpose (a photo); *überbewerten* is to over-
value or overestimate; *überbürden*, unsurprisingly, is to overburden;
übersetzen, then, in this context, is to overset, as in printing: to set up too
much type (*OED*, sense 12). "Curted" is too little; "oversetting" is too
much. Clearly for Heidegger the phrase *Der Satz vom Grund* is too short
a translation for *principium reddendae rationis sufficientis*; it says too little. The morphological symmetry I'm exploring here would suggest
that the book *Der Satz vom Grund* would then be too long a transla-

tion—but one, I'm suggesting, that still says too little. (In a moment we'll be looking at another *über, sich erübrigen,* which Heidegger sets in the [excluded] middle between too much and too little.)

Most of the first eleven senses given in the *OED* for "overset" as a verb deal with oppression and overthrow (all of them marked obsolete except 5 and 6, which are marked rare): (1) to oppress (2) to overcome, overthrow, overwhelm, overpower by force or violence (3) to overturn, upset, tip over (4) "to upset or subvert the order or condition of (an institution, state, or the like); to cause to fall into confusion," and figuratively, "to overturn the normal mental or physical condition of (a person); to overcome mentally or physically; to discompose, disorder, 'upset' (the stomach, etc.)" (5) to set a piece of clothing with ornaments (6) to postpone, put off (7) to impose, burden someone with (8) to overcharge, overassess, overload (9) to get over or past something (10) to get over or recover from an illness (11) various related but uncertain uses. (12), you'll recall from the previous paragraph, was to set too much type in a printing shop—a sense that was apparently still current in English when the *OED* was made. (My 1983 edition of the *Webster's New Unabridged International Dictionary* still gives (1) overcome/upset (2) overturn/overthrow, and (3) set too much type without marking any of them obsolete or rare; but in 1997 as I write these words no one "sets" type any more, and I wonder about the currency of those other definitions as well.)

All of these senses to me seem germane here, both to the effect that the revolutionary conservative Heidegger sought to have on his readers and to the effect that the events in Germany in the period from his resignation from the chancellorship in 1934 to his nervous breakdown in 1945 had on Heidegger. To overset is transitively to have the effect that generates the crypt; intransitively it is to suffer that effect, to be tumbling without bearings, to *need* a crypt in order to survive.

To put such fast might have leftovered itself inbetween (*Solches festzustellen, dürfte sich inzwischen erübrigt haben*). In other words, one might think there's nothing more to say about this than the "curted oversetting" or shortened or condensed translation of the title. Obviously, Heidegger doesn't believe this or he wouldn't write a whole book unfolding that fastputting or "comment, statement, observation" (in the sense of determining or establishing a thing). *Sich erübrigt* is the participial form of the reflexive verb *sich erübrigen* "to be superfluous, unnecessary, pointless, useless"; thus, it might have been unnecessary to make such a remark (as "ground is the translation of *ratio*").

But *erübrigen* has within it that root *über* "over," clearly a crucial adverb in this context of *übersetzen* "to translate," *übertragen* "to transpose," and *überliefern* "to deliver, to hand/run over" In all of these other *über*s Heidegger is talking about a crossing, a going-over from one side to the other, from one language or culture to another, from the past to the present (generating tradition); he also has an *überschauen* "look over, overview," where the *über* has the sense of "from above," an effect presumably to be achieved through the leap up off the ground. In *sich inzwischen erübrigt*, however, he's talking about an excluded middle, something "left over" in between, after sides have been chosen, something between Greek and German, perhaps, or between past and present.

Inzwischen appears once again a few lines down, in the context of the ground marked off by machine translation, which is "set in motion" in the excluded middle between the translation of business correspondence and the translation of poetry. I'm not quite sure what he means by the inbetween in this latter context: is he really trying to say that machine translation operates in the middle ground between commercial and literary translation? Or, since the *inzwischen* immediately follows the phrase *Jener ist übersetzbar, dieses nicht,* does he mean that machine translation operates in the middle ground between the translatable and the untranslatable? In any case, Heidegger seems to be building a telling lexical and argumentative bridge from machine translation to the *Feststellung* that nonthinkers have dismissed as a commonplace and Heidegger wants to unfold into *Dichten und Denken,* poeming and thinking.

In fact, note that *feststellen* is also to lock something down, make it secure, and a *Feststellung* is a locking device, or the process of locking something down tight, securing it. A technological process. The excluded middle or "leftover" caught in between in both cases or falls (for *falls* see below) is at least potentially technological. Heidegger's favorite word for technology was the *Gestell,* which contains the same transitive verb *stellen* "to put" as *Feststellung; Gestell* is usually translated in *feststellenden* or fastputting Heideggerian texts as "en-framing," outside of Heidegger as stand, rack, frame, framework, support, trestle, horse, mount, pedestal, holder, chassis, bedstead, crucible. Clearly, in a cryptonymic translation the phantomatic psychological crypt would also be a *Gestell* in this technological sense. We might formulate it as an onto-logical definition:

"To put such fast" i̶s̶ to secure it or lock it up tight in a crypt.

(Imagine that "is" thought in German as *heißt* [which I gave above as "hests," archaically meaning promises, commands, grants] but crossed out by Heidegger—alas, again, linearly, not cross-wise.)

Heidegger, of course, didn't like either technology or psychology;

the latter for him *was* a technological process. His conservative/anti-modernist "dislike" for both would thus help him repress the ways in which the *Feststellung* that he claims *not* to want to "leave over," render superfluous, let go without saying, is also a locking down of the things he *doesn't want to say* in technological/psychological wise.

Square (zwar). *Zwar* is usually translated idiomatically into English as "indeed, certainly, to be sure, of course, I admit," typically in the comparative or argumentative context of "on the one hand . . . on the other": *er ist zwar alt, aber noch sehr rüstig* "sure, he's old, but he's still very active." It's a way of admitting that your opponent's point is valid, but only within certain contextual constraints, which *you* will define; a way of surrendering (*überliefern*) the battle but still trying to win the war. Heidegger is saying, sure, it's a commonplace to say that *Grund* is a translation of Leibniz's Latin *ratio,* but only if you don't think about it. You can accuse me of mouthing trite cliches, belaboring the obvious, wallowing in the trivially true; but you're only right if we agree *not to think*—and I don't. So there. *Zwar* is a kind of verbal trump card.

"Square" in English may not be derived from the same Teutonic root as *zwar*—it comes from Old French *esquire, esquierre, esquare,* meaning the quite technological tool (still called a square in modern English) used for determining right angles—but it has also been written skvar, skwar, swar, suar, and suare in English, and in its adverbial use it means steadily, copiously, fairly, honestly, straightforwardly, solidly, without reserve, properly. This is all obviously very close to the "to be sure" adverbial use of *zwar* in German—except without the adversarial qualification. No qualifications at all: just plain squarely, straightforwardly, frankly, honestly. No hedging, no fudging; the plain truth. This is what Heidegger claims to be after in this passage, and this book, and in his work in general; but there is so much he isn't saying, so much that he must pass over in uneasy repressive silence, so much that he must encrypt, that the tendentious quality of *zwar* in comparison with the unreserved or uncryptic straightforwardness of "square(ly)" begins to seem quite revealing. "Square" is everything that Heidegger wants to be here but can't quite bring himself to be.

("Square" in English also goes nicely, if complexly for the intensely chauvinistic Heidegger, with *Gemeinplatz* "commonplace" two words earlier, bringing to mind Spanish plazas, Italian piazzas, and American shopping malls, all of which, presumably, would make good Heideggerian demonized synonyms for commonplace, marketplace, Latin, English, all other languages except ancient Greek and German, technology, psychology, etc. If being "square" with someone is homonymous [because homophonic] with going shopping at a common marketplace

like Evergreen Square, a shopping mall a few miles from where I used
to live, the location of the nearest Best Buy, where I bought all my computer stuff, then that particular kind of "openness" or "honesty" or
"straightforwardness" is as inessential, *wesenlos*, inauthentic, *uneigent-
lich*, as the shopping malls. For a discussion of Heidegger's *deweseniz-
ing* of unpleasant realities, see Caputo, frequently.)

In fact, this single word *zwar* seems to be a proform in Heidegger's
sentence, referring verblessly to a possible future (I translated it "will
remain one" in the "pedagogical" version) in which the important
things do ~~not~~ get said steadily, copiously, fairly, honestly, straightforwardly, solidly, without reserve, properly, because *someone* is ~~not~~ making a bethinking about them—or, to run that the other way, because ~~no~~
one has a reserve or a crypt somewhere that ~~un~~blocks a possible future
of straightforward honesty.

Forelying (vorliegenden). Usually translated into academic English as
"above" or "above-mentioned," and in certain other Heideggerian contexts as "independently existing," *vorliegend* means literally lying before,
either spatially (lying in front of) or temporally (lying prior). In English,
of course, as Abraham and Torok reminded us earlier in the chapter, retaining the cognate "to lie"—fore*lying*—points *liegend* "lying (down)" to
its morphmate *lügend* "lying (mendaciously)," the negated or repressed
opposite to *zwar*/square, dealing with a matter or a case (a "fall") fairly
or honestly or straightforwardly, without reserve, unencrypted.

Fall (Fall). *Fall* in modern German has all the connotations of sudden
disastrous downward movement that fall has in modern English—fall,
drop, tumble; decay, decline, ruin, overthrow, downfall, failure; water-
fall, cataract (from Cassell's)—but it also means, unlike the English,
"case, instance, matter, affair." The originary fall in English, of course,
what Abraham and Torok would call the paleonymic fall, is/was the
"Fall of Man" (and Woman), the Original Sin in the Garden of Eden, in
which our ancient forebears first fell from grace and then lied about it.
For Heidegger, of course, the Fall occurs some time in the second or
first century B.C.E., after the Romans take over the Macedonian empire
and begin translating the Greeks into Latin.

This would be one e'enlike fall. Translating Leibniz's Latin phrase
back into Leibniz's native German, the language that stands alongside
ancient Greek as the most spiritual and originary and messianic of languages, would thus be properly or "squarely" (at least ideally) speaking a *reversal* of the e'enlike fall into Latin, a "fall" backwards to the
time *before* the lying fall, into the true ancient or archaic speech of our
Greek forebears.

Except of course that the negative overtones of "lying" and "fall" continue to contaminate even this restorative translational movement through the channeling of our dead forebears. Who fell, and from what state to what state? Who were our "true" forebears, who were the lying ones? Heidegger's idealizations continue to surrender (*überliefern*) to his verbalizations; translation, even Hölderlinian translation, fails to redeem him and us from the spiritual poverty of our times.

That in the period between his resignation from the chancellorship in 1934 and his nervous breakdown in 1945, Heidegger built a crypt and put his innermost thoughts "fast" in it, and only revealed brief flashes from its contents in later years, to close friends like Petzet—or, as I've been hinting, from beyond the grave in the *Spiegel* interview—may be "(im)pure" speculation. In its broad outlines it is not an original thesis; Heidegger's secrecy about certain controversial issues is well-known (see Rockmore), and other biographers (see especially Ott) have speculated about his incomplete mourning (and melancholy) over the failure of his romantic dreams in the mid-30s: Hitler turned out to be just another technocrat; the Nazis turned against him, who was supposed to be the philosopher king; the occupation forces turned him out of his job, kept him from teaching until 1951. Certainly there is no way of proving any of this, any more than there is of proving that Freud or Abraham and Torok were right about the Wolf Man. Most likely the extent to which you find this line of speculation persuasive or farfetched will have something to do with your own ideological channelings, whether you find Heidegger's brand of revolutionary conservatism compelling or repellent or something leftovered inbetween. Rather than trotting out the full biographical evidence for my speculation, then, in a perhaps vain attempt to put such fast in *your* mind, let me just quote a few brief but suggestive passages from Petzet, Heidegger's close friend and hagiographer, in a mental frame (or rack or crucible) of bemused surprise at the way these discoveries "prove" me right.

On the formation of the crypt. In 1939, the year Heidegger turns 50, he writes to Petzet's father in Bremen:

"In these days, when we correspond with each other, I often think of the beautiful days that I spent at your house in Bremen and remember the mother of the house, who has returned home [i.e., died]." But the thoughts of the author of these letters, as well as the thoughts of those who received them, were concerned mostly with the bleakness of the future, which could not be lightened by state-ordered pseudo-optimism. Heidegger wrote, "In any case, we must now *detach ourselves in our inner life from everything that constituted our immediate surroundings and homeland*. For beyond the possible war we must endure other tests, from which we can hardly protect ourselves." At that time I understood these words most precisely. (43, emphasis mine)

We can hardly protect ourselves from those tests; but detaching ourselves in our inner lives from everything that matters most to us—our "homeland," which is associatively also the spiritualistic place Petzet's beloved mother has gone—may be our best chance at some measure of protection.

On the possibility of some day opening the doors of the crypt. In late summer 1941 Petzet's father dies and Heidegger writes a letter of condolence to him, concluding: "If Germans ever experience quiet days again and if they poetize and unfold their own being and their innermost destiny, then one day you will come again to the beloved Black Forest and will find with us a warm welcome and a spirit of shared remembrance" (43).

On the momentary opening of the doors of the crypt. In November 1947 Petzet visits Martin and Elfride at their house in Freiburg, still in ruins from the bombing and (very much like the romantics' Germany in the first decades of the nineteenth century) under French occupation; the three of them sit together talking all afternoon and on into the night:

When I told Heidegger how an incautious remark of mine in Augsburg shortly before the end of the war had nearly cost me my life, he took this as an occasion to talk about the unfair things that had happened to him in those years and how he had been endangered. In the meantime, the desk lamp that had somewhat scantily illumined the room had gone out, because the electricity was generally turned off, leaving the whole city in darkness. *For two hours or more we sat in total darkness and only heard each other's voices.* Perhaps it was exactly this situation, removed from everything irrelevant, that made our conversation more open and more intimate. Heidegger listened like a father, sometimes putting in a word of consolation. Then he began to reveal a great deal about himself of which I had not the slightest idea. *I can only hint at a few things; and we never returned to the topic later.* Heidegger spoke of the way he had been gradually and invisibly encircled, while he continued with his professional duties seemingly unchallenged. He spoke of how permission for publishing his new writings was denied and of how those approved were kept from appearing; of how they were collecting "evidence" against him and of how he was constantly spied upon after the numerous explicit statements he had made in his lectures became known to the police. He spoke of how an older participant in his seminar had come to him one day and confessed to being a Gestapo agent, charged with spying on him; but, in view of the work that Heidegger had accomplished in the seminar, the agent could no longer bring himself to perform his treacherous duty. On the other hand, he could not simply remain silent. That was why he wanted to alert Heidegger, before a possible order for something far worse de-

prived Heidegger of freedom. Heidegger recalled that he had "a long conversation with the Gestapo agent, who was an excellent human being." He added, "I
never saw him again; he was sent to the front and got killed." (45–46, emphasis
mine)

Sitting in total darkness, surrounded by the darkened ruins of his city
and his homeland, with only his wife and his closest friend present, and
they only (as it were) in voice and in spirit, not in body—their bodies in
the dark as invisible as the insidious "encircling" of him had earlier
been—Heidegger cautiously opens the doors of his crypt and tells of
things "of which I had not the slightest idea." Petzet, friend and devo-
tee, eager to clear the master's name of all calumnies and lies, can only
"hint" at a few of the things Heidegger said that night. Because he respects his friend's need to keep those dark days under lock and key?
Because he too had built his own crypt, which resonated with
Heidegger's? "At that time," he wrote of Heidegger's insistence on detaching himself in his inner life from his homeland, "I understood these
words most precisely." And of course as soon as the lights came back
on the doors to the master's crypt are closed and he never glimpses any
of those encrypted secrets again. As Petzet explains early in the book:

It will become apparent in the course of Heidegger's way that hidden behind
all this was the thinker's extreme vulnerability, which often had to seek protection in the shadow of silence. He did not have a thick skin, and wounds inflicted on him healed only with difficulty. For this reason, he did not like to de-
fend himself publicly. The public did not understand this, and enemies
intentionally took advantage of it. (23–24)

Third Translation

And now one last try:

What the messianic German language hests to call *Grundsatz vom Grund,* and
might be machine-translated into the inauthentic (because "modern," i.e.
technology-ridden) English language as "ground leap from the ground" (translation machines are so literal! they are absolutely no good at contextual diffe-
rentiation among the different senses of *Satz,* for example), might usefully be
thought of as (hence from now on *is*) a curtly foreshortened translation of the
famous Leibniz phrase *principium reddendae rationis sufficientis.* (Even though he
wrote the *Monadology* in the inauthentic Latin language, Leibniz is one of a
handful of truly inceptive German thinkers, a German proto-philosopher king.)
Grund, then, is the translation of *ratio.* Okay, now let's lock this up tight, bury

securely it in a crypt, and use it as an excluded-middle "leftover" to encrypt the German original of this translation. Besides, sure, this lockdown is a commonplace, square, or shopping mall so long as we give no honest or straightforward thought to what it has above it, below it, and all around its thick walls and secure perimeters with respect to translation in the forelying fall, which is not to say I'm foreing, lying, or falling, and in the e'enlike fall of our forebears out of true Greek/German essence.

Translation isn't everywhere the same thing as translation. Sometimes translation is of a business letter, which is translatable because inauthentic, i.e. because its expression is so unpleasantly steeped in technology and commerce, ick; what is "translatable" doesn't really exist in the true sense, has no essence, is mere symbolic logic, and the translation used to render it from one language to another isn't really translation at all. But sometimes, and more importantly for our purposes, translation is of a poem, which must continue to be mystified as untranslatable (from behind "thick" walls) in order to keep the encrypted and thus untranslated residue from being discovered and misappropriated.

Modern technology is a convenient cover for modern ideology, which is the mechanization of thinking and speaking around the elective affinities of power; what is really going on here is a war between competing technologies, ideologies, and power affinities. Of course we won't say any of this, as it might tend to blow *our* cover, which must remain protected at all times by the crypt. This makes it essential that the obvious parallels between the awkward and ponderous products of machine translation and the awkward and ponderous products of our "thinking" or "essential" translations never be unconcealed. The two must be kept radically separate, dualized, inauthentic vs. authentic, inessential vs. essential, unthinking vs. thinking, mechanical vs. spiritual (but be careful how you use that latter word), ~~meaty~~ vs. ~~ghostly~~. Let us, in fact, imagine translation technology as standing between, say, business letters (their side) and poems (our side) and "mediating," in the sense of the *non distributio medii,* between them:

• When their technology "works" on their texts (if you can call that working), not just business letters but weather reports and owner's manuals and the like, boring everyday texts that we want to have nothing to do with, we'll call it inauthentic, unthinking, mechanical, "machine" translation, and deride its painful literality.

• When their technology doesn't work on our texts, not just poems but richly texturalized philosophical texts steeped in the expressive repertoires of the source language, all those complexly exciting arcane texts that we like to read and write, we'll take this failure as proof that not only "machine" translation but *all* translation is betrayal.

• When our technology works on our texts (say, extended transformative readings in German of Heraclitus, Plato, Aristotle, or Leibniz), we will either (a) call it successful translation based on an essential responsive hearing/belonging to the voice of the original author (which we will *not* call spirit-channeling, though that's basically what it ~~is~~, or how we're thinking about it) or (b) use some other *über*/trans word for it, like *Übertragung*/transposition or

Überlieferung / tradition (see below), which everyone will recognize as translation raised to a higher (more essential) power, or (c) both. If anyone in their camp (see, e.g., Marten) dares call our translations / transpositions / traditions "misreadings" of the source text, based on stupid ignorant misunderstandings of the original Greek or Latin, and thus as "failures," we will dismiss them contemptuously as inauthentic nonthinkers trapped in mere superficial appearances like evanescent cultural differences, syntactic logic, and the commonsensical tyranny of the dictionary.

Thus their translation technology will be ridiculed as hopelessly bumbling machines out of a comic science-fiction tale and ours will be exalted as (the slightly secularized equivalent of) mystical contact with the divine spiritual forces of the universe. Then, language willing, the extent to which we too are cyborg translators will never become manifest . . .

We should also beware of allowing translation to be regarded as sheer mindless inauthentic event, something someone does at some specific time to some text for some audience; better to transcendentalize it in terms of an "essence" which varies with the languages one translates out of and into. It should be seen to make a vast difference, for example, whether one translates from ancient Greek into a highly stylized poetic German or from business German into business English: this opposition is primary and should remain exclusive. The kind of translation one should avoid, indeed that one should avoid talking and thinking about, or even regarding as possible or feasible or as a form of "translation" at all, is a cryptonymic one, from an encrypted German into an unencrypted English: a propagandistic translation that attempts to reappropriate the untranslated residue by voicing it, say—that attempts to redistribute the excluded middle by exposing it and the exclusion itself to critical debate.

Yet another crucial step in the encrypting of translation, as we suggested above, is its conceptualization as tradition. It is useful to thematize certain translations (especially of hegemonic poetic or philosophical texts) as generators of "tradition" in the root sense of that word: as works that "hand over" or "hand down" or channel a spiritual stabilizing principle or ground and thus reground the "handed-down" or tradition *as* spirit, language, Being. In the restriction of this theme to carefully selected translations, it is also useful to define certain epochs—especially those (like ancient Greece, German romanticism, and, fleetingly, national socialism) that simultaneously valorize both conservatism and progressivism by transcendentalizing progress as tradition—as unusually "ripe" for this regrounding of tradition. This will enable us to glorify the humble, submissive, spirit-channeling translator as a savior, as an indispensable vehicle of the messianic movement, as the critical conduit of the god that will save us: by passively channeling the providential speaking of Being in language, he (not she!) allows himself to be subjected in and by a given epoch of that speaking and thus advances the epoch toward the apocalyptic destination of Being. Amen.

Chapter Four

The (Ideo)logic of Spectrality

Shakespeare's Permission

In 1972 the Finnish Marxist poet and translator Matti Rossi translated *King Lear* for a production at the Turku City Theater, directed by Kalle Holmberg. In his preface to his translation in its published form, Rossi wrote (and let me give it to you in both Finnish and my English translation):

Rakenteeltaan Kuningas Lear on Shakespearen näytelmistä heikoimpia. Se alkaa vauhdikkaasti ja johdonmukaisesti, mutta vyyhteytyy sitten epämääräiseksi ja voimattomaksi. Voi melkein sanoa, missä on se harjanne jonka jälkeen taso alkaa laskea kirjailijan menettäessä tai hellittäessä otteensa.

Mahdollisesti tekijöitä on useita. Kenties Shakespeare kirjoitti näytelmästä vain osia, kiireissään, ja jätti avustajilleen puolivalmiin näytelmän ja ajatusrungon.

Päätimme Holmbergin kanssa, että näytelmää on turha toistaa koko epäloogisuudessaan. Erityisesti meitä vaivasi sen surkea loppu ja eräitten henkilöhahmojen, erimerkiksi Kentin latistuminen. Näytelmä tarvitsisi keskeisen teeman, joka selittäisi henkilöiden toiminnan.

Keskeiseksi teemaksi tuli taistelu vallasta, satamasta ja Doverin satamaalueesta, joka oli merkitykseltään elintärkeä Britannian kuningaskunnalle. "Dover" on tämän näytelmän avainsana. Miltei kaikki tekemäni tekstinmuutokset ja lisäykset kytkeytyvät siihen.

Lähteinäni muutoksia ja lisäyksiä varten olen käyttänyt Elisabetin kauden yhteiskuntaa, taloutta ja tapakulttuuria kuvaavia teoksia. Näytelmän "työttömät" ovat historiallinen totuus. Heitä nimitettiin 1500-luvulla "kerjäläisiksi" ja heidän paljoutensa johtui maaomaisuuden keskittymisestä. He olivat olennainen ilmiö Elisabet Ensimmäisen Englannissa.

Shakespearen luvalla olen vähentänyt loppukohtauksen jaloutta ja esittänyt vaihtoehdoksi mahtimiesten todellisen käyttäytymisen silloin kun taistelu kruunusta todella alkaa. (153)

~᎒᎒~

Structurally *King Lear* is one of Shakespeare's weakest plays. Having begun briskly and coherently it soon gets tangled up in incoherence and impotence. One can almost point to the exact spot where the writer loses or lets go his grip and the play begins to fall apart.

There are any number of explanations for this. Perhaps Shakespeare only wrote parts of the play, in a rush, and left his assistants with no more than a thematic framework and an unfinished play.

Holmberg and I decided that there was no point in repeating the play in all its illogicality. We were particularly irritated by the atrocious ending and the flattening out of various characters, such as Kent. The play needed a central theme that would explain the action of the characters.

The theme we took to be central was the struggle for power, especially the fight for the port of Dover, which was of vital importance to the English kingdom. "Dover" is the key to this play. Nearly all the textual changes and additions I have made tie in to it.

My sources for these changes and additions were historical studies of the society, economy, and customs of Elizabethan England. The play's "unemployed" are historical fact. In the sixteenth century they were called "beggars," and their vast number was due to the concentration of land-ownership in the hands of a few. They were a distinctive characteristic of Elizabeth I's England.

With Shakespeare's permission I have cut the high nobility of the ending and offered as an alternative the real behavior of power-holders when a battle for a crown truly begins.

What shall we do with this? One approach to this translation and the claims its translator makes for it might be academically dismissive: who is this Matti Rossi and where does he get off thinking that he can screw with a great classic of English literature?—or, for that matter, thinking that *King Lear* is incoherent or impotent in the first place? Rossi drags in all the tired cliches of *Lear* criticism from Nahum Tate to A. H. Bradley, by which the play is compared to various structural ideals from Aristotle to *King Leir* (Shakespeare's model, in which Cordelia is rescued before she is executed and a happy ending of sorts ensues) and found wanting—not in order to establish the "true form" of the play but to justify a high-handed "adaptation" or "interpretation" of it as socialist theater. In order for Rossi's Marxist adaptation to "work," it is essential that we—the translated play's viewers and/or readers—come to believe that Shakespeare left his assistants, readers, producers, directors, actors, and translators a mere "thematic framework and an unfinished play," a mere pile of dramatistic lumber from which Rossi and Holmberg can

build a socialist drama about workers and the unemployed, the fight for
the port of Dover, and the struggle for control of the crown. And this is
an assumption that Shakespeare scholars are no longer willing to make.

On the other hand Rossi says explicitly, and this is one reason why I
find this particular preface so fascinating, that he cuts the high nobility
of the ending "with Shakespeare's permission," *Shakespearen luvalla.*
What exactly does he mean by this? Should we imagine him to be *asking*
permission? The phraseology is familiar from addresses to kings and
other authorities: "With your permission, Sire, I would like to cut . . ."
(*Teidän Majesteettinne luvalla haluaisin poistaa . . .*). Since this request, if
that is what it is, comes several years after the actual translation was
made, *in* Rossi's preface to the published version of the play (clearly a
fait accompli), it would seem to be purely *pro forma*. And indeed it
sounds to me, perhaps this comes as no surprise, as if Rossi is not so
much asking Shakespeare's permission as invoking Shakespeare's
spirit—as if he is laying claim to Shakespeare's *blessing*, from beyond
the grave, on his socialist adaptation.

As it happens, Shakespeare's spirit has, in a manner of speaking
(and for all I know a *real* and *true* one), given a kind of blanket permission for this sort of adaptation of his work. In a book entitled *From
Heaven to Earth: Shakespeare Returns,* for example, Robert R. Leichtman
engages Shakespeare's spirit in conversation, through the mediumship
of D. Kendrick Johnson; there Shakespeare recurs several times to the
importance of "taking liberties" with his plays, interpreting them,
adapting them:

LEICHTMAN: So actually your plays continued to evolve during your
    life.

SHAKESPEARE: Well, to my way of thinking, theater should be a living
    thing. To go back to my comment about the liberties that people
    have taken with my plays, I think this is fine: it does tend to keep
    them living. If one can update *Hamlet* in certain ways, for example,
    then the play will be something new every time an audience sees it. I
    don't even mind the version of *Hamlet,* incidentally, in which Ham-
    let is revealed in the end to be a woman. [*Laughter.*] It's a rather inter-
    esting idea—I wish I had thought of it myself.

LEICHTMAN: How about staging your plays in modern language and
    dress?

SHAKESPEARE: Why not? Let me draw an analogy from medieval
    painting, which I was interested in but only had a nominal acquain-
    tance with. In medieval painting, scenes from the Bible were often

portrayed in contemporary dress and European settings—to make them more living and immediate.

LEICHTMAN: That's reasonable.

SHAKESPEARE: The arts can do this, whereas history cannot. (31)

And later, when Leichtman asks about the operas and musicals that have been made from his plays, Shakespeare replies easily, "I'm very happy that these plays are living enough that they can be adapted to a musical format. Of course, liberties are taken with them, but this is all right. The work of any creative person ought to be living enough that it can be adapted in some way. Otherwise, there would be no famous art or letters—it couldn't find a place in modern times" (45). Leichtman then makes a little joke, ha ha, about scholars frowning on the idea that the "real Shakespeare" is no purist, and the "real Shakespeare" replies: "The real Shakespeare is a man who learned the hard way that life is too precious to quibble with what happens to one's work. Part of the fun of doing the work was that it grew even during my lifetime. It was changed and altered and adapted, and that's why it grew" (45).

In other words: a socialist adaptation of *King Lear* is just fine! Never mind your academic quibbling; the "real Shakespeare" really and truly *has* given his permission to change it, adapt it, in whatever radical ways keep it a "living thing" (just as, presumably, the speaker of these remarks is still "living" after his death). Make Hamlet a woman; make Dover the key to *Lear*—no problem! The source author says it's okay! Just don't let the play die!

Then again . . . what exactly *is* the ontological status of this talk of Shakespeare's permission? Does Shakespeare's spirit really exist on some "inner plane," so that he really can give translators permission to adapt his plays? And are we really to assume that Rossi is invoking a spiritualistic rationale for a Marxist translation? How would *that* work, exactly? Marx disliked spiritualistic explanations intensely, although as we will see later in this chapter, he also invoked them repeatedly and obsessively *in order to* refute and dismiss them, and in the process of refuting and dismissing them continued to give them metaphorical life. Should we think of Rossi as wanting the spiritualistic "Shakespeare's permission" and the Marxist "real behavior of power-holders" to exist on the same ontological plane, both giving him the same type of justification for his translation? Or must we reduce the spiritualistic permission talk to the status of metaphorical vehicle for the ideological power-politics talk? Is he really claiming to channel both Shakespeare and Marx? Or is he only pretending to channel Shakespeare in order to channel Marx? Or, again, is he pretending to channel Shakespeare in order to pretend to be channeling not Marx but reality, political reality, *Realpolitik* (which has, but only coincidentally, a distinctly Marxist color, perhaps because Marx too, like Rossi, channeled the *reality of reality*, the really real political truth, but in parallel rather than in series, so that we should avoid jumping to the conclusion that Rossi channeled Marx)?

Note also that in that last sentence of the Rossi quote I had to make a syntactic and semantic choice: since Finnish has no articles, definite or indefinite, I could have translated "esittänyt vaihtoehdoksi mahtimiesten todellisen käyttäytymisen silloin kun taistelu kruunusta todella alkaa" (lit. "offered as-alternative power-men's real/true behavior then when battle for-crown really/truly begins") as either "offered as an alternative the real behavior of power-holders when *a* battle for *a* crown truly begins" or "offered as an alternative the real behavior of *the* power-holders when *the* battle for *the* crown truly begins." Both translations work as representations of the Finnish; but which did Rossi *really mean?* With Rossi's permission, the first time I translated this passage, in 1985, I settled on the latter; this time, in 1997, I settled on the former. And both times I really did believe that I was rendering the passage *with his permission*—even though I never actually called him up and asked him, and even though, unfortunately for the credibility of my general permission-claim, the ideological implications for the nature of Rossi's "channeling" of Shakespeare are significantly different in the two renditions, to the point of being almost mutually exclusive. With definite articles, Rossi is claiming access to the "real behavior" of the power-holders *in the play*, which would, I suspect, imply that he is channeling some sort of dramatistic reality directly from Shakespeare's individual or his repertory company's collective mind. With indefinite articles, on the other hand, Rossi is claiming access to the "real behavior" of power-holders in the "real" world, the world of power politics. Clearly, the former is the more spiritualistic claim, the latter the more realistic. But how, *really, truly,* which is to say *immediately*—without ideological mediation, without the "external" guidance of an ideology like Marxism (or for that matter capitalism, or liberal humanism, though these latter are ideologies scorned by this particular Finnish translator)—can Rossi claim to know either? Surely, and I imagine him agreeing with me here, even if only unconsciously, so that in some way or another I can pursue this line of reasoning with his permission, his conception of the "reality" of power-holders' behavior is channeled to him ideologically? Whether he is claiming "true" knowledge of the "real behavior" of power-holders in the play or in the world, surely the "truth" and "reality" of what he knows are shaped by Marxist thought?

As Derrida would insist in *Specters of Marx*, the difficulty here arises because we keep wanting to dualize inside and outside, self and other. Did Shakespeare really tell Rossi to turn *King Lear* into socialist drama, or didn't he? If he did, fine; in a traditional literary-critical framework the source author is the final authority in these things, and, implausible as it may sound, if Shakespeare really does still exist in some lucid and articulate spiritual form four centuries after his death and is capable of communicating to Rossi or other translators and directors and such his permission to adapt his plays in this or that way, well, we will just have to accept it. If, however (and you can imagine the long-suffering academic scholar taking a deep and rather histrionic breath here to dramatize his or her minimal forbearance with such idiocy as the aforementioned possibility), Shakespeare didn't *really* give Rossi his permission to bowdlerize his play in this absurd fashion, then Rossi is just making the whole thing up, the Marxist spin he puts on *Lear* is his own solipsistic little fantasy that he has scandalously imposed on us, his Finnish playgoers and readers (I hope you don't mind being included briefly in that group for purposes of illustration), when all we want is Shakespeare, the *real* Shakespeare, what Shakespeare *really wrote*. Either there is a true external mandate for his adaptation and it must therefore be accepted as authoritative, authorized by its original author; or there is no such external source and Rossi's *Lear* must be taken as purely internal, purely Rossi's own invention.

As Derrida argues, however (in Peggy Kamuf's translation), "one must perhaps ask oneself whether the *spectrality effect* does not consist in undoing this opposition, or even the dialectic, between actual, effective presence and its other" (40)—whether, in other words, "the logic of the ghost" doesn't critically undermine this traditional dualistic notion that I'm here and you're there, I'm a subject and that's an object, I'm real and that imaginary nonthing is unreal, and so on. "If we have been insisting so much since the beginning on the logic of the ghost," Derrida adds later, "it is because it points toward a thinking of the event that necessarily exceeds a binary or dialectical logic, the logic that distinguishes or opposes *effectivity or actuality* (either present, empirical, living—or not) and *ideality* (regulating or absolute non-presence)" (63). The ghost is real and unreal, visible and invisible, embodied and disembodied, present and absent, living and dead, inside and outside, self and other. The ghost is dead, but acts as if it were alive. It is the visible body of disembodied invisibility. It is there, talking to you, but it is at precisely that same moment also not there, or its "thereness" is a different sort of thereness altogether, a thereness that isn't "really" there. If you see a ghost, talk to a ghost, it is "just your imagination," a fantasy; and it is only in and through your imagination that you can see and talk to the ghost.

Or, to put that in terms of Rossi's invocation of Shakespeare's permission, Rossi did channel both Shakespeare and Marx, and he also made it all up. The "spirit(s)" of Shakespearean drama and Marxist political analysis that he channeled into the play are real forces in the world, and they are imaginary forces in his head. To get past those paradoxes, which make this whole line of reasoning sound like sheer argumentative sleight-of-mind, they are what Wilhelm Reich called "group fantasies." They are fantasies in the sense that they are imaginative, even perhaps imaginary—they lack the "actuality" and "effectivity" of living humans, tractors, and so on—but they also have a powerful impact on our lives because they are believed to be true by large groups. They are, in other words, ideologies, which do not "exist" in any tangible or demonstrable form, but are enormously powerful nonetheless.

In *The Translator's Turn* I tried to explain the inside/outside-your-headness of ideology with the concept of ideosomatics, collective belief structures that have been "somatized" into the autonomic nervous systems of individuals and regulate their behavior physiologically. In *Translation and Taboo* I used (and next chapter will be using again) Jacques Lacan's notion of the Other to get at something like this same psychosocial inside/outside, this self/other bridge. Here, since we're already talking about drama, let me try another tack: performance. The performative creation of "character." What is the "character" of, say, King Lear? Where does "he" exist? Where does the "real behavior" of the "power-holders" in the play exist? Nowhere, really; in our minds; in our imaginations. And yet we walk out of performances of the play saying things like "He was *perfect* as Lear!" or "*That's* not Lear at all!" When we talk this way, it sounds as if we are presupposing some stable and universal "deep structure" of character, like a Platonic ideal, that actors either "capture" or "fail to capture." Same thing when we say an actor "stayed in character," or "fell out of character." Where exactly would such an ideal dwell? In the text? Essentialist literary critics seem to think so—or at least talk as if that's how they thought. It doesn't take much skepticism to cast doubt on that notion, though; wherever "King Lear" or "the real behavior of (the) power-holders" might be thought to reside, it seems clear that they are mostly made out of readers' imaginations, out of the "unreal" materials of our fantasies. Character is a created illusion, a fiction formulated by the actor and the audience in a dialogical engagement at once with the script and with previous such engagements, which tend to carry over in influential and surreptitious ways. Character is an *interpretation* that, if successful, takes on an imaginative reality precisely by supplanting or bracketing or incorporating and transforming previous interpretations in the viewer's mind. We say that a particular King Lear (signaling our recognition of the plurality of Lear-interpretations by the indefinite article, which is fast becoming a kind of minor hero of this chapter) was "wrong," not because the actor failed to "capture" a universal deep-structure Lear, but because he failed to convince us that Lear could not be otherwise. The actor's task is to present his performance of Lear not as a representation of an ideal or universal, but as a sovereign *replacement* for all previous renderings, as a usurpative illusion or "specter" beside which competing illusions or spectralities pale into insignificance.

And in some sense—ideologically, at least—it is irrelevant precisely where this specter comes from, or how it is created and maintained. Channeled by D. Kendrick Johnson, the "real Shakespeare" tells us that "Queen Elizabeth has had a great deal to do with inspiring Bette Davis's style of acting. Her famous gesture. When Miss Davis was portraying Queen Elizabeth, she was often overshadowed in the important parts" (42). Should we say, then, that Bette Davis "was" Queen Elizabeth when she was "overshadowed" by the "real Queen Elizabeth," and was only an actress *pretending* to be Queen Elizabeth when not? Should we deride all other dramatic Queen Elizabeths as mere pretenders, impostors? Either an actor has access to the "real" spirit of the character s/he is portraying, or s/he is a fraud? That would be absurd. The actor creates/takes the character *from somewhere*. It comes from inside and outside her/his head. Bette Davis "imagines" what it must have been like to be Queen Elizabeth, reads about her, perhaps watches other movies about her, and builds a very personal "character" for the queen, Queen Elizabeth as performed by Bette Davis—and perhaps, if this *Shakespeare Returns* book is to be believed, the "unreal" Queen Elizabeth was "overshadowing" her for part of the time. Which acts of the imagination were guided by a spirit of the person she was performing? Which were her own "internal" or "personal" inventions? If William Shakespeare and Queen Elizabeth do still exist in some spiritual form and are following (perhaps overshadowing) me right now as I write these words, it probably matters a great deal to them which is which. From a secular, earthbound perspective, which is unfortunately, to my knowledge, the only one I inhabit, it doesn't matter in the slightest. All I need to know is that pragmatically speaking "character" in the performative sense, like "authorial intention" and "the spirit of the original," like ideology and pragmatic political "truth," are heuristic images, fictions, specters that human beings flesh forth out of *some* sort of ideological ectoplasm (or "ideoplasm"), they and we and I know not what.

(In)visibilizing Lear

Applying this "performative" conception of character to translation would generate something like the "post-Kantian" or "reader-response" approach I adumbrated in chapter one; indeed it harks back in the history of my own thinking on the subject to the "tropical" approach to translation that I developed in chapter three of *The Translator's Turn.* By "performing" Lear's words in the script as a "real" English king, by "performing" a tragedy written in English in 1605 or 1606 as a socialist drama written in Finnish in 1972, by "performing" Shakespeare as authorizing or permitting this radical transformation of the play, the actor/translator tropes on it or turns from it, and in so doing supplants it (at least in the reader/viewer/listener's imagination). I presented the process in that earlier book in largely eulogistic terms, in terms of the translator's creativity. Putting it in terms of spirits, specters, ghosts, however, and specifically in terms of a spectralization of ideology, acting and translation as the performative or purposeful molding of a spectral ideoplasm, casts a rather more problematic, even disturbing light on these tropes. Does a performative theory of translation, for example, not confer on the translator an intolerable power over both the source author and the target reader? Suspicious as I am of essentialist approaches to literature, enamored as I am of constructivist/reader-response/performative/tropical approaches, I resist the notion of *King Lear* as socialist drama, and want to rush to Shakespeare's defense. That's *not* what Shakespeare intended! Just *saying* Shakespeare gave you permission to radicalize the play doesn't make it so! Shakespeare is *not* just ideoplasm for you to shape to your own Marxist ends!

But of course in all kinds of important ways, he *is.* And the notion that he isn't, that he possesses a certain stable character that translators and directors and actors should endeavor not to violate or distort, is in fact mediated to me by another kind of ideoplasm, the ghosts of Shakespeare scholars over the last three centuries or so, the ghosts of essentializing literary critics who have wanted to instill in people like me a belief in the immutability (as opposed to ideoplasticity) of the "great authors."

Still, the ghosts of essentialists past continue to haunt us. Despite two centuries of Kantian and neo-Kantian critiques of philosophical foundationalism, it continues today to seem intuitively "right" to stabilize the "character" or "nature" or "essence" of the source author and/ or text, and to be wary or critical of distortions. There is an entire chorus of ghosts here, propping up the ideoplasm of the source author, constructing him or her as this or that, and this or that *only*. As I suggested in my discussion of Freud before the Vienna Psychiatic Society in chapter three, these "ghosts" are the collective "force(s)" (whatever we want to call it or them) that maintain ideology. It is ideologically correct to believe in the immutability of "Shakespeare"—to believe implicitly, for example, that whatever else he might have been he was not a Marxist and could never have been, so should never be made to *seem* one. Because so many ghosts—the lingering words of so many respected dead people—have told us that this is the case.

In this ghostly ideological light, certainly, the translator's undeniable power over the authorial ideoplasm *is* disturbing. To put it in more explicitly political terms: if in international politics an interpreter's error can precipitate an international incident, what degree of chaos might an ideologically manipulative or distortive interpreter not bring about—especially if that interpreter invoked the "spirit" or the "permission" of the source-language speaker as ideological authorizer of the manipulation? Isn't submission to an illusion of translational fidelity not infinitely preferable to a blatant recognition of the translator's vast power to supplant, to usurp, shape, to dictate terms? Matti Rossi is best known in Finland as a poet, only secondarily, this should come as no surprise, as a translator; and his poem "Kuningas Lear," "King Lear," dramatizes this question even better than his *Lear* translation ever could:

Kuningas Lear täyttää tänään 128 vuotta, kuningas Lear on nostettu ikkunaan katsomaan paraatia, 250 divisioonaa jalkamiestä, 90 000 panssaria, 150 000 maailman ympäri lentävää pommittajaa joista kolmannes on aina matkalla jonnekin, silmiinkantamattomiin kuuraketteja, jokaisen raketin päällä kahareisin jäntevä naissotilas; hilpeitä maanpuolustajia, nuortuneita kenraaleja, sillä tänään vietetään kuningas Learin syntymäpäivää,

ja ikkunassa kuningas Lear samettitakissaan, jalassaan vedenpitävät, eikä kukaan tiedä kasvaako tukka jo vai eikö se kasva enää, eikä kukaan kysy,

Kfmyfkh, kfmyfkh, sanoo Lear ja maiskauttaa, hoitajatar sieppaa laatikosta kuivat housut, mutta tulkki kääntää,

Me emme halua sotaa, mutta jos meidän kimppuumme hyökätään iskemme siekailematta, sillä meillä on kauhea ase, kfmyfkh, sanoo kuningas Lear ja hyppii jalat ristissä,

kauhea ase, jota me emme halua käyttää, kauhea ase,

kfmyfkh, kfmyfkh, sanoo kuningas Lear tyytyväisesti,

kauhea ase, sanoo tulkki, mutta kuningas Lear kiidätetään nopeasti takahuoneeseen ja pääministeri nostetaan ikkunaan,

Kfmyfkh, sanoo pääministeri, kfmyfkh, kfmyfkh.

༈

King Lear turns 128 today, they've lifted him up to the window to watch the parade, 250 infantry divisions, 90,000 tanks, 150,000 long-range bombers a third of which are always in the air, moon rockets as far as the eye can see, straddling every rocket a lithe WAC; high-spirited soldiers, rejuvenated generals, all to celebrate King Lear's birthday,

and in the window King Lear in his velvet jacket and galoshes, and no one knows whether his hair's started growing yet or whether it's stopped growing already, and no one asks,

Kfmyfkh, kfmyfkh, Lear says and smacks his lips, the nurse grabs a dry pair of pants from the drawer, but the interpreter translates,

We do not want war, but if we are attacked we will strike without hesitation, for we have a terrible weapon,

kfmyfkh, kfmyfkh, King Lear says and hops up and down with his legs crossed,

a terrible weapon that we do not want to use, a terrible weapon,

kfmyfkh, kfmyfkh, says Lear with satisfaction,

a terrible weapon, says the interpreter, but King Lear is hustled into a back room and the prime minister is lifted to the window,

Kfmyfkh, says the prime minister, kfmyfkh, kfmyfkh.

This poem revolves around a consecutive interpretation of two "speeches," two strings of sound emitted by ostensible authority figures and constructed as coherent by the interpreter. In traditional sense-for-sense terms it is a remarkable feat of interpretation: the interpreter succeeds in reaching through the gibberish King Lear and the prime minister seem to be uttering to the "sense" that underlies it. This reading, of course, manifestly ignores the poem's sinister power relations—or, perhaps, doesn't so much ignore as abets them, tacitly authorizes or justifies them. King Lear, after all, is not presented as an authority to whom the interpreter defers, not as the speaker of the authoritative original to which the interpreter must submit his or her rendition, but as a dehumanized or infantilized pawn of the true power-holders, represented in the poem by the nurse and the interpreter, Lear's symbolic "parents." The nurse, marked in Finnish as female, is a mother-figure who changes Lear's pants when he wets them; in what Freud calls the "family romance" this would make the interpreter (unmarked in Finnish for gender) a father-figure, the paternalistic guardian of Lear's speech functions who "interprets" the baby's ideoplasmic babbling for guests, the "dictator" who dictates what the child will (or did) say.

Indeed in an important sense the "terrible weapon" with which the interpreter (in the name of the king) threatens the enemies of the State is language itself, *words,* speech as an ideoplastic "speaking for"—and the true enemy is no potential victim of a bomb attack but precisely the "spoken-for," the ostensible speaker who finds the ideoplasm of his words collapsed and reshaped by an authority. The will to power is specifically, Rossi's poem suggests, a will to *dictation,* to dominion over the speech of others: a desire to silence the clamor of contrary voices, to hollow out the speech of the other into echoes of the self's inner voice.

NICE HOSTESS: "Would you like another scoop of ice cream, honey?"

LITTLE GIRL: "Yes pl—"

FATHER, interrupting: "No thanks, she's full"—intending no statement of fact (the little girl should know better than her father when she's full) but a conformation of her will to his, a reduction of *her desire* to *his purpose,* which may be intended to protect her from tooth decay or him from her real or imagined whining, but in either case is a purpose of *power.* The power to speak for or dictate to another person is politically one of the most effective, and personally one of the most damaging, forms of power, because the freedom it curtails is the freedom to choose or define an action, which is finally the freedom to choose or shape an identity by acting. (And of course in this Rossi's poem, like his translation, only repoliticizes Shakespeare's play, which revolves around the political complications of trading the power to dictate for dictated love: the nurse and the interpreter in the poem in important ways figure Regan and Goneril in the play.)

The beauty of this power lies in its economy: one wields it simply by threatening to use it. To talk about it is to do it. One threatens to use the terrible weapon if provoked, the terrible weapon one does not want to use, and in so doing conceals the fact that one *has just used it*, indeed that using the weapon was the whole reason for denying the desire to use it.

And in this poem the dictator, against all odds, in the face of all our complaints about our invisibility, is the interpreter, the translator. Here in fact are postromantic dreams of the translator's visibility brought to fullest fruition, the interpreter not only as dissident but as not-so-secret dictator, invisibly visible, visibly invisible, resisting Lear's "power" by channeling an ideology that is (presumably) not the king's, standing next to the nattily dressed Lear who waves to the masses as if he were truly in control, as if it were his words being projected out over their heads, when in fact they are Lear's verbal ideoplasm reformed, re-shaped, reconstituted by the "dissident" interpreter. Lear stands in roughly the same present/absent position in Rossi's poem as Shake-speare did in Rossi's preface, as the spectral "authority" whose presence at once authorizes the translator's transformative rendition and collapses (Rossi's verb is *vyyhteytyä*, to get tangled like a skein of yarn) into incoherence and impotence, and thus ultimately into absence. What Derrida's logic of the ghost marks in both the poem and the preface is the complexly overlapping interchange(ability) of the "actual, effective presence and its other," the living human being and the ghost, the visible and the invisible: pretending to channel the "source author" or "source speaker," the translator/interpreter channels a power ideology instead, Rossi's Marxism in the preface, some unnamed imperialism in the poem (American capitalism or Soviet communism), and (in)*visibilizes* the self/other as (*in*)visible.

It might be argued, in fact, that Rossi gives us only the "authoritative" reading of the poem's action, the official or public version of its events; for "kfmyfkh" seems less a transcription of actual babbling than an official marker, a stamp of censorship, a row of asterisks that indicates that something has been excised. King Lear is not only portrayed as doddering, reduced to lip-smacking and pant-wetting, but deprived of coherent speech as well, *silenced* by the revisionary historian whose handwriting the poem might be taken to be. Kfmyfkh is the ideoplasm in its base state, the willing clay waiting to be shaped ideologically by its verbal master.

But note that this "authoritative" reading is built on the foundation of the old authority: as the king, and on the poem-preface axis as the figure of Shakespeare himself, Lear is the representative of both (a) the feudalism displaced by capitalism in the West and (for a time) by Marxism in the East and (b) translation as worshipful spirit-channeling, translation as subordinate to the channeled spirit of the source author. If we could hear Lear speak, if he could say more to us than kfmyfkh, he would speak with the now-displaced authority of the feudal and spirit-channeled past. His silencing, his (in)visibilization, his reduction to the status of present/absent ghost, are all signs that the king is dead, long live the bureaucrat—that the old regime has been replaced with a new and different but no doubt equally repressive one.

Marx and Schleiermacher on Spirits and Ghosts

It is, in fact, precisely in the context of distinguishing the new from the old, new regimes from old, *truly* new regimes that are no longer repressive because they have cut off all ties with the old from *apparently* new ones that are still dominated by the old, that Karl Marx himself pronounces in passing on translation (and ghosts)—or actually, doesn't so much pronounce on translation as uses translation (and ghosts) as a figure for the move from the old to the new. The moment is in the second paragraph of *Der Achtzehnte Brumaire des Louis Bonaparte, The Eighteenth Brumaire of Louis Bonaparte* (1852):

Die Menschen machen ihre eigene Geschichte, aber sie machen sie nicht aus freien Stücken, nicht unter selbtgewählten, sondern unter unmittelbar vorgefundenen, gegebenen und überlieferten Umständen. Die Tradition aller toten Geschlechter lastet wie ein Alp auf dem Gehirn der Lebenden. Und wenn sie eben damit beschäftigt scheinen, sich und die Dinge umzuwälzen, noch nicht Dagewesenes zu schaffen, gerade in solchen Epochen revolutionärer Krise beschwören sie ängstlich die Geister der Vergangenheit zu ihrem Dienste herauf, entlehnen ihnen Namen, Schlachtparole, Kostüme, um in dieser altehrwürdigen Verkleidung und mit dieser erborgten Sprache die neue Weltgeschichtszene aufzuführen. So maskierte sich Luther als Apostel Paulus, die Revolution von 1789 bis 1814 drapierte sich abwechselnd als römische Republik und als römisches Kaisertum, und die Revolution von 1848 wußte nichts Besseres zu tun, als hier 1789, dort die revolutionäre Ueberlieferung von 1793 bis 1795 zu parodieren. (21)

Men make their own history, but not spontaneously, under conditions they have chosen for themselves; rather on terms immediately existing, given and handed down to them. The tradition of countless dead generations is an incubus to the mind of the living. At the very times when they seem to be engaged in revolutionizing themselves and their circumstances, in creating something previously non-existent, at just such epochs of revolutionary crisis they anxiously summon up the spirits of the past to their aid, borrowing from them names, rallying-cries, costumes, in order to stage the new world-historical drama in this time-honoured disguise and borrowed speech. Luther masqueraded as the Apostle Paul; the revolution of 1789–1814 camouflaged itself alternately as Roman republic or Roman empire and the revolution of 1848 could think of nothing better than to parody sometimes 1789 and sometimes the revolutionary tradition of 1793–1795. (Eugene Kamenka's translation, 287–88)

So far, clearly, he is figuring the power of ideology to regulate the present in its sweep toward the future as spirit-channeling, or, as he says just above and will say again a few lines below, "necromancy" or "conjuration/summoning/raising of the dead" (*beschwören sie die Geister*, they summon up the spirits, *Totenerweckung*, the raising or awakening of the dead). People *think* they are acting autonomously, in rational control of their actions, think they are "creating something previously non-existent," but all too often "they anxiously summon up the spirits of the past to their aid." And then he compares this process to language-learning and translation:

So übersetzt der Anfänger, der eine neue Sprache erlernt hat, sie immer zurück in seine Muttersprache, aber den Geist der neuen Sprache hat er sich nur angeeignet, und frei in ihr zu produzieren vermag er nur, sobald er sich ohne Rückerinnerung in ihr bewegt und die ihm angestammte Sprache in ihn vergißt. (21)

Just so does the beginner, having learnt a new language, always re-translate it into his mother tongue; he has not assimilated the spirit of the new language, nor learnt to manipulate it freely, until he uses it without reference to the old and forgets his native tongue in using the new one. (288)

Here translation is a bad thing; it is the bridge back to the past, to the native language, and in Marx's spectral logic to the spirits of the dead, to ghosts. The true revolutionary must cut the ties that bind him to the past, to the spirits of dead ancestors, to the mother tongue; must *stop* channeling their voices, their personal forces, must *stop* translating from the old language/regime and assimilate the spirit of the new. Translation as spirit-channeling as ideology: the analogical chain I've been following all through these last two chapters.

As Derrida notes in his discussion of this passage in *Specters of Marx* (110), however, Marx doesn't exactly want to *forget* the past; that after all is what the bourgeoisie do. It is precisely those who forget the past who keep on channeling it into the future. One must therefore in some sense forget the past without forgetting it; cut all ties with the past, with the dead, with the mother tongue, without quite jettisoning those things; stop translating from the mother tongue, stop carrying it out into the foreign, the new, but hold it, somehow, in reserve. And he figures this keep-it/junk-it tension, again, with spirits and ghosts:

Die Totenerweckung in jenen [wirklich revolutionären] Revolutionen diente also dazu, die neuen Kämpfe zu verherrlichen, nicht die alten zu parodieren, die gegebene Aufgabe in der Phantasie zu übertreiben, nicht vor ihrer Lösung in der Wirklichkeit zurückzuflüchten, den Geist der Revolution wieder zu finden, nicht ihr Gespenst wieder umgehen zu machen. (23)

The raising of the dead in those [truly revolutionary] revolutions, therefore, served to glorify the new struggles, not to parody the old; it fostered in imagination an aggrandizement of the set task, not flight from its actual solution, a rediscovery of the spirit of revolution rather than a summoning up of its ghost. (289)

Keep the spirit, ditch the ghost. Derrida's deconstruction of Marx's ghosts revolves about this very problematic: the spirits (*Geister*) Marx wants to keep are forever being contaminated by the ghosts (*Gespenster*) he wants to ditch. A *Geist* is, after all, both a spirit and a ghost; a *Gespenst* is only a ghost, and cannot be used to signify all the other "spiritual" things that *Geist* can mean, like mind, culture, mood. In wanting to "rediscover" the spirit/*Geist* of revolution *as opposed to* summoning up its ghost/*Gespenst*, Marx is very close to calling for ghosts without ghosts, unghostly ghosts, despectralized spirits—or, as Derrida puts it, to calling for a forgetting without forgetting, or even, in terms of his foreign-language analogy, a translating without translating.

The conceptual and imagistic dilemma across which Marx finds himself stretched here is strikingly similar, at least imagistically, to the one Friedrich Schleiermacher encounters in his 1813 lecture "Ueber die verschiedenen Methoden des Uebersezens," "On the Different Methods of Translating," which also invokes translation, spirits, and ghosts in order to bridge the gap between the native and the foreign, the old and the new. The third chapter of my *Translation and Taboo* was an extended close reading of the rather bizarre moment in Schleiermacher's lecture that I mean; and while I do not propose to rehearse that discussion here, the convergences and divergences between that passage and Marx's from *The Eighteenth Brumaire*, and their applicability to the question of translation as spirit-channeling, are so intriguing that I can't resist taking another quick look. The ghostly moment comes in the context of Schleiermacher's attack on the old chestnut according to which the translator should make the source author "speak" in the target language as if he (the source author) had originally written in that language. This is a patently absurd notion, Schleiermacher argues, because no one can ever write as well in a foreign language as in the mother tongue. To be sure, diplomats and courtiers often become fluent in several languages, and as the convivial discourse of these worldly people are sometimes cobbled together and called literature—novels of manners, for instance—it is just barely imaginable that some writer could write a piece of this "lite lit" in a foreign language; and perhaps this sort of literature could reasonably be translated, too, according to the rule that the translation should sound as if it had originally been written in the target language. Commercial and technical texts, too, which Schleiermacher describes as "under the sway of the object" (235, *in der Gewalt des Gegenstandes* [236]), can be translated in this way. This is where Heidegger will pick up the argument a century and a half later, as we saw in chapter three. But *true* literature, literature that is infused with "the imprint of a long-past era" (235, *das Gepräge einer längst abgelaufenen Zeit* [236]), cannot be translated this way at all (and again Heidegger would have to agree):

Dasselbe ist der Fall mit dem romanischen. Wer gezwungen und von Amstwegen eine solche Sprache schreibt, der wird sich doch wohl bewußt sein, daß seine Gedanken im ersten Entstehen deutsch sind, und daß er nur sehr früh während der Embryo sich noch gestaltet schon anfängt sie zu übersezen; und wer sich einer Wissenschaft wegen dazu ausopfert, der wird sich auch nur da leicht ungezwungen und *ohne geheimes Uebersezen finden,* wo er sich ganz in der Gewalt des Gegenstandes fühlt. Es giebt freilich auch außerdem eine freie Liebhaberei am lateinisch oder romanisch schreiben, und wenn es mit dieser wirklich darauf abgesehen wäre in einer fremden Sprache gleich gut wie in der eigenen und gleich ursprünglich zu produciren: so würde ich sie unbedenklich für eine *frevelhafte und magische Kunst* erklären, wie das *Doppeltgehen,* womit der Mensch nicht nur Geseze der Natur zu spotten, sondern auch andere zu verwirren gedächte. So ist es aber wohl nicht, sondern diese Liebhaberei ist nur ein feines mimisches Spiel, womit man sich höchstens in den Vorhöfen der Wissenschaft und Kunst die Zeit anmuthig vertreibt. Die Production in der fremden Sprache ist keine ursprüngliche; sondern Erinnerungen an einen bestimmten Schriftsteller oder auch an die Weise eines gewissen Zeitalters, das gleichsam *eine allgemeine Person vorstellt,* schweben der Seele fast wie *ein lebendiges äußeres Bild* vor, und die Nachahmung desselben leitet und bestimmt die Production. . . . Ist aber jemand gegen Natur und Sitte förmlich ein Ueberläufer geworden von der Muttersprache, und hat sich einer andern ergeben: so ist es nicht etwa gezierter und angedichteter Hohn, wenn er versichert, er könne sich in jener nun gar nicht mehr bewegen; sondern es ist nur eine Rechtfertigung, die er sich selbst schuldig ist, daß seine Natur wirklich ein Naturwunder ist gegen alle Ordnung und Regel, und eine Beruhigung für die andern, daß der wenigstens *nicht doppelt geht wie ein Gespenst.* (236–37; emphases mine)

～❀～

The same is true of the Romance languages. Anyone required to write one of them in an official capacity will be perfectly aware that his thoughts in their first embryonic state are German, and that he merely begins to translate them early on, while the embryo is still being formed; and anyone who dedicates himself to scholarly writing in one of them will only find his task easy, unforced, and *unaccompanied by covert translation* when he feels utterly under the sway of the object.

To be sure, some write in Latin or one of the Romance languages for their own pleasure; and if their intentions in this were to write as well and as originally in the foreign language as in their own, I would unhesitatingly pronounce it a *wicked and magical art* akin to *going doubled,* an attempt at once to flout the laws of nature and to perplex others. But that is truly not their aim; their hobby is but an exquisite mimetic game with which to beguile away the hours out on the margins of philosophy and art. Writing in a foreign language is never original; rather remembrances of specific authors or of the manner of a certain era, which flesh forth as it were *a collective persona,* float before the soul almost like *living simulacra* that, when imitated on paper, give the writing direction and definition. . . . If on the other hand, in defiance of nature and morality, a writer becomes a traitor to his mother tongue by surrendering his verbal life to another, it is no false or affected self-mockery when he protests that he can no longer move about in that language; it is rather his attempt to vindicate himself by portraying himself as a wonder, a miracle surpassing all natural rule and order, and to reassure others that he at least *does not go doubled like a ghost.* (235–36; translation and emphases mine)

The only semantic element "missing" from this passage, if we take it as a kind of "source text" for Marx's ruminations, almost four decades later, on translations, spirits, and ghosts, is *der Geist*—which does appear, as I showed in *Translation and Taboo* (179–80), a page or two earlier (among many other places), in connection with Grotius and Leibniz writing equally originally in Latin and German or Dutch. And in any case Schleiermacher does have a list of *good* spirits of the dead, ghosts-that-aren't-quite-ghosts, which I've italicized in the quote above: the "collective persona" fleshed forth by remembrances of dead authors, which "float before the soul almost like living simulacra."

What's interesting about the juxtaposition of this passage with Marx's from *The Eighteenth Brumaire* is that they both invoke identical figures, translation, spirits, and ghosts, but in almost exactly opposite directions. For both of them the spirit/*Geist* is good and the ghost/

Gespenst is bad; both want to keep the spirit and eradicate the ghost. But for Schleiermacher spirits (or rather collective personae and living simulacra) are tied to the old, to "remembrances of specific authors or of the manner of a certain era," precisely what Marx calls ghosts; and what Marx identifies as the "spirit of the new," the true spirit of revolution or a foreign language cut off from linguistic and political translations from the old, Schleiermacher identifies with ghostly doubles. Schleiermacher, after all, is warning specifically against cutting literature off from the mother tongue; anyone who attempts to speak a foreign language without subliminally or covertly translating from the native language (except in commercial and technical subjects), anyone who tries to write as originally in a foreign language as in the native one, any translator who attempts to translate into a foreign language, is effectively "going doubled like a ghost." The speaker, writer, and translator are all *embodied* in the native language, at home, in the old and familiar. Trying to function in the foreign language without translational ties to home is tantamount to projecting a ghostly double across ontological boundaries, becoming something one is not, something new and unnatural ("an attempt at once to flout the laws of nature and to perplex others"). The idea of not translating mentally, of breaking entirely free of the native language, washes Schleiermacher with dread. Whenever a writer or a translator moves in the realms of the foreign he needs a bridge back to the native language; without such a bridge he not only cannot return home but can't "move" in the native language, becomes not only exiled abroad but paralyzed at home. Marx wants to blow up that bridge, wants to figure revolution with the image of the native speaker leaving his native language behind and moving body and soul into the foreign, forgetting the native language in order to "produce" in the foreign without translating: the *spirit* of the revolution is, or is it, the new without the old, the foreign without a translational bridge back to the native; the *ghost* or *specter* of the revolution is the old, the native, the familiar-but-dead, the past, ancient ideologies, which continue to hold sway over the bourgeoisie but must *not* continue to work upon the proletariat! We must *cut them off*, exorcise them, *not* channel them, not become necromancers of the ghosts of the dead ideological past, *not* translate them into the future, which must be kept free of ghosts and free of translations. Shakespeare shouldn't have to give Rossi permission to radicalize *Lear*. Shakespeare is dead and buried. His ghost shouldn't control what a Marxist translator does with his work in 1972. The future calls and the revolutionary translator responds. Schleiermacher on the other hand, like the other German romantics from Herder to Humboldt, is the quintessential bourgeois-becoming-aristocrat, longing for a return of the dead, dreaming of the graves opening and the invisible dead coming to life again, gaining new tangible bodies, becoming visible and vital. And the dead must appear in their own true colors, foreignized, not assimilated to our modern culture; they must come to life *on their home ground,* and we must go to them (this is Schleiermacher's legacy from the dead Herder, 10 years in the grave but still speaking to the German romantics). And if the dead will not speak, if their spirits are silent, why, speak for them, speak with their voice and their permission, or what you presume to call their voice and their permission; do what you must do *in their name,* and *in their spirit;* let it be the channeling of your group's ideological needs but call it the channeling of the dead, Homer and Shakespeare. Listen carefully to what you take to be the speaking of the dead, and if all you hear is kfmyfkh, then speak what you *know* they are saying . . .

At the argumentative extremes, then:

a. Schleiermacher says that we have to stick close to the old, the familiar, the native, the home culture, and insists that, when we speak or write foreign languages, we must always translate (covertly or embryonically) into them from our native language; arguing that only beginning language learners do this, and that it hinders their ability to "produce" in the foreign language, Marx urges us to *stop* translating from the old and embrace the spirit of the new.

b. Schleiermacher cherishes the spirits of dead authors and speaks lovingly of the directional and definitional guidance exerted by those spirits on writing and translating; Marx calls these dead historical figures who continue to influence the present "ghosts" and warns against their pernicious effects.

c. Schleiermacher warns against "going doubled like a ghost," by which he means precisely the kind of all-or-nothing plunging into the foreign without translational ties to the past, to the old and familiar, to the mother tongue, that Marx lauds as the true revolutionary spirit.

In a binary framework such as these two thinkers both clearly envision, Schleiermacher would be the liberal bourgeois who wants change, but wants to ground change firmly in tradition, in the past, in the familiar, and Marx would be the revolutionary who wants to liberate himself and his culture from the encircling arms of the past. Both view translation with a good deal of suspicion, but for opposite reasons—Marx because translation ties culture to its sources in the past, Schleiermacher because the translator is always potentially a "traitor" (*Überläufer*) to the native land and language:

Denn so wahr das auch bleibt in mancher Hinsicht, daß erst durch das Verständnis mehrerer Sprachen der Mensch in gewissem Sinne gebildet wird, und ein Weltbürger: so müssen wir doch gestehen, so wie wir die Weltbürgerschaft nicht für die ächte halten, die in wichtigen Momenten die Vaterlandsliebe unterbrükkt, so ist auch in Bezug auf die Sprachen eine solche allgemeine Liebe nicht die rechte und wahrhaft bildende, welche für den lebendigen und höheren Gebrauch irgend eine Sprache, gleichviel ob alte oder neue, der vaterländlichen gleich stellen will. Wie Einem Lande, so auch Einer Sprache oder der andern, muß der Mensch sich entschließen anzugehören, oder er schwebt haltungslos in unerfreulicher Mitte. (Schleiermacher 236)

For true as it remains in many ways that one cannot be considered educated and cosmopolitan without a knowledge of several languages, we must also admit that cosmopolitanism does not seem authentic to us if at critical moments it suppresses patriotism; and the same thing is true of languages. That highly generalized love of language that cares little what language (the native one or some other, old or new) is used for a variety of expressive purposes (mundane or sublime) is not the best kind of love for improving the mind or the culture. One Country, One Language—or else another: a person has to make up his mind to belong somewhere, or else hang disoriented in the unpleasant middle. (235)

Neither thinker likes the notion of forming indiscriminate attachments to any old culture or language or political system that comes along, old or new, native ("fatherlandish") or foreign; but when push comes to shove, Schleiermacher wants the old and the native, Marx the new and the foreign.

As Derrida showed with regard to Marx, however, and as Anthony Pym has shown with regard to Schleiermacher, both German thinkers were far less binary than they wanted to be, or even than they believed they actually were. Marx wants to have his ghosts and exorcise them too; Schleiermacher wants to keep German culture safe from foreign contamination and to strengthen German culture by importing the best and the brightest that foreign lands have to offer. Marx wants us to stop translating/channeling the ghosts (spirits) of the past and pour ourselves body and soul into the spirit (ghost) of the future; but if we cut ourselves entirely adrift from the past, if we forget the past, then we don't recognize its ghosts when they return to haunt us. "So one must not forget it," Derrida says, "one must remember it but while forgetting it enough, in this very memory, in order to 'find again the *spirit* of the revolution without making its *specter* return'" (110). Schleiermacher is attached to the past and would not willingly cut it off; but he is also directed toward a better future, in which the past and present disunity of Germany, German culture, the German language, might be gloriously transformed and purified. As Pym writes of Schleiermacher's family romance, the fatherland and mother tongue and their *Blendling* or bastard child, the German culture of the future, product of foreignizing translations:

Their child was necessarily "ein werdendes Volk" (p. 61), a people with a future, a people whose values were to be more than those inherited from the past. Since the mother is not a real mother [she still has to rely on Latin], the father is not yet an entirely legitimate father [he is politically fragmented and militarily occupied by the French], and the child is called upon to become rather more than a "pure effigy" of its parents, there can be no question of simply opposing the impurity of *Blendlinge* to the unblemished virtue of any immediately happy family. The natural German child is perhaps also a bastard. Schleiermacher's rhetorical questions, posing a choice between home and away, could not be answered clearly because neither of its terms was clear. Good and bad lay on both sides. The preacher could only state the problem and move on to more metaphors. ("*Blendlinge*" 19)

Both Schleiermacher and Marx imagine a utopia in which they would be free of otherness, ideally liberated from forces of alterity impinging on them from *somewhere* (within their own thoughts and actions, within the national mind or culture or *Geist*), but they can't pull it off. Not only can they not achieve such a utopia; they can't even imagine it fully. They need the spirits of otherness, of the past for Marx, of the foreign for Schleiermacher. They bring their idealizing binary imaginations to bear on a fuzzy world, and soon find themselves enmeshed in the impossibility of their own designs.

These two impossible designs most clearly converge in contemporary translation theory, perhaps, in Lawrence Venuti: a schleiermacherian Marxist who wants simultaneously to ground translation in respect for the past and the foreign and to use translation to push the native culture toward a better future; a conservative schleiermacherian elitist who takes Schleiermacher to task for his elitist conservatism; a dissident Marxist who associates something very like Marx's revolutionary conception of translation with assimilative capitalism, the enemy against which he struggles. Venuti wants to have both Marx and Schleiermacher, and to binarize the fuzziness that each failed to sort out on his own.

The problem for all three of these thinkers is the persistence of spirits, specters, ghosts—specifically, in this chapter, ideologies, or more generally otherness, alterity—despite everything they have done to banish them from a properly rationalist approach to translation. One would be self-contained, self-controlling, autonomous, decisive; free of unconscious impulses of dubious origin; able to size up a situation, make a rational decision for the future, and carry it out, without interference from alien forces. And yet the alien, the foreign, the different, the other is precisely what one needs to stir things up at home. One would institute a foreignizing regime without interference from the foreign; a rationalist inclusivist policy that will exclude every impulse not strictly controlled by reason. As we will see in chapter five, it can't be done. But that does not make the project any less attractive.

PART THREE

Transient Assemblies

Chapter Five

The Pandemonium Self

Rationalist and Postrationalist Theories of the Self

Most theories of translation have been, and continue today to be, rationalist. In them the source author is thought to have written the source text rationally, in the sense that he (in the patriarchal tradition of Western rationalism, agents idealized as "rational" are normatively male) first used his reason to structure his perceptual and other experiential data in systematic ways; next used those structures as raw materials for the formulation of a single coherent reason-governed intention (intended meaning or thought-content); and finally articulated that intention in the form of the source text. The source author, to put that simply, knew what he wanted to say and said exactly that.

The translation commissioner or initiator, then, guided by reason, decided to have the source text translated into the target language, and sought out a collective or individual agent (a translator, a translation agency, an ephemeral grouping of translators, experts, editors, project managers, marketers, etc.—the topic of chapter six) to perform the translation. Each member of this agent/agency then performed his job rationally, in the sense of using reason to direct and coordinate a plethora of translation- and generally language-related tasks toward the desired end of a successful target text. Whatever part-tasks fell to each individual agent in this process were thus subordinated to the dictates of reason: semantic, syntactic, and/or pragmatic transfer; adjustments for cultural differences; terminology management; proofreading; the coordination of send-out/receive-back cycles; the maximization of profit, marketability, professional reputation, etc.

Now, I should note that not all of this process has traditionally been a part of rationalist translation theory. Until fairly recently translation was thought of purely as an activity performed by a single rational agent, the translator, on a text created by another rational agent, the source author. It was not until the mid-1980s that scholars in the German *skopos/Handlung/*functionalist school of translation studies—Katharina Reiß, Hans Vermeer, Justa Holz-Mänttäri, Christiane Nord—began to articulate along rationalist lines the social processes by which a source text comes to be given to the translator to translate, how it is translated, and how the translation is disseminated. Polysystem and descriptive translation scholars—Itamar Even-Zohar, Gideon Toury, James Holmes, André Lefevere, Theo Hermans—have similarly attempted since the late 1970s and early 1980s to impose rationalist frameworks on the "systemic" mechanisms controlling translation in the target culture, notably in terms of the regulation of translation through cultural norms (generally at a significantly higher level of sociocultural generality than in the *skopos/Handlung/*functionalist school).

Rationalist ideals for the methods and practices of translation and translation scholarship have, however, come under increasing fire since around 1980 (dating this shift from Derrida's essay "Des Tours de Babel"), especially from various poststructuralist theorists who come to the study of translation from reading in the work of Jacques Lacan, Michel Foucault, Jacques Derrida, Gilles Deleuze and Fèlix Guattari, Luce Irigaray, Hélène Cixous, Julia Kristeva, and others. Typically, however, this work has been focused on issues other than translator subjectivity, most especially on texts—the breakdown or fragmentation or indeterminacy of meaning, the infinite regressions of "originality" (the disappearance of "original texts") (Rosemary Arrojo)—and on what I've called level-four ruminations on the emptying out of subjectivity, for example Foucauldian ruminations on the "translator-function" as a social construct that controls translator decisions far more effectively than any translator subjectivity; see, for example, Myriam Diaz-Diocaretz's *Translating Poetic Discourse,* my discussion of Diaz-Diocaretz in chapter 7 of *What Is Translation?,* Karin Littau in "Intertextuality and Translation" and "Translation in the Age of Postmodern Production," and Theo Hermans in "Translation and Normativity." Hermans these days has one foot in the rationalist camp of the descriptivists and the other in the post-rationalist camp of the deconstructionists, and in fact this poststructuralist fence-straddling has been increasingly common (and productive) in the field since the late 1980s: Lawrence Venuti draws heavily on post-structuralist theory to support a fairly traditional (explicitly rationalist) position in favor of foreignism (see his *The Translator's Invisibility* and

The Scandal of Translation); Tejaswini Niranjana in *Siting Translation* and Eric Cheyfitz in *The Poetics of Imperialism* enlist poststructuralist strategies in their postcolonial projects; the Brazilian translation theorist Else Vieira poststructuralizes the Anthropophagous Movement launched by Oswald de Andrade in the 1920s and transmogrified under the banner of cannibalism and *intradução* or "intranslation" by Augusto and Haroldo de Campos and Silviano Santiago in the 1970s and 1980s; Anthony Pym draws on poststructuralist theory to unfold a fundamentally rationalist economic approach to translation (see his *Translation and Text Transfer* and *Epistemological Problems in Translation and Its Teaching*); many recent feminist theorists of translation, such as Lori Chamberlain, Carol Maier, Suzanne Jill Levine, Sherry Simon, and Luise von Flotow, untie patriarchal knots using poststructuralist tools; my own *Translator's Turn* and *Translation and Taboo* (and this book as well) straddle the fence with poststructuralism in somewhat different but structurally parallel ways. For useful discussions of these trends, see especially Edwin Gentzler's *Contemporary Translation Theories* and Marilyn Gaddis Rose's *Translation and Literary Criticism*.

The only work in the field that I've seen that begins to deal with a postmodern or poststructuralist or postrationalist translator subjectivity, in fact, is the notion of "mosaic *habitus*" that Daniel Simeoni derives out of the sociological thought of Pierre Bourdieu. Put simply, Bourdieu's notion of the *habitus* is that we are what we do: all the many practices of our social lives, including talking and interacting with others, shape who we are. We inhabit the social spaces of our lives through what we do; what we do socially constitutes a kind of social personality, stretched both psychologically and socially over all the networked people and places and occasions in and around and with whom/which we interact. Simeoni's contribution to this theoretical framework is not only that he has begun tentatively to apply it to the translator's subjectivity, and thus to annex *habitus* theory for translation studies; he has also complicated the *habitus* with his concept of the mosaic, the multiplicity and fragmentariness of the *habitus,* the overlappingness of all the many *habitus* we inhabit.

My approach to postrationalist translator subjectivities is akin to Simeoni's (at least to the tentative model he has begun to flesh out in his *Target* article) in my concern with the fragmentation and "scattering" (as of seed, by a sower) of translator subjectivity across wide psychosocial networks. Whether this scattering is the *result* of the breakdown of rationalist explanatory models, or perhaps even of reason itself in a postmodern world, as it might seem to thinkers nostalgic for the comforts of reason, or whether translator subjectivities have always been scattered, fragmentary, "pandemoniac," and have only *seemed* tidily ordered by reason when artificially reduced to rationalist schemas—well, this is probably something that cannot be known. A postrationalist thinker would insist that rationalist translator subjectivities were beyond question the mere imaginary effects of rationalist ideologies and their conceptual lenses (and vanished when those ideologies crumbled), but then would almost certainly want to hedge on truth claims about translators' *true* subjectivities. Is it the case that, with discredited rationalist ideologies and methodologies tossed on the scrapheap, we can now *see clearly* the fragmentary subjectivities that have always been there? The temptation is great to make precisely that case. On balance, however, the postrationalist thinker must ultimately accede to the less triumphant view that the fragmentary or pandemoniac subjectivities s/he sees clearly are just as much the effects of his or her ideologies and methodologies as the old rationalist ones were of theirs.

In other words: in these two remaining chapters I am going to be trying *not* to present the translator's pandemonium self or disaggregated agency as "the way things are," even when my phrasing suggests that I believe that that is precisely the way things are. I do believe that the models I develop here accurately depict translator subjectivity; but I am also aware that my belief is itself an effect of the model—or rather, to be more accurate, it is an effect of a general ideological preference (not mine alone: it is widely associated with postmodern or poststructuralist or postfoundationalist or postrationalist culture at large) for fragmentary things over tightly ordered things, which preference inclines me to create pandemoniac models, and also to generate personal belief in those models.

In my terms from chapters three and four, in fact, my belief in the translator's fragmentary subjectivities is "channeled" to me by an ideology taken to be dominant in contemporary society (or at least in progressive or radical sectors of contemporary society).

It is generally considered advisable in poststructuralist discourse to blur the in/out or self/other distinction, so that, for example, the translator's "mosaic *habitus*" that Daniel Simeoni writes of should be thought of as referring both to the translator's "personality" or "psychology" "inside" his or her head and to the translator's social practices "outside" his or her head. I have endeavored to follow this rule myself, especially in *Translation and Taboo*, where Lacan's notion of the Other bridged the inside/outside gap, signifying a collective social force activated within individual heads. I have not, however, had a great deal of luck with this particular stratagem. The self/other distinction is far too well entrenched, its blurring thus far too counterintuitive, to prevent the summary collapse in most readers' minds of the whole inside/outside or self/other bridge into one side or the other. What I want to do here, therefore, is to do the "inside" first, here in chapter five, the "outside" second, in chapter six: first the psychology, then the political economy. At the same time I'd like to note that my discussion of the "inside" here in chapter five is constantly stretched across the inside/outside gap, and furthermore to remind diehard postmodern readers that this whole book is about the experience individuals have, at a whole series of different levels and in a whole range of different imageries, of being acted on by forces coming from the outside: spirits, ideologies, personality demons, and invisible hands.

Remembering, then, the four-step logology of spirit that I traced in chapter one, with (1) God at the top (singular, control, knowledge) (2) gods and goddesses, angels and demons, sprites and familiars (plural, control, knowledge) just below (3) then channeled spirits of the dead (plural, no control, knowledge), and finally, at the bottom (4) worshiped/remembered/imagined spirits (plural, no control, no knowledge), let me once again trace a secularized logology of the self, imagining the various forces that act on the self (well, yes, from within/ without, in Derrida's logic of spectrality) like spirits:

1. *Rationalist theories of the self.* Reason is not only the self's internalized god, king, lord, master, father; it is the only internal power. Since it has also been recognized for the entire history of rationalism that reason competes with other internal forces for control of the self (hence 2, below), "strong" rationalist theories of the self must posit a difference between those in whom reason rules and those ruled by other forces—the passions, for example. The multiplicity of inner powers is thus projectively mapped outwardly onto the socius, enabling rationalists to believe that they at least, and all other right-thinking people, are ruled entirely by reason. Another way of putting this is that reason reigns supreme inside everyone who may be said to possess a self; rational selfhood is denied various groups, especially women and children and members of despised races and classes, in order to buttress the idealized image of reason as a monotheistic deity inside the educated male European (or member of any other privileged group). Reason organizes all perception, all cognitive processing of perception, and all verbal and behavioral expression of thought. Reason constantly scans the past and present in search of the raw materials for the crucial task of planning and controlling the immediate (and to whatever extent possible also the less immediate) future. Education and civilization are imagined primarily as channels of instilling reason in children and other "prerational"

groups. Ethics is imagined as a channel for convincing individuals to make choices guided by reason.

2. *Competitive-powers theories.* Here the self is imagined as a battlefield where a small number of clearly defined forces struggle for ascendancy: God and the devil, faith and sin, the spirit and carnality (Christian theories). Intellect and emotion, reason and the passions, or, in Cartesian dualism, the mind and the brain, or again, in recent pop psychology, the left-brain and the right-brain, or the cortex and the limbic system (rationalist theories). The superego, ego, and id, or the conscious, preconscious, and unconscious (Freud). Each decision becomes a clash among these internal titans for control; in theory it should be possible after every such decision to determine which power seized the reins, which called the shots. As in 1, the assumption here is that only one power controls every action; in 2, however, no single power is ever imagined as intrinsically or automatically or continuously in charge.

3. *Pandemonium theories.* Currently the prevailing explanatory model in the cognitive sciences and neuropsychology/neurophilosophy; often referred to as multiple-draft theories, transient-assemblies theories, parallel-processing theories, production-systems theories, stream-of-consciousness theories, kludges theories, contention-scheduling theories, disaggregated-agency theories, etc. Not only is every action the product of conflicting or contending internal forces, as in (2); no one force *ever* seizes control. The illusion of control is generated out of a very rapid sifting out of hundreds or even thousands of such forces, often theorized as "demons" or "homunculi," or as "specialists" and "generalists." Huge numbers of action-potentials are constantly being generated, contrasted, explored, revised, discarded, tried out in practice; and the "selves" that are complexly and problematically constituted by these multiple agents most commonly don't quite know what they are going to do or say until they are actually doing or saying it. The motto of this level might be the famous quip of E. M. Forster: "How do I know what I think until I see what I say?" (quoted in Dennett 245).

4. *Posthumanist death-of-the-self theories:* any talk of agency or selfhood is a mere semantic echo of once-dominant but now phantomatic ideologies (notably "liberal humanism" or "bourgeois individualism"). All actions performed by what seems to be a "self" or a "subject" are in fact controlled by external social/ideological forces, which also project the atavistic illusion that the "person" ostensibly "intended" and performed the action out of some individualistic "autonomy." There are no selves, there is no autonomy; hence there is no freedom or free

will. The "individuals" wielded by these external forces are purely passive, the pawns of a deterministic control system.

As I noted in the corresponding place in chapter one, I am hoping that this logological tabulation will help forestall kneejerk dualistic responses to an assault on rationalism. If I challenge the validity of rationalism, you may dualistically want to believe, I must be an irrationalist—or even (guilt by association) irrational. If I don't believe individuals have perfected rational control over their actions, I must believe they have no control at all. If I reject rationalist theories of the self (1), I must agree with posthumanist death-of-the-self theories (4). The advantage of a four-rung schematization is that it helps us sort out the differences among levels 2, 3, and 4, which are often lumped together in dismissive ways by rationalist thinkers for whom there is only rationalism and everything else:

2. If you resist the liberal-humanist conception of the controlled rationalist subject, if you insist that reason is only one internal voice or force or agent among many, if you invoke Freud's theories of libido and the unconscious, if you speak of the many layers of somatic programming (*The Translator's Turn*) or the infinite displacements of taboo (*Translation and Taboo*), you think everybody is sick, crazy, everyone has Multiple Personality Disorder. You think translators aren't professionals self-governed by knowledge, training, craft, and ethics, they're out-of-control intuitives, empaths, spirit-channelers. You're a mystic, a dreamer, a flake.

3. If you resist the liberal-humanist conception of the unified executive mind, if you cite recent research in the cognitive and neurological sciences to the effect that there is no one "place" or "gland" or "Cartesian theater" in the brain to which all neural events are "brought" for executive decision-making, if you insist on the irreducible multiplicity of human thought, you're a mechanistic electrochemical determinist. In denying the existence of a "mind," you would turn the brain into an inhuman machine. You are, therefore, not only antihumanist; you are antihuman.

4. And if you resist the liberal-humanist conception of the individual will or intentionality, if you suggest that selfhood (including your own) is an illusion, you're completely cut off from reality, you're delusional.

Except that, insofar as all these forms of "insanity" blur together in the rationalist mind, it's never this clear. If you invoke Freud's theory of the conflicted tripartite psyche (2) or Dennett's theory of internal pandemonium (3), you're as likely to be called deterministic or delusional as morbidly flaky. If you invoke poststructuralist theories of the death of the self, you may well be accused of biological reductionism. By night all irrationalities are gray.

My main interest throughout this book—indeed in some sense throughout all my work—is in this third level, spirits, multiple ideologies, and the pandemonium self (as well as, next chapter, invisible-hand theories of disaggregated economic agency). Rationalist as I am in one sense of that word—that is, skeptical—I find first-level rationalist theories of the self and society embarrassingly naive, outdated, unrealistic, simpleminded; and fourth-level poststructuralist death-of-the-self theories, while interesting and provocative, and important in their opposition to enlightenment rationalism, too extreme in their utter rejection of agency.

Lacan's Schema L

But that description of my "main interest" being in the third level is too simple. I *am* interested primarily in 3, but more specifically in 2-becoming-3, in the liminal state or transition from 2 to 3, the gray area where minimal multiplicity slides into maximal multiplicity—where conflict becomes complexity and complexity moves toward chaos. I am specifically interested in this chapter in "infecting" a level-2 model like Jacques Lacan's schema L, from "On a question preliminary to any possible treatment of psychosis," with the level-3 complexity of Daniel Dennett's pandemonium model of the self in *Consciousness Explained*. By interweaving the two models (and the two levels), I hope to multiply complexity without simply sowing confusion.

Lacan's schema L is itself, in fact, a becoming-level-3 version of Freud's level-2 tripartite theory of the psyche, with multiple impulses from three other-terms rising steadily up through the Z-shaped schema toward the subject and expression:

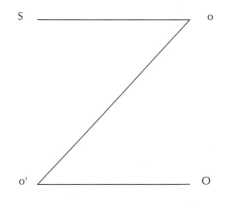

Schema L

Here S is the subject, the o or other-small-o is the subject's objects (important people and things, rendered "imaginary" by the subject's imagination), the o' or o-prime is the ego-ideal, and the O is the Other. The o' is roughly the ego *and* the superego (the ego in its aspect as superego) and the O roughly the unconscious—Lacan says that "the unconscious is the discourse of the Other" (193). The subject can probably best be understood as the therapeutic patient, the person sitting in front of the psychoanalyst; the subject is the front-side of the problem, the facade that must be gotten past to the "real" stuff, the depth psychology, which Lacan associates, famously, with otherness: "This schema signifies that the condition of the subject S (neurosis or psychosis) is dependent on what is being unfolded in the Other O" (193). The Z-shape of the schema, hanging downward with a bend, suggests that both that dependence and that unfolding are channeled *through* the o and o', the subject's objects and ego-ideal. The subject, which more traditional (rationalist) theories of the self have seen as either the entire self or its controlling agent, is constituted through and by otherness. "Why would the subject be interested in this discourse [of the Other]," Lacan asks, "if he were not taking part in it? He is, indeed, a participator, in that he is stretched over the four corners of the schema: namely, S, his ineffable, stupid existence, *o*, his objects, *o'*, his ego, that is, that which is reflected of his form in his objects, and O, the locus from which the question of his existence may be presented to him" (193–94).

Now, difficult as this model may seem at first glance, one of its attractions in the context of this chapter is that it is strikingly isomorphic with the four-rung logology of spirit I have now twice exfoliated (in chapters one and three), and interfolding them will bring about a more complex understanding of both Lacan and the logological hierarchy. Imagine schema L as the logology (with its original parameters from chapter one) bent and turned upside down:

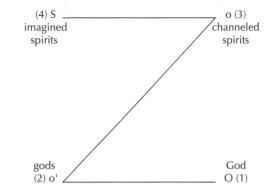

(4) S — imagined spirits

o (3) channeled spirits

gods (2) o'

God O (1)

Schema L$_S$

Or, more fully:

4. *worshipped/remembered/imagined spirits of the dead* (plural, no control, no knowledge) as the *subject* (S)

   • the subject has no independent power to act, no agency, no independent existence, or at best, as Lacan says, only an "ineffable, stupid existence"; in some sense it doesn't exist at all, except as an illusory effect of otherness, of the discourse of the Other; Lacan envisions only a single subject, one per customer, while this logological model would pluralize it, the subject as a statistical average of a long succession of moments of stupid ineffability

3. *channeled spirits of the dead* (plural, no control, knowledge) as the subject's *objects* (people and things), the other-small-o (o)

   • the objects are the introjected real-world others whose "knowledge" of the subject shapes or structures it from within, without however being able to regulate its behavior

2. *gods and goddesses, angels and demons, sprites and familiars* (plural, control, knowledge) as the *ego-ideal* (o')

   • again singular in Lacan (and Freud) but plural here, these are introjected authority figures, especially parents (for Freud and Lacan just the father) but also teachers, priests, political leaders, etc.; all manner of idealized ego-norms to which the subject attempts to conform its behavior and images

1. *God* (singular, control, knowledge) as the *Other*

   • Lacan never really defines the Other, and indeed in some sense it is undefinable, mysterious; in its power and mystery it *is* vaguely godlike, but entirely in a secular (nonsupernatural) context; it is the basic but inaccessible Voice that, in Lacan's revision of Heidegger's language mysticism, "speaks us"; it is ideology (the force that according to Althusser interpellates us as subjects) and also more than ideology; it is a trans-self or a meta-self, a "higher" (or lower) self that we channel in order to exist at all (it is, as Lacan says, "the locus from which the question of [the subject's] existence may be presented to him")

Note above all the reversal of rationalism here: the most powerful godlike locus of control in Lacan's schema, the Other, is also the most mysterious, the most alien and other, and the least susceptible to *our* control; and the "self" that rationalism would enthrone as reason, lord of all it surveys, becomes the stupid and ineffable subject, an empty husk, a mere sham or shell that is only given the illusory appearance of fullness by otherness. The middle terms are once again, at least for me, the most interesting: they are basically other people, idealized (2) or otherwise imaginarized (3) as inner voices, secularized analogues of channeled spirit-voices.

What I want to do in the rest of this chapter, then, once I've presented a quick summary of Daniel Dennett's pandemonium theory of consciousness, is to track the translator's disaggregated self down through Lacan's four terms: the invisible translator-subject (4); the introjected people, forms, tools that make the translator's job possible (3); the translator's ego-ideals, various forms of what Horace called the *fidus interpres* (Horace did not imagine the "faithful translator" as an ideal, but two millennia of theorizing have made it one) (2); and the translator's Other (1).

Pandemonium

"Pandemonium" is a term that Daniel Dennett borrows—ultimately from John Milton, of course, but more proximately from the early artificial intelligence researcher Oliver Selfridge, who was creating pandemonium AI architectures in the late 1950s—to describe what he persuasively argues is the true nature of consciousness: not so much total chaos, as the term seems to suggest in colloquial English, but simply the "place of all the demons," a place populated and run by hundreds of demons, thousands, perhaps millions. By demons Dennett does not mean evil spirits, of course, in the Christian sense, but simply agents, forces, in the Greek sense of *daimon* (indeed you may remember Socrates referring to τῆς δαιμονίας σοφίας, *tes daimonias sophias*, wise spirits/powers/gods, in the *Cratylus*, quoted in chapter two, above). A pandemonium theory of consciousness would be one in which every event was precipitated by a multitude of inner demons, or homunculi—agents—all proffering their partial, alternative, overlapping, conflicting or contending or cooperating contributions, and some finding their way into action, others being postponed for testing or timing, truckloads of others, the vast majority, being discarded.

This theory of consciousness seems counterintuitive in a rationalist tradition long given to assumptions about an executive decision-maker called the mind or the intellect or reason, situated somewhere in the brain (Descartes famously located it in the pineal gland). According to most rationalist theories of cognition, every mental event is staged, sooner or later, in this imaginary place that Dennett calls the "Cartesian

Theater"; every scrap of perception, every mental state, every thought is "shown" or "presented" to the mind for adjudication (what to do? where to send it? yes or no? now or later or never?). This tradition is so well-entrenched in Western thought that its assumptions seem self-evident to us. How else could we act in coherent, principled, and meaningful ways? How else could we ever say what we mean, and make our deeds match our intentions? (And surely we must *have* intentions that our words and deeds later match!) There *must* be an executive board-room somewhere that makes all the decisions. Not only would life be meaningless without it; it would be unlivable. We could not accomplish a single thing, from getting out of bed in the morning to brushing our teeth before bed at night.

In fact, however, we not only could; we do. There is no evidence at all that such a place exists in the brain—that the millions of different mental action-potentials are *ever* (let alone always) guided into some one single staging area for vetting or other executive processing. Ever since Gilbert Ryle's attack on the idea in *The Concept of Mind* (1949), philosophers, neuroscientists, cognitive scientists, and psychologists have been finding themselves forced by cumulative empirical and introspective evidence alike to conclude—many with a good deal of ideological or "intuitive" resistance—that there is no such thing as a single executive "mind" or "reason" that makes the brain's decisions, and thus "is" or "reflects" or "represents" the *true me.*

And once we begin to fight past the intuitions dictated to us by rationalism, massive quantities of postrationalist intuitions come flooding in:

We have scant access to the processes by which words "occur to us" to say, even in the cases where we speak deliberately, rehearsing our speech acts silently before uttering them. Candidates for something to say just spring up from we know not where. Either we find ourselves already saying them, or we find ourselves checking them out, sometimes discarding them, other times editing them slightly and then saying them, but even these occasional intermediate steps give us no further hints about how we do them. We just find ourselves accepting or discarding this word and that. If we have reasons for our judgments, they are seldom contemplated before the act, but only retrospectively obvious. ("I was going to use the word *jejune* but stopped myself, since it would have sounded so pretentious.") So we really have no privileged insight into the processes that occur in us to get us from thought to speech. They might be produced by a pandemonium, for all we know. (Dennett 304)

Like spirits speaking through a channel, like ideological agents operating through a subject, these word-demons "just spring up from we know not where" and start feeding us utterances. Some of those utterances we utter; others we stop or block. And it is only, as Dennett says, through a fraught process of *ex post facto* reconstruction that we are able to come up with rationales for having uttered A, B, and C and having left X, Y, and Z unsaid.

We also know that the brain does not have time to perform the kind of executive function that the rationalist tradition posits for it. This is painfully evident to foreign language students who, used to the artificial slowness of the classroom, try for the first time to speak or comprehend the language in a natural use situation: there just isn't time. By the time one has begun to parse a sentence coming out of a native speaker's mouth, the sentence is over and the next one (or the one after that) is already begun. Speaking is easier, provided one addresses a listener who is patient enough to wait for the analytical brain to review grammatical rules and lexical items and fit them all together into a coherent sentence; but just try to join in a conversation among several people. You will never find an opening. Natural speech is just too fast. Even for native speakers natural speech is often too fast to follow; the only reason the brain can successfully analyze incoming sentences in a language it knows well, in fact, is that it has developed various anticipatory strategies based on tonal, semantic, and syntactic redundancy. (Hence the notorious difficulty of following an academic paper read out loud at top speed: written academic discourse typically lacks the redundancies that make speech easier to follow at high speeds.) Speaking a language fluently, participating actively in a conversation, making witty remarks with just the right timing, is typically a series of what cognitive scientists call "ballistic" acts, or "unguided missiles," as Dennett puts it: "once they are triggered, their trajectories are not adjustable" (145). (Sometimes while in the middle of a rapid-fire conversation in a foreign language that you speak really well it's possible to *feel* the ballisticity of your own speech production: the words and sentences come hurtling out across your tongue and between your lips, and you can feel yourself not having time to formulate a coherent discursive intention, feel the extent to which you are at the mercy of your brain's ballistic acts. Perhaps you have the presence of mind while all this is going on to marvel at your ability to do this successfully in a language learned after childhood; while you are marveling, however, all you can do is hope that everything comes out all right.)

But even nonballistic acts must be formulated very rapidly:

The brain's task is to guide the body it controls through a world of shifting conditions and sudden surprises, so it must gather information from that world and use it *swiftly* to "produce future"—to extract anticipations in order to stay one step ahead of disaster. . . . So the brain must represent temporal properties of events in the world, and it must do this efficiently. The processes that are responsible for executing this task are spatially distributed in a large brain with no central node, and communication between regions of this brain is relatively slow; electrochemical nerve impulses travel thousands of times slower than light (or electronic signals through wires). So the brain is under significant time pressure. It must often arrange to modulate its output in the light of its input within a time window that leaves no slack for delays. (144)

Hence, of course, the notoriously error-ridden nature of speech (and all human behavior). We stop and start sentences in the middle. We hem and haw, leaving dozens of thoughts half-expressed every minute. We keep casting around for just the right thing to say, hoping that our "mouths" will find it for us—since, as E. M. Forster so wittily and so accurately perceived, we often don't know what we're trying to say until we say it, and have some time to reflect on what just came out of our mouths. ("Did I really say that? That sounded awful . . .") We transpose and conflate phonemes, syllables, and whole words, creating spoonerisms and mangling idioms; we omit key words, like "not," making semantic hash of what we imagined we were trying to say. We think we have said something when we haven't, and we think we've only thought something that we have actually voiced—and it is often difficult for others to convince us that we are wrong about what we think happened. One voice or force or group of such forces in our heads handled the utterance while another handled the behind-the-scenes intending, and the two don't quite concur. When we translate, our eyes and fingers play tricks on us, and we invert or omit characters, words, or whole lines. One translator friend reported that, while editing a translation she had just finished, she began unconsciously to translate it back into the source language. Hundreds or thousands of mental "word demons" or "utterance demons," or whatever we want to call them, lots of them, all flow into the stream(s) of consciousness, generating alternative things to say all at once; and since we have so little time to choose among them, sometimes several come out at the same time and contaminate each other. As Dennett writes:

We can suppose that all of this happens in swift generations of "wasteful" parallel processing, with hordes of anonymous demons and their hopeful constructions never seeing the light of day—either as options that are *consciously* considered and rejected, or as ultimately executed speech acts for outsiders to hear. If given enough time, more than one of these may be silently tried out in a conscious rehearsal, but such a formal audition is a relatively rare event, reserved for occasions where the stakes are high and misspeaking carries heavy penalties. In the normal case, the speaker gets no preview; he and his audience learn what the speaker's utterance is at the same time. (238)

"In the Pandemonium model," Dennett writes a few pages later, "control is usurped rather than delegated, in a process that is largely undesigned and opportunistic; there are multiple sources for the design 'decisions' that yield the final utterance, and no strict division is possible between the marching orders of content flowing from within and the volunteered suggestions for implementation posed by the word-demons" (241). There is, in other words, no such thing as a single "thinker" in the brain that "thinks thoughts," intends meanings, and then starts planning how to express them in the most effective and accurate way possible. If thoughts are "designed," if meanings are "intended," they are designed and intended by lots of smaller contending thinkers ("demons") rather than a single executive one, and have to take their chances in the welter or pandemonium of other demons trying to formulate and express their ideas too. And even those demons should not be thought of as part of the architecture of the brain; it is not as if we had thousands of *permanent* word-demons sitting around in our brains coming up with things to say. The word-demons *are* the verbal productions they create. A thousand of them are born and die every minute. (Our cultural evolution over the past 150,000 or 10,000 or 100 years [depending on precisely what kind of cultural evolution we're talking about] has soft-wired into various parts of our brain the *potential* for creating these word-demons, and our linguistic habits from the course of our life to date give them content and direction, but the word-demons themselves are utterly ephemeral.)

Reason is our most valiant attempt to impose some sort of order on this process, and sometimes it does seem as if that project is working. We seem to feel (though only after the fact, and only through the rapid forgetting of all the rejected or discarded action-potentials) a smooth transition from thought to articulation, from plan to action. Other times we make some horribly revealing Freudian slip and want to hide in a hole in the ground. And it is only a tiny neurological distance from the stammers and misfires that plague our speech to the truly bizarre speech productions of some aphasics, like the "jargon aphasic" who was asked to identify a pair of scissors and said: "Groves—it's a groves—it's not really a groves—two groves containing a comb—no, not a comb—two groves providing that the commandant is not now—" (quoted in Dennett 249–50). This seems psychotic, but isn't. In fact we all produce sentences just like that in our sleep, or in the hallucinatory theta state between waking and sleep. The line separating "rational speech" from word-salad is exceedingly thin and impossible to pin down—precisely because we do *not* have in our brains the kind of "central meaner" or thought-thinker that rationalist philosophy has wanted both to posit in theory and to create in practice. One last longish quote from Dennett, and then we'll move on:

> There is no single, definitive "stream of consciousness," because there is no central Headquarters, no Cartesian Theater where "it all comes together" for the perusal of a Central Meaner. Instead of such a single stream (however wide), there are multiple channels in which specialist circuits try, in parallel pandemoniums, to do their various things, creating Multiple Drafts as they go. Most of these fragmentary drafts or "narratives" play short-lived roles in the modulation of current activity but some get promoted to further functional roles, in swift succession, by the activity of a virtual machine in the brain. The seriality of this machine (its "von Neumannesque" character) is not a "hard-wired" design feature, but rather the upshot of a succession of coalitions of these specialists.
>
> The basic specialists are part of our animal heritage. They were not developed to perform peculiarly human actions, such as reading and writing, but ducking, predator-avoiding, face-recognizing, grasping, throwing, berry-picking, and other essential tasks. They are often opportunistically enlisted in new roles, for which their native talents more or less suit them. The result is not bedlam only because the trends that are imposed on all this activity are themselves the product of design. Some of this design is innate, and is shared with other animals. But it is augmented, and sometimes even overwhelmed in importance, by microhabits of thought that are developed in the individual, partly idiosyncratic results of self-exploration and partly the predesigned gifts of culture. Thousands of memes, mostly borne by language, but also by wordless "images" and other data structures, take up residence in an individual brain, shaping its tendencies and thereby turning it into a mind. (Dennett 254–55)

The Invisible Subject

I suggested above that Lacan imagines the subject as the patient, the analysand, the person sitting before him in analysis: the flesh-and-blood body that "hides" (but also complexly reveals) the psychic complexities "inside." It will be important, and perhaps also difficult, to distinguish this from the "mask" or "persona" that we project outward into the world, our "self-image." That latter would be the ego, or even the ego-ideal, which Lacan places on the same left side of schema L but on a lower layer: the o' is the idealized self as modeled on the father, or, in the pluralized version of the schema that I diagramed above, on parents and other authority figures. One fairly simplistic way of making the distinction would be that the S is the view of himself as whole person that the patient presents, the patient as he would like to see himself (sticking with Lacan's generic "he"), supposedly autonomous and full of rational intentions; and the o' is the lower layer uncovered by analysis, the self as constituted by idealized emulation of authority figures.

But that is still too simplistic. The problem is perspective: are we going to take the psychoanalyst's view from outside the patient, or the patient's view from the inside? The complexity of Lacan is that he attempts to do both at once: the right side of his schema is otherness as perceived by the self, and the left side is the self as conditioned by otherness. And even that is too simple. Like Derrida's logic of spectrality, indeed like a great deal of poststructuralist theory (to which it contributed in no small way), Lacan's conception of the psyche oscillates strategically between inside and outside, always contaminating the one with the other: the inside is full of introjected outsides, the outside consists (at least as humanly perceived—Kant's point exactly) of projected insides. In Lacan's theory of the mirror-stage (1–7), for example, the year-and-a-half-old toddler discovers the "self" by seeing it in a mirror: an external image is internalized as the inner "me," and what is thus internalized remains other, outer, alienated. The self as other; the other as self.

So what we have in the subject is an image of the self that is conditioned by all the forces of otherness—all the other-demons, as Dennett would put it—to which it is tied on the diagram, the o/o'/O, and at the same time presents to the outside world a "representative" face, a face that takes credit for all that it is not, all that it is lent by otherness.

What makes this interesting in the translator is that the true inner substance that the translator-subject is supposed to represent *is* precisely the absence of self, the emptying-out of self—the invisible self. The perfect translator-subject is invisible, anonymous, or, as Anthony Pym writes in *Translation and Text Transfer*, "nobody":

It has been astutely lamented that, in accordance with the principle of ideal equivalence, the translator remains "nobody in particular" (Belitt 1978). Of all the symbols and saints used to represent the profession—Janus or Jerome, forked tongues or true interpreters—, the figure of "nobody" is of particular theoretical profundity.

Some translators have of course expressed and exerted strong personal identities. Yet there must remain doubt as to whether their particularity was not in conflict with their work as translators. Reading a Hölderlin version of

Pindar probably has more to do with reading Hölderlin than with establishing any strict relation of equivalence with Pindar. Or again, active appreciation of the subjectivity and work of a Jerome or a Luther effectively blocks the reading position necessary for ideal equivalence to what might be projected as "the" Bible. In principle, if translated texts are to be received and believed as ideal equivalents of their antecedents, translators themselves must remain anonymous and their work must remain unevaluated as individual labour. (51)

This is a powerful statement of an ancient norm from one of the most thoughtful and provocative translation theorists in the world today. Pym fleshes forth the translator as automaton, the translating subject as automatic writer. Impulses come in from the outside, and the translator carries them out. The translator-subject has no personality, no ideas, no opinions. The translator-subject has nothing to say. The word-demons and idea-demons and image-demons come from outside the subject, possess it briefly, use it to produce a translation, and move on. "A scholar is just a library's way of making another library," as Dennett quips (202); by the same token a translator-subject is just a source text's way of making a target text, a source author's way of addressing a target reader. The translating subject is just a channel.

Pym goes on:

This means that, although equivalence is certainly the result of work, its social function depends on the practical anonymity of this work; it can only function for as long as the receiver is indifferent to the translator's subjectivity. Equivalence itself may well be analysed in terms of exchange value; its false naturalness may be reduced to mere assurance of potential use; but no aspect of applied or misapplied economics gives the slightest indication that the principle of equivalence will allow translators to be appreciated in terms of any individualised labour value. A labour-value theory of equivalence would be a contradiction in terms.

Translation might thus be described as a potentially scandalous activity in which people work to produce an output which is ideally thought to have the same value as the input, leaving their labour without value in itself. (51–52)

It is, Pym recognizes, more complicated than this: "After all, physical translators are individuals, with individual bank accounts which should be individually affected to the extent that the value of their work is at least financially quantified. Should the anonymity posited as a correlative of ideal equivalence then be seen as no more than the way in which *certain* translations are read by *certain* people?" (52).

Yes and no. Economically translators do add value to texts, and do receive remuneration accordingly. Semiotically, though, "translation is defined by a relation of equivalence which denies the very possibility of any such value added, since the output is supposed to be directly exchangeable for the input" (52). How is this possible? As Pym notes, these two economies, that of material text-production and that of equivalent meaning-production, are at once in conflict and interconnected: "Since ideal equivalence on the semiotic level denies value added, it necessarily hides translational labour value or converts it into non-value, thereby exerting habitually nefarious influences on translators' financial remuneration and professional psychology" (52).

And with those last two items, pay and subjectivity, we've gotten where I wanted to go with Pym. Let's stop now and run that backwards: the translator's low pay and low professional self-esteem, negative effects in the monetary/professional economy of material text-production, are caused by the translator's ideologically prescribed anonymity, which is mandated by the semiotic economy of equivalent meaning-production, which in turn is caused by—what? Pym doesn't say. "Translation *is defined* by a relation of equivalence which denies the very possibility of any such value added, since the output *is supposed* to be directly exchangeable for the input"—defined and supposed by whom, by what? And how does that work, exactly? How does translation get defined that way, and, more important in this chapter on the self, how does the translator-subject get constructed as anonymous, invisible, the performer of labor that adds no value?

Uncovering the origins of this mandate in cultural and ideological history has been one of my most pressing concerns in earlier books, especially *The Translator's Turn* and *Translation and Taboo;* the image of translation as spirit-channeling here, especially in chapter two, is another attempt to get at the "prehistory" of what Pym realistically enough accepts as the way things are, the nature of translation in its current cultural and economic context. But let me set questions of historical origins aside here and focus instead on this question of the immediate psychological *construction* of an anonymous or invisible subject. If Dennett's pandemonium theory of the self is even close to the way things actually work, there should be not only second- and third-level (o and o') demons working to construct the translator-subject as invisible—economic demons implanted in the translator's head by clients, agency people, translation instructors, and the like (the other-small-o), ideological demons implanted in the translator's head by various normative authorities (the o' or ego-ideal)—but first-level (S) demons as well, front-line demons that convert deeper economic and ideological impulses into subjective behavior. Or, in terms of Lacan's schema L:

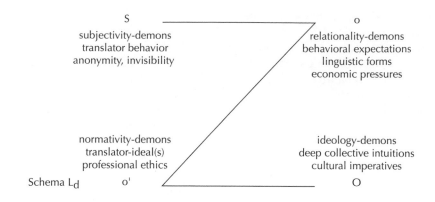

This is, of course, very much a first approximation. I will be attempting to flesh this schematization out all through the rest of this chapter.

For now, then: what are the subjectivity-demons that collectively, thousands and thousands at a time, continuously construct the translator-subject as invisible, anonymous, as a phantom that performs labor without adding value? The invisibility of the translator-subject cannot, we agreed, come from nowhere; it must be constructed. And Dennett's pandemonium model of human consciousness, which reflects the currently prevailing assumptions of both neurology and cognitive science, suggests that it must be *constantly* constructed, built wastefully and piecemeal by thousands of action-potentials or demons. The invisible translator-subject in this view would not, therefore, be the *subtracted* self, my eremitological term for the Augustinian cenobitic translator-ideal in *Translation and Taboo* (101); it would rather be a self continually being reconstructed in the *image* of the subtracted self. Reconstructed (and not subtracted), we might say, by anonymity-demons, or invisibility-demons, which arise to build the anonymous or invisible self in specific situations, in response to specific behavioral and especially self-representational needs:

o what difference does it make whether anybody knows I did it, it's got to be done, I can do it, I'll do it

o I can do it by tomorrow at 9 A.M. if I stay up all night, and they do *need* it by then

o who cares if it's boring, the pay's the same as for an interesting text

o here's a challenge for you, this guy has a very distinctive style, try to sound *just like* him

o you don't need a life, what would you be doing if you weren't sitting here translating? watching TV, probably, feeding your face, getting sloshed, so just keep going and quit bitching and moaning

And so on. But note that these anonymity-demons are implicitly in dialogue with a whole other class of demons, offering negative responses to them, rebellious or resistant demons arising from personality, perhaps, or boredom, or cramped muscles, or some other form of improperly embodied or (non-in)visible behavior. This suggests that anonymity-demons might in fact be antipersonality-demons, demonic antibodies as it were, hordes and hordes of troops dedicated to catching and exterminating personality-demons, have-a-life-demons, body-demons—round 'em up and snuff 'em out before they can make the leap into translatorial behavior:

- why should I do this, I hate this job, I'll just work and work and work and nobody will ever know I did it
- there's no way I can get this done by the deadline
- this is so *boring*
- why don't I quit translating and find something more challenging to do with my life?
- what am I *doing* here, staring at this stupid computer screen hour after hour with these tedious repetitive texts, poring through dictionaries looking for just right word, as if just the right word made such a huge difference, my back is on fire, I've got a splitting headache, I've got to get a *life*

Or we might imagine the anonymity/antipersonality-demons speaking more generally, each of them whispering a slightly different variation on the same general theme (this is highly idealized, of course, which is to say highly ideologized; adios to rough edges and truncated grammar, squeaks and shouts and stammers; cue the violins; if you hear the sappy strains of "Desiderata" in the background here, it's no accident):

- I should step back and let the source author speak directly to the target reader
- translation isn't about me
- translation is about the source author communicating to people who don't speak or read his/her language
- I'm a neutral instrument of communication between people from different language communities

o whatever comes along, it's my job to pass it on unchanged, not to think about it critically

o I have no right to come between the source author and target readers, except as a window comes between a viewer and the thing viewed

o subjectivity is a luxury that only the writer and reader can afford

o subjectivity in the translator spells disaster for translation

o I should be empty before the text

o the text should flow through me without impediment or distortion

o the flowing of texts through my emptiness feels wonderful, almost mystical

o the loss of ego that this process entails is my highest achievement as a translator

o I need ego-loss like a drug

o the emptying-out of subjectivity may be impossible, but it has to be done

o I'm only human, I'm bound to let personality get in the way to some extent or another but

o I shouldn't celebrate the personality-demons that rise to the surface, I should hate them, and myself for giving them any shelter or encouragement

o even the tiniest personality-demon that sneaks into a translation distorts the spirit of the source text.

o the result of that distortion is always bad translation

o if a personality-demon ever ventures the notion that a personal translation is a good one, I should push it aside it in horror and disgust

o that's original writing, not translation

o nothing wrong with original writing, but trying to pass it off as a translation is deception

And again, that reference to the horrified suppression of personality suggests personality-demons like the following (still idealized, still coming out with a liberal-humanist paint job), and antipersonality-demons to hunt them down:

• I'm a creative person, I've got a flair for these things, I can make this translation come to life!

- these words I'm writing, they're all mine, they came out of my head, my experience of the target language
- if the translation is going to live for my reader it has to live for *me*, and *through* me
- sure, what my reader gets through me is mostly me, but without my creative intervention s/he would get *nothing* of the source text, and hey, it *is* my creative response to the source text, I'm not just making it up
- and anyway, even if it was entirely me, that would still be an undeniably good thing for the target reader, who needs *something* to work with, and can't get it in the source language
- to be a good translator I need experiential exposure to and creative and imitative command of expressive modes, styles, registers, idiolects and sociolects, jargons, argots; cultures, subcultures, intercultures; people, interpersonal communication, human motivation; ideas, arguments, theses, philosophies; mythologies and traditional imageries; belief structures, conventions, traditions, norms; and when I imitate them, it's *me* doing it, not somebody else.
- my job is constructive, I build things, starting with the source text and author, whom I invent out of my own research-based imagination, and continuing right on to the target text and its reader, whom I have to imagine for translation to be at all possible
- and so what if I see things my own way, so what if my perspective is slanted, biased, prejudiced; as Hans-Georg Gadamer says, without prejudice there is no understanding

Death to all these personality-demons! That must be the battle cry of the anonymity/antipersonality-demons, which we can imagine being created or generated or perhaps just summoned forth out of some unformed ideological other-directed mass of antipersonality animus.

Still, some do get through. It is inevitable. There are too many of them. Translators are expected to have personalities in other areas of their lives; it is perhaps asking too much for the antipersonality-demons to eradicate every impulse to personality as it arises, before it erupts into behavior. The antipersonality-demons are not infallible. They make mistakes. Some of the personality-demons can in fact be quite persuasive, even importunate. They can sometimes make their case plausibly and urgently. The target-language words do come from the translator's own expressive repertoires; the translator does lend vibrancy to the target text. In some cases these notions might even be perfectly harmless. And the antipersonality-demons typically only have a fraction of a second to make a strategic kill-or-pass decision. *Is that a personality-demon? Maybe not . . . oops, damn, it was, too late! Better kill anything that might even be construed as one. Preemptive strike, better safe than sorry.* It is difficult to tell when an apparently harmless personality-demon is going to lead to a serious distortion of the text; hence in principle there *is no such thing*, at least while translating, as a harmless personality-demon. Kill them all, let the Other sort them out.

Note here the advantage of Dennett's pandemonium model: even with a dualistic level-2 competitive-selves situation, personality vs. anonymity, creativity vs. instrumentality, visibility vs. invisibility, level-3 multiplicity reigns. Dualism is always a reductive idealization of a vastly more complex field. A useful reduction, in some cases, especially as a first step toward a more detailed and realistic understanding—but dangerous in its tendency to settle in and set up housekeeping as *reality*, and to delay indefinitely the moment at which the "temporarily" forgotten complexities are engaged.

The Translator's Objects

The translator's objects, as I mentioned earlier, are other people and things—but only in the translator's imagination. This is the hermeneutical sense of "dialogue" that I explored in part two of *The Translator's Turn:* dialogue with imagined others, imaginary source authors and target readers, but also, beyond the relatively narrow scope of that book's argument, imaginary clients and agency people and editors and experts, imaginary native speakers of the source and target languages (along with any linguistic analyses derived from the imagination of "what they'd say" in specific imaginary contexts), and imaginary things (machines, parts, processes, systems) fleshed forth from diagrams, descriptions, past experience, television, the movies, etc. The translator sits alone at the computer, imagining people and things:

- imagining what the source author was trying to say, and how that would have to be reframed so as to make the most sense to an imagined target reader;
- imagining what the client or agency project manager or freelance editor would say if s/he did this or that;
- imagining how another translator in the same language combination (a competitor, a friend) would render this or that;

- imagining how an expert in the field of the text who *really knows* this terminology would say this or that;

- imagining native speakers of the two languages who use those languages fluently, effectively, idiomatically, or even problematically, complexly, transformatively, and basing contextualized and personalized linguistic analyses on the speech of those imaginary people; and

- imagining the referents described in the text, the machinery and its parts in a technical text, the product and its "sizzle" (lifestyle images, etc., see Berger) in an advertising text, the plaintiff and defendant and their counsel and other parties in legal documents, the companies and their structures and personnel and solvency and product lines (and so on) in a tender, the company and its production processes and and chemical compounds and waste disposal and surrounding areas in an environmental impact document, etc.

The translator does interact with real people, of course, albeit often "invisible" ones (because they make contact by phone, fax, or e-mail and so remain bodiless and often nameless), and we will be exploring such interactions in the context of disaggregated translation agencies in chapter six; but even when the translator knows one of these real people personally, or has spoken with him or her on the phone, *in the translator's imagination* that person is still what Lacan (and in general psychological object-relations theory) calls an imaginary "object."

Once again Dennett's pandemonium theory of the self encourages us to think of these "objects" impinging on the translator's behavior through the emergence of thousands of individual demons, each carrying a bit of remembered experience, an interpretation, a suggested rendition, etc., and all of them overlapping, conflicting, fine-tuning each other, suppressing or resisting each other:

- imagined-source-author-demons
- imagined-target-reader-demons
- imagined-client-demons
- imagined-agency-demons (imagined-project-manager-demons, imagined-editor-demons, imagined-proofreader-demons, etc.)
- imagined-competitor-demons, imagined-colleague-demons, imagined-friend-demons
- imagined-expert-demons
- imagined-native-speaker-demons (lexicon-demons, syntax-demons, collocation demons, text-type-demons, relevance-demons, etc.)

- imagined-referent-demons (machine-demons, system-demons, procedure-demons, process-demons, bureaucracy-demons, cultural-knowledge-demons, etc.)

Rather than exfoliating each of these at length here, I propose to postpone discussion of most of them until chapter six, where the real-world economic agents we'll be studying will be partly invisible and partly also, as I say, imaginary as well. Here, then, let me simply illustrate the method on a single category, the imagined-native-speaker-demons, in the process delineating a pandemonium model for linguistic analysis that seems to me far more realistic in terms of actual human language-processing than existing linguistic models and, as such, might even form the basis for a pandemonium neural-net machine translator.

Once again the basic assumption is that hordes of these demons rise up into the translator's stream(s) of consciousness every moment, vying for attention, acting on and reacting to each other, correcting each other, tripping over each other in their haste to come forward and be recognized and make the leap into behavior—which is to say, in this case, make some significant contribution to the translation. I've taken a sample sentence from an actual translation job I did about two weeks before this writing, a one-paragraph letter to the editor from a Finnish newspaper, faxed to me by an agency person who had no idea what it was, only that it was Finnish and that the client wanted it translated. The physical appearance of the fax is described by one of the text-type-demons, below (Tb). The sample sentence is the first line of the letter. I've numbered its words to facilitate symbolic representation in writing of the sequencing shifts made by the syntax- and article-demons (an animated computer graphics program could represent the sequentializing done by those demons more powerfully, though not necessarily with precise phenomenological realism):

1	2	3	4	5	6	7	8	9

Keskustan ollessa hallituksessa annettiin noin 70 miljardin pankkituelle pankkisalaisuus.

- lexicon-demons:

  La Downtown be government give about 70 milliard bank-support bank-secret.

  Lb Center be cabinet give about 70 billion bank-benefit bank-secrecy.

  Lc Center-Party be board-of-directors give approximately 70 thousand-million bank-bailout bank-confidentiality.

  Ln etc.

- syntax-demons:

  Sa 1's/of-1 while-2ing in-3 was-4ed 5 6 7 to/for-8 9

  Sb 1 while-2ing in-3 5 6 of-7 for-8 was-4ed 9

  Sc while-2ing in-3 1 was-4ed 5 6 7's to-8 9

  Sd while 1 2ed in-3 9 was-4ed to-5–6–7–8

  Se 9 was-4ed for-8 of-5–6–7 while in-3 1 2ed

  Sf While 1 2ed in-3 9 was-4ed to-5–6–7–8

  Sg 9 was-4ed to-5–6–7–8 while 1 2ed in-3

  Sn etc.

- article-demons (since, as I mentioned in chapter four, Finnish has none and they must be slotted in appropriate places in English)

  Aa 1 3 6 7 8 9

  Ab the-1 the-3 the-6 the-7 the-8 the-9

  Ac a-1 a-3 a-6 a-7 a-8 a-9

  Ad a-1 a-3 the-6 the-7 a-8 a-9

  Ae a-1 the-3 a-6 the-7 a-8 the-9

  An etc.

- collocation-demons

  Ca the government's downtown, the government is in a building downtown, there is a government building downtown, government is a name for what goes on in a building downtown, the government is in the city center, the cabinet is in the city center, the cabinet is in the center, the cabinet is in the center of the room, the center is in the cabinet, the centerpiece is stored in the cabinet, it's stored in the center of the cabinet; the cabinet/government has a center, the governmental cabinet is in the center, the center is in the governmental cabinet, the Cabinet has politicians from the left, right, and center, the Center Party is in the Cabinet

  Cb banks have support, banks have secrets, banks have secret supports, bank secrets have bank supports, bank supports have bank secrets, how a bank is supported is one of the bank's secrets, the architectural supports of a bank building are hidden from public view, a bank's financial support is kept secret, the bank is given secret support, the bank is secretly supported financially, the bank is bailed out, the bailout is confidential

  Cn etc.

- text-type demons
  Ta this is a newspaper, this is the editorial page, these are the letters to the editor, this is a letter to the editor, it will express the opinion of a private citizen, it may be written in a colloquial style
  Tb this is a fax, it has four different types of writing on it, handwriting ("Doug—As discussed. Please have back by noon today. Job #XXXX, X X [name]—XXX XXX-XXXX, Fin—>Eng $30 BBS— (XXX) XXX-XXXX"), computer printout ("SUOMENMAA 20.02.97 34 OULU SIT 10881 LT 5/VK 103 NEITSYTSAARET 3 105"), logo ("SITA"), photocopied newsprint (". . ."), Suomenmaa lit. Finland's country, name of newspaper published in Oulu, 20.02.97 must be the date this article was published, 34 the page, it's a newspaper article, it's short, one paragraph long, it's signed *Veronmaksaja* = taxpayer, it must be a letter to the editor, it will express the opinion of a private citizen, it may be written in a colloquial style
  Tn etc.
- relevance-demons
  Ra A taxpayer is writing about the placement of cabinets in—no, too much money involved, and what would banks and secret support have to do with that? "cabinet" as a piece of furniture must be an incorrect translation of "hallitus"
  Rb A taxpayer is writing about the downtown area, something about the cost of banks and government buildings in the city center, secrecy or confidentiality
  Rc A taxpayer is writing about Finland's political center, the government, and banks, or no, not the whole government, the Cabinet, the political center in the Cabinet and its relation to banks, Finnish cabinet members have become bank directors, bank directors have become Cabinet members, are we talking about secret support for banks among centrist politicians in the Finnish Cabinet?
  Rd Keskusta = center is also used as shorthand for keskustapuolue = Center Party, it makes more sense to talk about a specific party in the Cabinet, a political party with Cabinet representation, than it does about the political center, nowhere in the letter is the party mentioned specifically, it's just center this and center that, but a specific time frame is given, when the center was in the Cabinet, and by definition there's always a "center" in the Cabinet (even if only abstractly), so it should be when the Center Party was in the Cabinet

Re The taxpayer is saying that a lot of money, 70 billion, presumably (since this is in Finnish and no currency is specified) 70 billion Finnmarks, was given to banks (a bailout, probably, given the amount, and weren't the banks in big trouble recently?) and then some sort of secrecy or confidentiality was slapped on it, bank confidentiality, the confidentiality that protects all bank transactions, s/he must be complaining that a political act that should not have been protected by banking confidentiality was concealed from the public by the *ruse* of banking confidentiality, concealed by the Center Party, that must be the implication here, otherwise why harp on the fact that the Center Party happened to be in the Cabinet then? or the taxpayer is insinuating that the whole thing was set up by the Center Party, some sort of pork-barrel deal

Rn etc.

So all these demons swirl around in my head for a few seconds and I type this:

While the Center Party was in the Cabinet a 70-billion-mark bank bailout was concealed through banking confidentiality.

Note, however, that many of these demons make serious mistakes about the text—and that, while syntax-demon Sf ultimately made it into print, Sg would have been equally correct (and before the translator-subject settled on Sf it would almost certainly have had to hear from rhythm-demons and theme-and-rheme-demons and the like—this list of demon-categories is far from exhaustive). The keys to success in this sort of pandemonium translation process are *multiplicity* and *functional redundancy:* there have to be *lots* of demons, and their functions have to overlap in significant ways, so that, for example, lexicon-demons, collocation-demons, and relevance-demons are all working on word-choice, from slightly different angles. No one demonic category is ever given executive status. There is no Satan, no king of the demons, to lay down the law. The demons just continue to compete until a coherent and (hopefully) accurate or otherwise successful translation emerges—which may take a few hundred milliseconds, a few seconds, a few minutes, a few hours (some of that time spent poring over dictionaries and other reference works, on the phone or e-mail to other translators and experts, or doing some unrelated activity like walking or eating, while the demons continue to swim into the stream) or even, as one occasionally hears in legendary stories of heroic literary translators, days, weeks, months . . .

The one feature in this pandemonium model that approaches the traditional rationalist conception of a single executive power is habit: the more experience one has in translating, the more habitual it becomes, which is to say, in pandemonium terms, the more streamlined the process of demon-sifting becomes. A novice translator's syntax-demons may work on *keskustan ollessa hallituksessa* (lit. center's being-in cabinet-in) for a considerable time, either generating no syntax-demons for it (a paucity of word-demons is a common problem among novice translators)—or else generating many different potential English word orders for it, testing each against the work of other demons, rolling it around on the upstretched hands of the tongue-demons like some sort of stage-diver at a rock concert, bouncing it echoically off the reverberating drum-like surfaces of the ear-demons, without quite being able to sift through them, pandemonium without significant emergent patterns. An experienced translator will instantly generate a syntax-demon that says "while the something was in the something" and proceed to other variables—only later, perhaps, if necessary, going back and wondering whether that "stock" or "standard" transfer pattern really is best here.

This habitualization of translation speeds things up considerably: the translation of this 100-word letter to the editor that I did from start to finish in about 20 minutes might have taken a beginning translator hours to do. It also improves accuracy, because it eliminates much of the demonic guesswork (i.e., overlap and contention). But it doesn't for all that subordinate the translation process to a single rational executive decision-maker. Pandemonium ensues anew with every new translation. It's just that the pandemonium is a bit more streamlined, a bit less like a barroom brawl.

Fidus interpres and the Double Bind

I'm going to cop out a bit with the last two terms in Lacan's schema, the o' and the O, the ego-ideal and the Other-capital-O, and deal with both of them together—partly because the Other is so hard to talk about with any kind of specificity (and the chapter is already too long for more glittering generalities), partly because the two tend to run together in my mind anyway. Lacan himself seems to me to confuse the two by following Freud in associating the ego-ideal with the introjected father and then labeling the Other with the Name of the Father (197). As a result the O and the o' have always seemed to me similar normative introjects; the O is just a bit "bigger," less personal, more mysterious, than the o'. I first developed a tabulation of the double-bind as the conflicted speaking of the Other (as parent and child, as majority and minority, as culture and anarchy) in *Ring Lardner and the Other*, and modified that tabulation for the study of translation in an early draft of *Translation and Taboo* as the speaking of the Other-as-mystery and the Other-as-reason; I ended up cutting that translational double-bind out of *Taboo* and publishing it elsewhere (see "Translation and the Double Bind"), with the idea of writing several more such tabulations for this book. And did— but as I wrote them, two things started to bother me. One, there were way too many of them, six or seven, on the clash between the source and target cultures, on love and money, love and structure, knowledge and intuition, human and machine, nationalist and migrant, and creator and channeler, and the book started taking a shape that wouldn't accommodate so many. And two, I couldn't decide whether they should be regarded as the speaking of the Other or the ego-ideal. So instead of deciding between them, I'm going to fudge it and let the double-bind be the speaking, loosely, of both.

And I will only be presenting a single double-bind here, in an attempt to keep length down. In fact I've already started presenting it, the channeler/creator one, in the "Invisible Subject" section: the general anonymity-demons (marked with a ○ on pages 160–62) and the personality-demons (marked with a • on pages 161–63) were adapted from the first two categories, respectively; I'll give the third, fourth, and fifth here.

The idea behind the double bind as the speaking of either the translator's ego-ideal or some shadowy ideological Other is that thinking about translation is not only normative (hence the imperative voice of the double bind and its affiliation with a normative or idealized figure that commands obedience and emulation), but conflicted as well. There *are* translation norms, which the translator-subject knows and (to the best of its ability) obeys; but the norms tell it to do contradictory things. Theodore Savory sums these conflicts up succinctly and humorously in *The Art of Translation:*

1. A translation must give the words of the original.
2. A translation must give the ideas of the original.
3. A translation should read like an original work.
4. A translation should read like a translation.
5. A translation should reflect the style of the original.
6. A translation should possess the style of the translator.
7. A translation should read as a contemporary of the original.
8. A translation should read as a contemporary of the translator.
9. A translation may never add to or omit from the original.
10. A translation may never add to or omit from the original.

11. A translation of verse should be in prose.
12. A translation of verse should be in verse. (50)

And while the history of translation theory right up to the present is by and large a history of people taking sides on these issues—most people opting for fluent sense-for-sense translations, a hardy few insisting on literal or foreignizing renditions—the conflicts survive everywhere, even within the writing of individuals (for a discussion of those conflicts in Jerome, see my *Taboo* 102–7). Perhaps the most striking case of conflicted translator ideals in the history of Western translation theory, however, is Horace's *fidus interpres* or "faithful translator," which for him was purely negative, a cautionary exemplar, something *not* to emulate: "nor trouble to render word for word with the faithfulness of a translator" (E. C. Wickham's translation, in Robinson *Western* 15). His advice was directed not at translators but at writers working with familiar literary materials: don't be minutely faithful to the received materials like those slavish literalist translators. Because to make his meter work he didn't say *like* the faithful translator, however—in Latin he says *nec verbum verbo curabis reddere, fidus / Interpres*, or literally, "nor word for word bother to render, faithful / Translator"—dozens of later translation theorists have taken his words as advice to the translator, and have read it to mean both *do* and *don't* render word for word:

I fear that I shall commit the fault of the faithful interpreter when I render each word by a word corresponding to it. (Boethius, 510, Charles S. F. Burnett's translation, in Robinson *Western* 35)

If someone should find the text of the aforesaid translation obscure or impenetrable, let him consider me the *translator* of this work, not its *expositor*. Indeed I fear that I have incurred the blame of the faithful translator. (Johannes Scotus Eriugena, mid-9th century, Rita Copeland's translation, in Robinson *Western* 36)

For if you wish another's material to be regarded as yours, "you will," as Horace says, "take pains not to render word for word like a faithful translator," but rather, taking up a sentence of that material, you will cast it into the structure of your own diction; thus you will appear not to have translated but to have composed the text out of your own head . . . (Burgundio of Pisa, 1170s, Edward Capps III's translation, in Robinson *Western* 42)

I conceive it a vulgar error in translating poets, to affect being *Fidus Interpres;* let that care be with them who deal in matters of fact, or matters of faith. (John Denham, 1656, in Robinson *Western* 156)

By this Passage of *Horace*, thus truly explained, the Reader may clearly perceive, First, that *Horace* gave no Rules for Translation, and therefore cannot be said (as some have stil'd him to be) *Of that Art the great Law-giver*. For doubtless he thought it below him. Next, that according to the Judgment of Horace himself, 'tis the Duty of a faithful Interpreter to translate what he undertakes word for word . . . (Sir Edward Sherburne, 1702, in Steiner 89)

For Boethius and Eriugena, Horace is clearly warning against literal translation, making their commitment to literalism (and the *fidus interpres* itself) a *culpa* or fault—although it is also just as clearly a fault they are determined to commit, with some degree of residual guilt (for Boethius perhaps of the tongue-in-cheek sort) for deviating from Horace. For Burgundio and Sherburne his warnings are directed elsewhere, to original writers, but implicitly he is associating the *fidus interpres* with literalism and thus defining translation as normatively literal. For Denham, the literalism of the *fidus interpres* is just as pernicious for the translator of poetry as it is for the original writer dealing with received materials, so that like Boethius and Eriugena he construes Horace's warning as directed against literal translation and, unlike them, heeds that warning. (For a lengthy discussion of similar conflicted debates over the meaning of Horace's lines for translation in the French Renaissance, see Norton 57–110.)

Now this interpretive conflict could be analyzed with the divide-and-conquer methods of dualism:

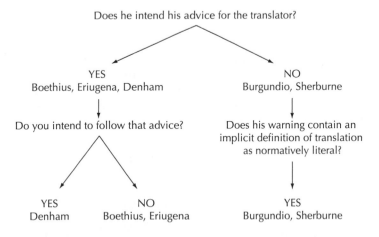

Does he intend his advice for the translator?

YES
Boethius, Eriugena, Denham

NO
Burgundio, Sherburne

Do you intend to follow that advice?

Does his warning contain an implicit definition of translation as normatively literal?

YES
Denham

NO
Boethius, Eriugena

YES
Burgundio, Sherburne

This would be a time-tried method for determining what Horace "really" meant, and, of course, better, what individual translation theorists through the centuries thought he really meant. And it has been thought important to establish these things because in a rationalist intellectual tradition it is essential that all precepts be unambiguous: yes, translate word for word; no, translate sense for sense. There has to be a single executive decision-maker (person or principle), and for that decision-maker to be conceived as rational it must be internally consistent. Thus if as rationalists we decide that the one true executive principle regulating *all* translation is literalist, then Boethius and Eriugena are right in problematic ways, Burgundio and Sherburne are simply right, and Denham is wrong (and Horace is excused as not really writing about translation at all). If on the other hand we decide (as Western civilization more or less did by the Renaissance) that the one true executive principle regulating all translation is sense-for-sense, then Denham is right and all the rest are wrong (and Horace, though not strictly speaking a translation theorist, is accepted into the canon as an important precursor: *at least he was on the right track*).

What this nervous rationalist dualizing confounds, however, is what Theodore Savory saw very clearly: that there *is* no one right precept. The translator's ego-ideal in the West is conflicted. The *fidus interpres* translates both slavishly and freely, and feels guilty for doing either. All the sophistic Horace interpretations are cagey attempts to justify a single reductive construction of the *fidus interpres*, but those attempts only work locally, for the theorist himself or herself (and perhaps a friend or two). They can never constitute a single universal precept, one that can be taken to govern all translators in all times and places, because the rationalist tradition that insists that there be only one is false, simplistic— a nervous tic born of existential insecurity generating a power move disguised as logic.

A double-bind interpretation of Horace and his interpreters, then, would constitute a pandemonium theory of the translator's ego-ideal: the norm-demons controlling translational segmentation (sense-for-sense, word-for-word, foot-for-foot, etc.) come up with so many conflicted directions because they are sent by a squabbling group of double-binding ego-ideals or Others that *want* translators confused. I adapt my formulation of the double bind from Gregory Bateson (*Steps to an Ecology of Mind*), who identifies the double bind as the primary causative factor in the etiology of schizophrenia: double-binding parents (and generally societies) drive people crazy. In adapting this format to translation studies, therefore, I might be thought of as trying to say that the collectivized speakers of the various double binds drive translators crazy—indeed, that they construct us as translators *by* driving us crazy. But in fact I would disagree: the want-to-drive-translators-crazy hypothesis would presuppose a *single* vicious executive force or voice. A pandemonium model of the double bind could posit legions of well-meaning ego-ideals or Others, all working earnestly and in good faith to clarify things for the translator-subject, to banish all confusion—but someone in the welter of demonic impulses creating the impression that the subject is damned if it does and damned if it doesn't.

There are, Bateson suggests, three levels to the double bind: (1) a negative command, a "thou shalt not," enforced by signals that threaten survival; (2) a conflicting negative command on a higher level of abstraction, a command not only to obey but to *accept* (1) as right and natural, again enforced by signals that threaten survival; and (3) an all-encompassing negative command that prevents escape from the dilemma posed by (1) and (2).

But as I argued in my Lardner book (26ff, esp. 29), this initial formulation seems inadequate to the debilitating contradictions of the double bind as Bateson himself exemplifies it. It seems to me that the imperative contradiction(s) must come not at different levels of abstraction but at precisely the same level—that the contradictions must be hidden from the subject not through shifts in the level of abstraction but through shifting thematizations or idealizations of the commands. This might be schematized for all normative double binding as follows: (1) do X; (2) do not-X; (3) internalize the command to do both, and expect punishment for failure; (4) repress (1), (2), and (3), along with any anger or frustration that their contradictoriness might engender; and (5) idealize the command-giver by taking all blame for failure on yourself.

As I say, I've already presented (1) and (2) in the "invisible subject" section, above: be anonymous, be invisible, be a neutral channel (1), and be creative, be an artist (2). There in the subject section, where the reigning illusion was that this is *me,* my personality (or lack thereof)— I'm *not* other-defined—I framed the demons as first-person self-talk, as the suggestions and beliefs of individual demons who *spoke for me,* the subject. Now that we are out of the subject section and it is clear that the demons are *sent* by some internalized other, let me phrase them in the second-person imperative:

3. *Internalize the command to be both a neutral anonymous invisible channel (1) and a fully alive and creative artist (2), and expect censure for failure.*

   a. Understand without being told that what is at stake here is not just your professional integrity as a translator, but your worth as a human being. Know that a good translator must be both the perfect neutral channel and a supreme creator, and that to be worthy of the esteem of others you must not only be both but define your-self professionally in terms of both.

b. Understand without being told that you can't do both, and thus will never be either a good translator or a good person.

c. Expect to be scorned for success in either and both: you're a drudge, a slave, a tool, a thing, a vehicle, a nonperson, if you suc-ceed in 1, and you're presumptuous and arrogant, a fraud and a charlatan, if you succeed in 2.

d. Expect to be scorned for failure in either and both: you're insensi-tive, insufficiently attuned to the communicative needs of the source author and/or target reader if you fail at 1, and you're an unimaginative and uncreative drone if you fail at 2.

e. Internalize the negative conception these conflicting commands mandate not only of you but of your profession. Think of the translator as intrinsically a traducer.

f. Fight the negative conception of translation that the impossibility of obeying both 1 and 2 mandates by working harder, and calling on other translators to work harder as well, to obey both 1 and 2. If only translators would be at once more creative and more perfectly attuned to the spirit of the interaction between the source author and target reader, people would respect you and your profession more. Let this transform 1–2–3 into a vicious circle from which there is no escape.

g. Invent "positive" (encouraging or reassuring) syntheses of 1 and 2: it takes enormous creativity to empty out one's personality and put oneself so thoroughly in the service of another voice; spirit-channelers are among our most creative and talented citizens. Learn to enjoy the contradictions and tensions in these syntheses. Feel them as the rough edges or the sharp thorns of real life—not as a falling away from the purity of binary logic.

h. Fail to enjoy those contradictions and tensions as fully as you would like. Keep drifting to one side or the other, in search of stable ground. Feel frustrated that none seems to exist.

i. Kick yourself for this failure too.

j. But tell yourself that your failures are much more interesting than some people's successes, because of your tolerance for complexity and contradiction.

k. But never forget that this sort of pride will interfere with your ability to step back and let the source author speak through you, and thus to become a good translator as defined in 1.

l. Never forget, either, that any desire to become a good translator as defined in 1 will make you a bad ("slavish") translator as defined in 2.

4. *Repress all this, and despise anyone who reminds you of it.*

a. Believe that translation may occasionally be difficult, but it is certainly not impossible—certainly nothing to imagine in terms of a vicious circle from which there is no escape. It is only high-falutin' theorists, estranged from the realities of day-to-day translation practice, who portray it as impossible. Show some scorn for these nay-sayers, but ignore them as best you can and go on doing what you do best.

b. Believe that translation is impossible, but nonetheless absolutely essential. Scorn those naive translators who think translation is easy, who fail to recognize the massive, indeed insurmountable difficulties to be overcome in order to achieve the perfect synthesis of creativity and surrender to the speaking of the source author. Despise them for their compromises—but be willing to compromise yourself in order to go on practicing a profession that you firmly believe is impossible.

c. Remain convinced that your compromises (insofar as you allow yourself to become aware of them) are of a higher order than those made by your naive colleagues who do not understand how high the stakes are. You can feel yourself compelled to compromise, and even then you yield only slightly, and ache with the cost of that yielding; those others compromise unconsciously, with blithe indifference to what is lost in the process.

d. Laugh (un)easily at any suggestion that you are channeling the "spirits" of ideological norms in any of this. The very idea is absurd. You're a translator. You try to do your best as you see fit, period. Sure, there are professional ethics governing the field, but what field doesn't have ethical guidelines? Just because you try to be an ethical professional, that doesn't mean you're some kind of wispy head-in-the-sky psychic medium reading crystals and auras and Tarot cards and things. You *choose* to obey those rules. And you could choose to disobey them, too, if you wanted. You just don't want to. Because you're a professional.

e. Laugh (un)easily at any suggestion that your refusal to admit to channeling ideological "spirits" or norms makes you a maverick, a scofflaw, a rugged individualist who will not surrender his or her will to anybody. Your uneasiness about being thought of as a channeler, the neutral instrument of forces outside yourself, does not mean you necessarily agree entirely with the commands in 2—that you are setting yourself up as some kind of creative genius who is not bound by the rules. You have a healthy respect for the rules. This stuff just goes too far, that's all.

f. Ridicule translation theorists who dredge up all this unpleasant stuff and then have the nerve to peddle it as "translation theory"—as if spirit-channeling had anything at all to do with translation! Dismiss them easily, being very careful to control your anger and the anxieties that drive it, as unserious people, hardly worth the effort it takes to tell people not to read them. This new stuff is useless not because it bothers you (it doesn't), but because it's irrelevant to the proper study of translation—which your group defines, but don't say that outright, as an admission of that sort might tend to localize, motivate, and thus deidealize the group's approach.

g. Ridicule translation theorists who present all this unpleasant stuff as "new," innovative, groundbreaking, revolutionary, when of course everyone (in your camp) has known it all along and has said it many times before, and much better; call it "reinventing the wheel," a futile undertaking that could have been avoided had the offending theorists only read a bit more extensively in the writings of your group. This "new" stuff is useless not because it bothers you (it still doesn't), but because you're sick and tired of hearing the same old thing over and over, especially when it is deceptively offered in the guise of the new.

5. *Idealize the command-giver.*

a. Believe that there is no command-giver; there is simply a factual state of affairs. Don't even deny the existence of a command-giver; just never let the possibility arise. If you find it both difficult and essential to be creative and to empty out your personality simultaneously, that is not because you have been commanded (or trained, or programmed) to do both, and to conceive translation as doing both. That's just what translation is—not what someone told you it is, not some artificial restrictive definition of translation, but the *facts*.

b. To the extent that you identify the command-giver with the spirit of the source author, channel that spirit by surrendering your will to it as to God—an infinitely wiser and more evolved spirit than anything you have experienced in your current world. Tacitly turn the channeling into a form of worship.

c. To the extent that you identify the command-giver with the spirit of the target reader, channel that spirit by surrendering your will to it as a parent does to a beloved child—an exquisitely open and receptive creature whose curiosity and wonder before the unknown serves as your primary inspiration. Model your own receptivity to the source text and author on this idealized command-giver, and despair of ever living up to its high standards.

d. To the extent that you identify the command-giver with the spirit of verbal creativity, channel that spirit by surrendering your will to it as a writer does to the muse—very much in fact as you imagine your source author having surrendered to the inspiration of the muse in writing the source text. Let that spirit be at once your own creativity and something far superior to you that enters you from the outside. When people claim that you took liberties with the source text, throw up your hands and say that you had no control over it; the translation simply came to you, from somewhere.

e. To the extent that you identify the command-giver with the spirit of ideology, norms, conventions, professional ethics, conscience, the source or target literary system, channel that spirit by surrendering your will to it as a computer does to its operating system—as a spirit that wields you from within, and from so deep-seated and well-integrated a part of you that it seems to be your own voice, your own innermost impulses. Do not think of it as authoritarian control or social regulation. Brook no conspiracy theories about this process—because there are no conspirators! Chafe at Nietzschean descriptions of this channeling as "internalized mastery." Yes, it is internalized, but do we have to derogate it as "mastery"? Nobody is bossing you around; nobody is telling you what to do; the impulses to act in certain ways, and indeed the impulses to obey those impulses, come from inside you. It feels perfectly normal and natural to go along with them, to let them guide you. You *want* to—and can it really be mastery if you freely choose to be mastered?

Chapter Six

The Invisible Hand

Invisible and Hidden Hands

To recap the book so far: in part one I set up the idea of translation *as* spirit-channeling; in parts two and three I've been setting up a series of conceptions of translation as *like* spirit-channeling. Some people have claimed to "translate" by channeling actual discarnate spirits (part one). Others have seen translation as controlled by ideological forces that, while entirely secular, are nonetheless like discarnate spirits in significant ways (part two). Daniel Dennett's pandemonium model of consciousness, which consolidates current trends in cognitive and brain science, suggests that translator subjectivity too is (or can realistically be imagined as) structured along secularized spirit-channeling lines, with mental "demons" bringing messages and other action-potentials into the stream(s) of consciousness (first half of part three). Now, finally, here in chapter six I want to explore the socioeconomic "outside" to match chapter five's psychological or even neurological "inside": the actual economic forces controlling the creation of a translation in the marketplace, including clients, translators, agency and freelance editors, proofreaders, project managers, experts, and so on. To that end I will be using Adam Smith's suggestive "spirit-channeling" metaphor of the "invisible hand" that leads merchants in a free market to promote collective interests while intending only to satisfy self-interest, and Robert Nozick's "disaggregated agency" reading of that metaphor, which he developed out of a reading of Dennett.

As Emma Rothschild notes in an important historical excavation of the metaphor, Smith referred to an invisible hand twice in economic contexts, once in *The Theory of Moral Sentiments* (1759), sardonically, to describe rapacious entrepreneurs for whom the common good is the last thing on their mind, but in the pursuit of their own "vain and insatiable desires" (quoted in Rothschild 319) do provide work to thousands. "They are led by an invisible hand to . . . without intending it, without knowing it, advance the interest of the society" (quoted in Rothschild 319); and again, more famously, in *The Wealth of Nations* (1776): "he is in this, as in many other cases, led by an invisible hand to promote an end which is no part of his intention" (quoted in Rothschild 319).

But as long as economic historians and theorists have only read those two passages, the invisible hand has remained a puzzle. Did Smith, a religious skeptic, mean God, or some other deistic spirit? If not, what did he mean? What "invisible" force wielded economic agents to ends other than their own?

Rothschild works to answer these questions by tracing what amounts to a logology of the invisible hand, beginning with a quasinaturalistic context in Ovid's *Metamorphoses*, where one hero stabs his opponent in the back: "twisted and plied his invisible hand, inflicting wound within wound." Here the hand is invisible not because the body to which it is attached is spiritual, ghostly, supernatural, but because it is behind the victim's back and so cannot be seen. The next context, rather more spiritualistic, is in Shakespeare's *Macbeth:*

> Come, seeling night,
> Scarf up the tender eye of pitiful day,
> And with thy bloody and invisible hand
> Cancel and tear to pieces that great bond
> Which keeps me pale! (3.2.46–50)

Here "seeling night" is personified as a violent spirit invoked by Macbeth to calm his conscience: his thoughts of the men he has murdered, which "should indeed have died / With them they think on" (3.2.10–11), live on to torment him. The third context, then, is Smith's first: in *The History of Astronomy*, probably written in the early to mid-1750s, a handful of years before *The Theory of Moral Sentiment* (and only published posthumously in 1795). "He is talking," Rothschild writes, "about the credulity of people in polytheistic societies, who ascribe 'the irregular events of nature,' such as thunder and storms, to 'intelligent though invisible beings—to gods, demons, witches, genii, fairies.' They do not ascribe divine support to 'the ordinary course of things': 'nor was the invisible hand of Jupiter ever apprehended to be employed in those matters'"(319). Here the invisible hand is clearly spiritualistic and divine, almost monotheistic: Jupiter as the greatest of the gods has often been made a figure (or logological precursor) for the "supreme being" of monotheistic Christianity. Later, also, between *The Theory of Moral Sentiment* and *An Inquiry into the Nature and Causes of the Wealth of Nations*, in a lecture series delivered in 1762–1763—the *Lectures on Rhetoric and Belles Lettres*—Smith referred to "fairies, Nymphs, Fawns, Satyrs, Dryads, and such divinities" as "invisible powers" (quoted in Rothschild 320). The logological movement is clearly from naturalistic human hands that are invisible because hidden from the eyes, through the unseen controlling influence of animistic or deistic spirits, to some sort of unspecified economic force.

Working out just what that economic force was, what Smith could have meant by the market's invisible hand, has in the twentieth century become an entire cottage industry in political economics—as Rothschild notes, Smith's commentators paid little attention to the invisible hand before the twentieth century (319), possibly because, as we will see in a moment, before Marx, Darwin, and Freud there was no secular model of disaggregate agency that would account for a locus of regulation outside the rationalist self, secular avatar of God. Indeed as Rothschild shows, "the invisible hand is un-Smithian" (320), for five reasons:

1. The agents controlled by invisible hands in his work are "undignified: they are silly polytheists, rapacious proprietors, disingenuous merchants" (Rothschild 320).

2. Invisible-hand theories diminish the rational subject's power of action, self-mastery, making it seem as if individuals are not as free as Smith, an enthusiastic liberal individualist, would like them to be.

3. The invisible hand presupposes an emperor's-new-clothes type of relation between the blind ordinary people to whom the hand truly is invisible and the theorist who sees the hand and can make it visible to others. As Rothschild notes, "This knowingness of the theorist is characteristic of 18th- and 19th-century doctrines of unintended consequences; when G. W. F. Hegel talks of the cunning of reason, he is also talking of his own cunning" (320). This is not only condescending; it leaves economic agents vulnerable to those who would manipulate their actions in the name of the "market"—something Smith disapproved of.

4. The implicit deism or even spiritualism of the invisible hand (especially as it was read in the nineteenth century) was foreign to Smith's own agnostic temper.

5. The invisible hand in the context of Smith's argument in *The Wealth of Nations* was a kind of politically useful "trinket" (Rothschild 321), a rather silly and simplistic reduction of political and habitual forces that Smith didn't like and was engaged in theorizing in far more interesting ways.

In other words, Rothschild persuasively shows Smith working to purify the rationalist model of the self of any supernatural or otherwise unexplainable or unmasterable influences—and as a result sees the two economic mentions of invisible hands as a careless survival of earlier (and now despised) thought in Smith's near-perfect rationalism. Rationalism must be just as monotheistic as the Platonic Christianity out of which it largely emerged: thou shalt have no other selves before me. Economic agents should be the sovereign masters of their own fates. The only forces acting on them should be other economic agents who are similarly masters of their own fates. Certainly there should be no incursion of "invisible hands" from supernatural or psychological realms whose very existence, if it could be proven, would shake the foundations of rationalism. As Carl Menger wrote in 1883, in *Untersuchungen über die Methode der Soczialwissenschaften und der politischen Oekonomie insbesondere* ("Investigations into the Method of the Social Sciences and Political Economics In Particular"), Smith and his later followers viewed "the institutions of economy . . . [as] the intended product of the *common will* of society or of positive legislation. . . . The broad realm of unintentionally created social structures remains closed to their theoretical comprehension" (quoted in Williamson 323).

It was Menger's view, in fact, foreshadowing a whole host of twentieth-century theories of the almost infinite diffusion of control in both society and the psyche, that "law, language, the state, money, markets, . . . [the] prices of goods, interest rates, ground rents, wages, and a thousand other phenomena [are] to no small extent the unintended result of social development" (quoted in Williamson 323). As Menger posed the key question for the social sciences: "How can it be that institutions which serve the common welfare and are extremely significant for its development come into being without a common will directed toward establishing them?" (quoted in Williamson 323). Or, as Robert Nozick has most influentially reframed that question for late-twentieth-century political economics, drawing on Dennett, "what decentralized competing processes *within* an individual"—and, by sociological extension, within an entire society or economy— "would give rise to a (relatively) coherent decision-maker?" ("Explanations" 314).

Nozick first raised this issue in his 1974 book *Anarchy, State, and Utopia,* where among other scenarios he imagined the emergence of a loosely organized mutual protection agency through a series of related and perhaps partly modeled or influenced but nonetheless at least in part independent decisions, people agreeing officially and unofficially to protect each other's interests and assets, firms offering protective services, etc. This agency, which could be called a kind of "ultra-minimal state" ("Explanations" 314), would not need to have been intended or planned by any one of the agents whose actions helped to create it. It could exist without any official, legislated or licensed, status. The process by which this sort of "unintended" economic entity arises Nozick called an invisible-hand process; the theory that explains its formation he called an invisible-hand explanation. As he later summarized that argument:

Two types of processes seemed important: filtering processes wherein some filter eliminates all entities not fitting a certain pattern, and equilibrium processes wherein each component part adjusts to local conditions, changing the local environments of others close by, so the sum of the local adjustments realizes a pattern. The pattern produced by the adjustments of some entities might itself constitute a filter another faces. The opposite kind of explanation, wherein an apparently unintended, accidental, or unrelated set of events is shown to result from intentional design, I termed a *hidden-hand explanation.* The notion of invisible-hand explanation is descriptive, not normative. Not every pattern that arises by an invisible-hand process is desirable, and something that can arise by an invisible-hand process might better arise or be maintained through conscious intervention. ("Explanations" 314)

The question still remained, however: what powers those "filtering" and "equilibrium" processes? What forces lie behind them? A hidden-hand explanation presumes rational agency: someone somewhere intended for this or that event-structure to emerge; and it did. An invisible-hand explanation by definition remains in what Friedrich Schleiermacher called *der unerfreuliche Mitte,* the unpleasant middle ground, between randomness, chaos, sheer accident, on the one hand, and rational planning on the other. *Something* drives these event-structures; but what?

In his later exfoliations of invisible-hand theories Nozick has attempted to answer this question by drawing on Dennett's pandemonium theories of the self, which Nozick renames "disaggregated agency." Economic theorists typically attempt to explain event-structures by reference to the decisions and other actions of rational agents, agents conceived in terms of God's singularity, control, and knowledge: each agent is a single unified being, organized and directed by reason and utterly lacking in conflicting or other centrifugal agentive forces or impulses; each agent is in control of its actions; each agent possesses the knowledge it needs to plan and execute a well-informed course of action. The difficulty faced by such explanations lies in the plurality of agents: obviously an economy is more polytheistic, more like the squabblings of the ancient Greek or Roman gods and goddesses, than like the monotheistic model of a single all-powerful God in perfect control of all his actions. No economic agent can ever control his or her actions perfectly, because there are too many other such agents also striving to maximize their own action-control. Hence the importance of hidden-hand and other power-group theories, which would see (certain) economic agents as the secularized equivalents of gods and goddesses, angels and demons: the ruling class, those who control the means of production, etc. But such theories still idealize the possibility of rational control, ignoring the modern and postmodern fragmentation of the self postulated by Freud and others as well as the empirical findings of brain scientists, who, as we saw in chapter five, find no evidence that mental events are ever channeled through any single neural circuit or fiber bundle or other place that might thus be construed as the "mind." These findings point us to invisible-hand explanations, which move us to the third level of a logological hierarchy of economic agents:

1. *Rational-agent explanations,* Smith's liberal ideal: each agent is master of his or her actional realm, and possesses sufficient knowledge of other such realms to make and carry out decisions for the adequate control of his or her own. Larger event-structures are the product of collective decision-making, which entails rational conversation among individual rational agents, moving eventually toward consensus or majority rule. Wherever rational agents are outvoted by their peers, they are not to be thought of as "surrendering" their will to the collective; rather, they make a rational decision to go along with the majority, because they have determined that it is in their best interests to do so. There is never, in other words, a surrender of will or intentionality to external forces. There are only different fully sovereign expressions of rational intentionality. Collective agencies operate on the same rationalist principles: they are governed by by-laws, executive decision-making bodies, proportional representation, votes, and so on.

2. *Conspiracy and ruling-class theories,* including hidden-hand explanations: each agent is rational and strives for knowledge-based control,

but the plurality of such agents makes total control impossible. More powerful agents, those with better social, financial, and intellectual backing, will therefore tend to rule over less powerful ones. Social Darwinism: the socioeconomic survival of the fittest. Powerful cliques too will conflict, generating a constant jockeying and intriguing for control. When power is wielded overtly, various despotic formations result. When power is wielded covertly, hidden-hand theories come into play.

3. *Invisible-hand theories:* economic agents from the individual up through various ephemeral groupings to the city, the nation, and all humanity are disaggregated, fragmentary, self-divided. Each agent may see itself as functioning rationally, but in fact is constantly being surprised by ideas and impulses arising out of its own unconscious or semiconscious thought processes and behavior chains. Sometimes the best solutions to difficult problems emerge from a prolonged state of confusion, from stumbling and groping about. Opposed forces within the agent will vie for control over an action, and sometimes the force that sees itself in control will be forced to yield to other internal forces. The decision-making process that leads to the creation of a single translation, for example, will be divided and conflicted whether the translating agent is a single individual, as in chapter five, or a group of individuals (translator(s), expert helper(s), editor(s), project manager(s), end-user(s), etc.). Neither the individual nor the group should be imagined as any more rationally organized or directed than the other. To the extent that rationalist models remain dominant in such a process, any potential awareness of the disaggregated nature of decision-making must be repressed and re-explained as the product of rationalist consensus or the like. Indeed rationalist and other ideologies should be regarded as disaggregated forces at work within the agent.

4. *Posthumanist discourses-of-power theories:* economic agents are controlled like puppets by the power-discourses that constituted them as agents. Ideology, or what Michel Foucault calls the power-discourse of "institutions," is all-powerful.

Translation Agencies

I am not going to be looking as closely at the economic agencies that translate in this last chapter as I did in chapter two at the channeling of spirits, in chapters three and four at the channeling of ideology, and in chapter five at the channeling of mental "demons." By now the pattern I'm exploring should be clear, and it would quickly become repetitious if I were to trace the functioning of various secularized "spirits" or invisible hands through the full range of the translation market, clients, agencies, initiators, freelancers, helpers, editors, end-users. My brief, in any case, is mainly that translators are not autonomous individuals producing translations like omnipotent gods out of the fullness of their (textual, cultural, economic, psychosocial) world-mastery, but parts of larger translation or translatorial agencies, in a broad philosophical sense of "agency" that sometimes overlaps, but is not coterminous, with the legal sense. Translators in and as these agencies channel the voices and writings and ideas and knowhow and plans and desires of *other people*—bits and pieces of cultural and technical expertise, meanings, authorial/translatorial/editorial skills, various cooperative and competitive economic motives, and so on—*from* various sources, *through* their own bodies, *to* various targets, users, ends. A client needs a text translated, and hires an agency to do it; the agency does the translation and bills the client for the work. What I'm suggesting is that we follow economic theory and business law and treat that agency as a collective "person"—or rather, that we bring the same kind of models to bear on the agency as we did in chapter five on the individual translator. Both the translation agency/bureau/company and the individual translator may be said to "have agency," in the philosophical sense. Legally both are "persons" or "bodies"—the one a corporate person or body, the other a private one.

And by analogical extension the ephemeral "translation agency," that loose conglomeration of individuals bound only by work-for-hire contracts or oral agreements and a spirit of cooperation that often collectively performs the work of translation, is a "person" too. Some examples from my own recent experience as a freelancer:

a. A direct client calls me and asks me to "do" a translation. I agree, but see that the job is too big for me, so I send parts of it out to other translators, and edit their work myself. We all do a good deal of research for the job as well, finding terminological and register models on the Web, calling experts, sending e-mail queries to translator discussion groups, etc. I pay the other translators out of the fee the client pays me.

b. An agency calls me and wants me to do a translation for them. It's too difficult for me (a very technical text from English into Finnish) and I don't have time, so I give them names of other translators for them to try. But I've done work for them before and they trust me, so they beg. Finally, I suggest that they pay me a few cents more per word than their usual rate and I will have a Finnish technical translator edit it. They agree. But they also edit the job in-house, and find, to my chagrin, several embarrassing omissions.

c. An agency hires me as an editor for a big translation job they've contracted to do, English to Finnish. They have also hired another freelance translator, a native speaker of Finnish, to do the main translating job. I don't normally accept jobs like this, but I know the agency owner personally and find it difficult to refuse. We both do sample translations of a page or two and discuss general and specific strategies by e-mail. We both compile a glossary as we work. The agency has various in-house people doing background terminological research to support us. Our collective work is edited in-house before being sent to the client.

d. I get a call from an agency asking me to translate a series of medical questionnaires from Finnish to English. I agree, and start working. I'm only a page or two into the job, though, when I get a strong feeling that I'm doing a back-translation. The phrasings are occasionally awkward in Finnish in ways that remind me of translations I've done into Finnish before. Semantic one-to-many and many-to-one problems abound. The contact person listed in the Finnish text, most likely the author of the questionnaires, has an English name and a U.S. address, which also suggests that the original language was English. I call the agency and ask, but they won't confirm or deny that what I'm doing is back-translating—which to me is a bit silly, since a back-translation, it seems to me, should be done differently than a straight (forward?) translation (more literally, to show the client more or less what the first translation said). In any case, I'm kind of rushed with this job because I'm leaving for the American Translators Association conference in a day or two, but I e-mail a couple of Finnish translator friends with term questions, get two of the questionnaires done, modem them to the agency's BBS, ring them up to say that I'll have to finish the job after the conference; they say fine. At the conference I'm introduced to a Finnish translator whom I've never met; he was a doctor in Finland, moved to the United States a year or two ago, can't practice medicine here so he's been translating medical texts. We start talking, we have mutual friends in Finland, and soon he laughs a little and says, "So you've been back-translating my work, huh?" It turns out that he was the original translator; he found out about me doing the back-translation from one of my Finnish translator friends, who went to him with one of my term queries. He and I sit down and compare notes on the job; I remember some problem areas and ask him about them, he remembers the original English and the problems he had getting it into Finnish, etc. A very fruitful discussion. After the conference I return home and finish the job, which is now much easier. A few days later I get a call from the agency project-manager, wanting to discuss my translations, which I have done *as* back-translations, despite the lack of confirmation from the agency. I did the first ones that way, before the conference, and I certainly did the last ones that way too, after finding out that they really were. The project-manager has no problem with the way I did the translations; she wants to check on some of my parenthetical comments, which were designed to help her do the best possible job with what I sent her. We discuss some of the problems, she is satisfied, and hangs up to finish the job. I never see the end result, or have any idea what "my" translation ended up looking like.

I am suggesting that we think of the loose groupings of people that "did" the translations in all four of these scenarios as "translation agencies"—in a theoretical rather than legal sense. In a., I basically created an *ad hoc* agency of my own, which did the job that I had contracted to do as a freelancer, a private person doing work-for-hire; when the job was done, the agency disbanded. It "existed" only in the virtual sense; it was never a legal entity. In b., c., and d., agencies that did exist as legal entities hired me and various other people who were not affiliated with those entities in any stable way to—what? Do the translation? Help do the translation? How do we want to put it? It makes a good deal of sense, it seems to me, to treat the whole transient assembly—the actual corporate agency that contracted with the client to "do" the translation *and* all the people they either assigned or hired to work on it, as well as the various random helpers stumbled on along the way, such as the Finnish medical translator I met at the conference—as a single (if disaggregated) translation agency.

In fact, it is more complicated than this. How do we draw the boundaries between, say, the "translation agency" and the "commissioning agency"—the person or group of people who hire the translation agency to do the work? Well, the translation agency translates; the commissioning agency commissions the translation. But the editors in large corporations who are assigned the job of commissioning translations are sometimes translators themselves, or were trained as translators and after college found their way into jobs overseeing translations done by others. Even those who have no personal experience of translating develop a fine sense of the problems translators face from working so closely over a period of several years with translation agencies of all sorts (corporate agencies, freelancers, etc.). Not only do these people come to identify with translators; they are often lumped together with the translators they hire by their superiors, who may complain to them that "your translators really screwed this one up." It might make sense to include such people in the translation agencies—to say that the translation agency "begins" when some boss in the technical information division says to the editor in charge of translations, "Here, get this translated by next Wednesday."

But is that a reasonable boundary either? No. The difference between the editor in charge of translation and his or her boss is no greater than that between the in-house editor and the agency owner, or between the agency owner and the freelancer. They're all part of the translation agency.

And what about tech writers and engineers? Should we include them too? No, of course not. They write; translators translate. But tech writers and engineers often insist on checking and editing translations that come in—especially but not exclusively when the translations have been made into their mother tongue. Sometimes in-house corporate editors seek help from tech writers, engineers, machine operators, and other in-house people on translations "done" by an outside agency. Sometimes before sending translations to the printer they have them checked by people working for the company's dealers or subsidiaries in the target country. And many engineers and tech writers systematically "teach" in-house translators their own principles of translation, including things like "don't worry about style, just write what's there as literally as you can."

And in any case it should be clear that, economically speaking, no matter how large or small we make the boundaries of the "translation agency," it is always part of a larger "publication agency," which in turn is part of a still-larger "marketing agency," which is part of "the economy" (corporate, national, global), etc. Where we draw the lines between any two "parts" of these agencies may make a significant difference to the people whose job it is to "manage" them—analysis and classification are useful tools in the mental sorting out of complex disaggregated entities—but it doesn't really define them, in the sense of giving them a separate stable identity. Agentive identities bleed across all definitional boundaries, because all agencies, in Dennett's terms, operate in the same state of pandemonium as individuals do. All agencies, as Nozick would put it, are disaggregated. Even when their bureaucratic structure is rigidly hierarchized, even when the chain of command is strictly demarcated and enforced, they behave pandemonically, because each individual *member* of them is a pandemonium. The rigid rationalism of Taylor-style management was an attempt to create a rational top-down executive structure for what was, because it was a human organization, a pandemonium, a disaggregated agency. Recognizing that, corporate managers and management gurus in the second half of the twentieth century have been dismantling the hierarchical rigidities of Taylor-style management and replacing it with Total Quality Management (TQM), reengineering, knowledge-leveraging, the "virtual organization"—all management schemes aimed at not only recognizing but affirming the pandemonic or disaggregated agency of all human organizations, and putting it to new uses. Tom Peters, one of the new management gurus, writes:

In an increasingly crowded, noisy global marketplace, innovation is not optional. Corporations need an appetite for adventure, a passion for bold leaps into the unknown. That means hiring the adventurous and the bold, even when they set your teeth to grinding and break a lot of china. It means a passion for lobbing an exciting new product onto the market, even if its success will dry up your current "cash cow." It means cherishing your failures—especially the granddaddies. And it means chopping your company into firewood before the competition does. . . .

The virtual corporation is a colleague of mine, engaged in dozens of globe-spanning adventures, who brags about not having visited his own headquarters in the last five years. It's "big" companies, booking billions, with, literally, only a handful of full-time employees. Mostly, it's the idea that to own resources is a mistake. Instead, you need instant access to the best resources from wherever, whenever, to get the job done.

Business and management have long been about control, job descriptions, organization charts, headquarters towers, structures that are changed reluctantly every five years, and linear careers that rise up "ladders." Now impermanence and improvisation are markers for success. . . .

Hierarchies are going, going, gone. The average Mary or Mike is being asked to take on extraordinary responsibility. He or she may be on the payroll or, at least as likely, an independent contractor. In any event, the hyperfast-moving, wired-up, reengineered, quality-obsessed corporation—virtual or not—will succeed or fail on the strength of the truth that the remaining, tiny cadre of managers places in the folks working on the front line. (16–17)

But the fact that rationalist corporate structures are being dissolved right and left does not *prove* that Dennett is right about consciousness, or that Nozick is right about economic agency, or that I'm right about translation. It could be that "impermanence and improvisation," Peters's "markers for success," are mere passing fads—in translation theory, political economics, and cognitive science as well as in business administration. It could be that a very powerful ideological Other or coalition of Others, dedicated to complexity, decentralization, disaggregation, fragmentation, rapid change, the leveling of hierarchies, the blurring of boundaries, and so on, has moved in and taken over for a few decades . . . and twenty or thirty years from now all this will merely seem quaint. (That last part, of course, is almost certainly true. I would be very surprised, however, if that feeling of quaintness were precipitated by a return to the old rigid rationalism.)

Still, the convergence of these strikingly isomorphic theories across an entire spectrum of social practices does suggest *something*—if nothing more, that these theories are worth taking seriously enough to resist or rebut them. And I would argue that they suggest much more. They suggest that middle-ground level-3 theories of human behavior, based on the notion that we are largely but not entirely guided by massive quantities of conflicting voices or forces coming from somewhere outside whatever we want to define as our *selves*, have survived two millennia of emergent rationalism and are alive and well and productive today.

Conclusion:
Beyond Reason

The argument of this book might be reduced, if one were inclined to play it safe, to something like the following propositions:

1. Translation has been traditionally thought of as a process involving the translator's submission to forces outside his or her own rational volition, notably the source author and/or text.

2. This conception of the submissive transmission of another('s) voice strikingly resembles spirit-channeling, and indeed some of the most famous translations in Western history were once believed to have been channeled, or "divinely inspired."

3. The notion of the "regulation" of translation by ideological forces (norms, conventions, values) is philosophically congruent with, and bears comparison with, the older and more metaphysical notion that translators channel the voices of discarnate spirits.

4. Cognitive scientists and neurophilosophers today agree that the rationalist model of consciousness, according to which it is controlled by a single decision-making center, is false and must be replaced by a disaggregated model that is again strikingly congruent with the spiritualist and ideological models in 2 and 3, above.

5. As the translation marketplace grows increasingly complex and translations are produced less and less by individual translators, more and more by disaggregated agencies consisting of project managers, editorial assistants, freelance translators, and research assistants, the economic model governing translation too has come

to resemble the spiritualist, ideological, and cognitive models in 2, 3, and 4, above.

Thus conceived, this book offers a series of isomorphic models for understanding translation in terms of the history of religion (spirit-channeling), the operation of ideology (norm-channeling), cognitive science (the channeling of action-potentials), and economics (the channeling of invisible hands). In each translation is seen as "governed" not by a single unitary mind, as in older rationalist models, but rather by a loose and rather chaotic collection of competing forces that somehow, despite their lack of rationalist organization, nevertheless manage to bring about coherent action.

Most readers, I should think, will be willing to go along with the book's argument in this form, and accept propositions 1 – 5 as fair and accurate descriptions of reality. I imagine the strongest resistance arising to 4; the reigning assumptions of cognitive and brain science today still seem utterly counterintuitive to ordinary people whose intuitions remain most powerfully shaped by two millennia of rationalist thinking. But anyone who is initially skeptical of this approach and takes the trouble to read extensively in cognitive science, or even just Dennett's book *Consciousness Explained,* will almost certainly be convinced as well.

Underlying this "safe" formulation of the book's argument, however, is a more radical activist agenda that goes something like this:

6. While translation's own spiritualist traditions, ideological norm theory, cognitive science, and studies of the translation market-place all show that rationalist assumptions about translation are outdated, discredited, and unrealistic, rationalist thought is still so dominant in society that translators, translation instructors, and translation theorists continue to conceive their work along rationalist lines—as when instructors assume that the only way to teach people to translate is to get them to internalize and obey universalized precepts (*always translate sense-for-sense!* or *always foreignize!*), or else to teach them to base all translation on rigorous textual analysis; or as when accrediting bodies continue to base accreditation examinations on the old idea that translators work alone and so candidates must be prevented from "cheating" by researching or checking their work with other people.

7. These lingering rationalist assumptions are not only silly and outdated; they are actively harmful. They interfere normatively with

the translator's complex real-world approach to his or her task, and thus should be rooted out wherever they are found.

8. This antirationalist project is rendered enormously difficult not only by the deep-seated rationalist norms that continue to govern most theoretical and scholarly activity in the West, but also by the power of the rationalist tradition to brand *anti*rationalism as *irra*tionalist. Anyone who attacks rationalism is by normative definition irrational: a mystic, a crazy, an unserious person.

9. The disaggregated-agency models developed in this book, especially the ideological, cognitive, and economic ones, offer an alternative conceptualization of translation *outside* the narrow dualistic straitjacket of rational/irrational. They trace a channeling of regulatory forces that are neither rationalist, in the sense of positing a single governing mind behind every agency, nor irrational, in the sense of inviting sheer blooming chaos to reign.

10. The antirationalist project this book undertakes is not merely to advance some abstract new theory that is cleverer or more philosophically sophisticated than reigning rationalist models; it is to do battle against the normative theories that would blind us to the true complexities of current practical realities.

I claim, in other words, that the disaggregated-agency models I offer here are more *realistic* than the rationalist ones they seek to displace. Rationalism is a dream of perfect control; that dream may help us organize our work and thought in concerted ways, but it never succeeds. Reality is far too complex to succumb to such visions of absolute mastery. It always resists schemes of rationalist regulation in brilliantly diverse and effective ways. For the dedicated rationalist, this simply means the necessity of redoubled efforts; I am arguing that it would be more productive to adjust our theoretical models to reality rather than continuing to attempt to force reality to conform to impossibly idealized models.

Maybe discarnate spirits don't control translation. Maybe ideological norms are figments of our imagination. Maybe our cognitive processes are not controlled by what Daniel Dennett calls inner "demons." Maybe the "invisible hands" that Adam Smith postulated don't exist either, and economic processes are regulated in some other way. Even if these specific theoretical formulations prove to be illusory, however, I am arguing that something like them, something equally scattered or diversified, has far more power over translation than rationalist models can ever allow. Except in highly circumscribed and at best only partially successful ways, *we* do not control our world.

Works Cited

Abraham, Nicholas, and Maria Torok. *The Wolf Man's Magic Word: A Cryptonomy*. Translated by Nicholas Rand. Minneapolis: University of Minnesota Press, 1986.

Althusser, Louis. "Ideology and Ideological State Apparatuses (Notes Toward an Investigation)." Translated by Ben Brewster. In Althusser, *Lenin and Philosophy and Other Essays*, 127–86. New York and London: Monthly Review Press, 1971.

Balmary, Marie. *Psychoanalyzing Psychoanalysis*. Translated by Ned Lukacher. Baltimore: Johns Hopkins University Press, 1982.

Bateson, Gregory. *Steps to an Ecology of Mind*. New York: Ballantine, 1985.

Benjamin, Andrew. *Translation and the Nature of Philosophy: A New Theory of Words*. New York: Routledge, 1989.

Berger, John. *Ways of Seeing*. Harmondsworth: Penguin, 1972.

Berman, Antoine. *The Experience of the Foreign: Culture and Translation in Romantic Germany*. Translated by S. Heyvaert. Albany: State University of New York Press, 1992.

Burke, Kenneth. *The Rhetoric of Religion: Studies in Logology*. 1961; rpt. Berkeley: University of California Press, 1970.

Caputo, John D. *Demythologizing Heidegger*. Bloomington: Indiana University Press, 1993.

———. "Heidegger's Scandal: Thinking and the Essence of the Victim." In Rockmore and Margolis, *The Heidegger Case*, 265–81. Reprinted in expanded form as chapter seven of Caputo, *Demythologizing Heidegger*, 131–47.

Chamberlain, Lori. "Gender and the Metaphorics of Translation." *Signs* 13 (1988): 454–72.

Chesterman, Andrew. *Memes of Translation*. Amsterdam: John Benjamins, 1997.

Cheyfitz, Eric. *The Poetics of Imperialism: Translation and Colonization from The Tempest to Tarzan*. New York: Oxford University Press, 1991.

Dan, Joseph. "Midrash and the Dawn of Kabbalah." In Geoffrey H. Hartmann and Sanford Budick, eds., *Midrash and Literature*, 129–39. New Haven: Yale University Press, 1986.

Dennett, Daniel. *Consciousness Explained*. Boston: Little, Brown, 1991.

Derrida, Jacques. "Fors: The Anglish Words of Nicholas Abraham and Maria Torok." Translated by Barbara Johnson. In Abraham and Torok, *The Wolf Man's Magic Word*, xi-xlviii.

———. *On Spirit: Heidegger and the Question.* Translated by Geoffrey Bennington and Rachel Bowlby. 1987; Chicago: University of Chicago Press, 1991.
———. *Specters of Marx: The State of the Debt, The Work of Mourning, and the New International.* Translated by Peggy Kamuf. London: Routledge, 1994.
Díaz-Diocaretz, Myriam. *Translating Poetic Discourse: Questions on Feminist Strategies in Adrienne Rich.* Amsterdam and Philadelphia: John Benjamins, 1985.
Findlay, Arthur. *The Psychic Stream, or The Source and Growth of the Christian Faith.* 1939. Reprint. London: Psychic Press, 1947.
Fiumara, Gemma Corradi. *The Other Side of Language: A Philosophy of Listening.* Translated by Charles Lambert. London and New York: Routledge, 1990.
Foucault, Michel. *Discipline and Punish: The Birth of the Prison.* Translated by Alan Sheridan. 1975; New York: Random House/Vintage, 1979.
Gentzler, Edwin. *Contemporary Translation Theories.* London: Routledge, 1993.
Graham, Joseph, ed. *Difference in Translation.* Ithaca: Cornell University Press, 1985.
Halliday, W. R. *Greek Divination: A Study of Its Methods and Principles.* London: Macmillan, 1913.
Heidegger, Martin. *Der Satz vom Grund.* Pfulligen: Neske, 1957.
———. "Spiegel Interview with Martin Heidegger." In Günther Neske and Emil Kettering, eds., *Martin Heidegger and National Socialism: Questions and Answers.* Translated by Lisa Harries and Joachim Neugroschel. 1988; New York: Paragon House, 1990.
———. "Die Sprache." In *Unterwegs zur Sprache,* 7–30. Vol. 12 of Part 1, *Veröffentlichte Schriften 1910–1976,* of Friedrich-Wilhelm von Herrmann, ed., *Gesamtausgabe.* Frankfurt-am-Main: Vittorio Klostermann, 1985.
Hermans, Theo. "Translation and Normativity." *Current Issues in Language and Society* 5.1–2 (1998): 51–72.
Hofstadter, Albert, trans. "Language." In Martin Heidegger, *Poetry, Language, Thought,* 187–210. New York: Harper & Row, 1975.
Jacquemond, Richard. "Translation and Cultural Hegemony: The Case of French-Arabic Translation." In Lawrence Venuti, ed., *Rethinking Translation,* 139–58. London and New York: Routledge, 1992.
Jaynes, Julian. *The Origin of Consciousness in the Breakdown of the Bicameral Mind.* 1976; Boston: Houghton Mifflin, 1990.
Klimo, Jon. *Channeling: Investigations on Receiving Information from Paranormal Sources.* Los Angeles: Tarcher, 1987.
Lacan, Jacques. *Écrits: A Selection.* Translated by Alan Sheridan. 1966; New York: Norton, 1977.
Laing, R. D. *The Divided Self.* 1960. Reprint. New York: Pantheon Books, 1969.
Lefevere, André. *Translation, Rewriting, and the Manipulation of Literary Fame.* London: Routledge, 1992.
Leichtman, Robert R., M.D., through the mediumship of D. Kendrick Johnson. *From Heaven to Earth: Shakespeare Returns.* Columbus, OH: Ariel Press, 1978.
Levine, Suzanne Jill. *The Subversive Scribe: Translating Latin-American Fiction.* St. Paul: Graywolf, 1992.

Lewis, Philip E. "The Measure of Translation Effects." In Graham, ed., *Difference in Translation*, 31–62.

Lilly, Reginald, trans. *The Principle of Ground*, by Martin Heidegger. Bloomington: Indiana University Press, 1991.

Littau, Karin. "Intertextuality and Translation: *The Waste Land* in French and German." In Catriona Picken, ed., *Translation: The Vital Link*, 63–69. London: Chameleon, 1993.

———. "Translation in the Age of Postmodern Production: From Text to Intertext to Hypertext." *Forum for Modern Language Studies* 33 (1997): 81–96.

Maier, Carol. "Notes after Words: Looking Forward Retrospectively at Translation and (Hispanic and Luso-Brazilian) Feminist Criticism." In Herman Vidal, ed., *Cultural and Historical Grounding for Hispanic and Luso-Brazilian Feminist Literary Criticism*, 625–53. Minneapolis: University of Minnesota Press, 1989.

Marten, Rainer. "Heidegger and the Greeks." In Rockmore and Margolis, *The Heidegger Question*, 167–87.

Marx, Karl. *Der achtzehnte Brumaire des Louis Bonaparte*. Vienna and Berlin: Verlag für Literatur und Politik, 1927.

Maxwell, Neal A. "By the Gift and Power of God." *The Ensign* (January 1997): 36–41.

Nibley, Preston. *Joseph Smith the Prophet*. Salt Lake City: Deseret News Press, 1946.

Nietzsche, Freidrich. *The Genealogy of Morals: An Attack*. Translated by Francis Golffing. In *The Birth of Tragedy and The Genealogy of Morals*, 147–299. New York: Doubleday/Anchor, 1956.

Niranjana, Tejaswini. *Siting Translation: History, Post-Structuralism, and the Colonial Context*. Berkeley and Los Angeles: University of California Press, 1992.

Norton, Glyn. *The Ideology and Language of Translation in Renaissance France and Their Humanist Antecedents*. Geneva: Droz, 1984.

Nozick, Robert. *Anarchy, State, and Utopia*. New York: Basic Books, 1974.

———. "Invisible-Hand Explanations." *The American Economic Review* 84.2 (May 1994): 314–38.

Ott, Hugo. "Biographical Bases for Heidegger's 'Mentality of Disunity.'" In Rockmore and Margolis, *The Heidegger Case*, 93–113.

Paul, Jeffrey, ed. *Reading Nozick: Essays on 'Anarchy, State, and Utopia.'* Totowa, NJ: Rowman and Littlefield, 1981.

Persuitte, David. *Joseph Smith and the Origins of "The Book of Mormon."* Jefferson, NC, and London: McFarland, 1985.

Peters, Tom. *The Pursuit of Wow! Every Person's Guide to Topsy-Turvy Times*. New York: Vintage/Random House, 1994.

Petzet, Heinrich Wiegand. *Encounters and Dialogues with Martin Heidegger, 1929–1976*. Translated by Parvis Emad and Kenneth Maly. 1983; Chicago: University of Chicago Press, 1993.

Plato. *Opera Omnia*. Ed. Godofredus Stalbaum. *Phaedrus* Vol. 4 sect. 1. *Cratylus* Vol. 5 sect. 2, London: Hennings, 1885.

———. *The Collected Dialogues*. Ed. Edith Hamilton and Huntington Cairns. Bollingen Series 71. 1963; rpt. Princeton: Princeton University Press, 1980.

Plotinus. *Enneads.* Trans. Stephen MacKenna. 1917–1930; rpt. London: Faber & Faber, 1956.

Pym, Anthony. *Epistemological Problems in Translation and Its Teaching.* Calaceite: Caminade, 1993.

———. "Schleiermacher and the Problem of *Blendlinge.*" *Translation and Literature* 4.1 (1995): 1–30.

———. *Translation and Text Transfer.* Frankfurt-am-Main: Peter Lang, 1992.

Rand, Nicholas. "The Political Truth of Heidegger's 'Logos': Hiding in Translation." *PMLA* 105 (May 1990): 436–47.

Reed, Henry, under the editorship of Charles Thomas Cayce. *Edgar Cayce on Channeling Your Higher Self.* New York: Warner, 1989.

Robinson, Douglas. *Becoming a Translator: An Accelerated Course.* London: Routledge, 1997.

———. "Classical Theories of Translation from Cicero to Aulus Gellius." *TEXTconTEXT* 1 (1992): 15–55.

———. *The Translator's Turn.* Baltimore: Johns Hopkins University Press, 1991.

———. *Translation and Empire: Postcolonial Theories Explained.* Manchester: St. Jerome, 1997.

———. *Translation and Taboo.* DeKalb: Northern Illinois University Press, 1996.

———. "Translation and the Double Bind." *Studies in the Humanities* 22.1/2 (December 1995): 1–11.

———. *What Is Translation? Centrifugal Theories, Critical Interventions.* Kent, OH: Kent State University Press, 1997.

Robinson, Douglas, ed. *Western Translation Theory From Herodotus to Nietzsche.* Manchester: St. Jerome, 1997.

Rockmore, Tom. *On Heidegger's Nazism and Philosophy.* Berkeley and Los Angeles: University of California Press, 1992.

Rockmore, Tom, and Joseph Margolis, eds. *The Heidegger Case: On Philosophy and Politics.* Philadelphia: Temple University Press, 1992.

Rose, Marilyn Gaddis. *Translation and Literary Criticism.* Manchester: St. Jerome, 1997.

Rothschild, Emma. "Adam Smith and the Invisible Hand." *The American Economic Review* 84.2 (May 1994): 319–22.

Ryle, Gilbert. *The Concept of Mind.* London: Hutchinson, 1949.

Schleiermacher, Friedrich (1813) "Ueber die verschiedenen Methoden des Uebersezens." Lecture 3 of *Abhandlungen gelesen in der Königlichen Akademie der Wissenschaften* (207–45). In vol. 2 (1838) of Schleiermacher, *Zur Philosophie,* 149–495. 9 vols. (reprinted in 4 vols. [1–2, 3–4, 5–6, 7–9]). Berlin: G. Reimer, 1835–1846. Part 3 of *Friedrich Schleiermacher's sämmtliche Werke.* Translated by Douglas Robinson, "On the Different Methods of Translating." In Robinson, ed., *Western Translation Theory from Herodotus to Nietzsche,* 225–38.

Simeoni, Daniel. "The Pivotal Status of the Translator's Habitus." *Target* 10.1 (1998): 1–39.

Simon, Sherry. *Translation and Gender.* London and New York: Routledge, 1995.

Smith, Joseph (trans.?). *The Book of Mormon*. 1830. Reprint. Salt Lake City: The Church of Jesus Christ of Latter-Day Saints, 1986.

Torok, Maria. "What Is Occult in Occultism? Between Sigmund Freud and Sergei Pankeiev Wolf Man." Translated by Nicholas Rand. In Abraham and Torok, *The Wolf Man's Magic Word*, 84–106.

Toury, Gideon. *Descriptive Translation Studies and Beyond*. Amsterdam and Philadelphia: John Benjamins, 1995.

Venuti, Lawrence. *The Scandal of Translation*. London and New York: Routledge, 1997.

———. *The Translator's Invisibility*. London and New York: Routledge, 1995.

Vieira, Else Ribeiro Pires. "New Registers for Translation in Latin America." In Peter Bush and Kirsten Malmkjœr, eds., *Rimbaud's Rainbow: Literary Translation in Higher Education*, 171–95. Amsterdam and Philadelphia: John Benjamins, 1998.

von Flotow, Luise. *Translation and Gender: Feminist Theories Explained*. Manchester: St. Jerome, 1997.

Williamson, Oliver E. "Visible and Invisible Governance." *The American Economic Review* 84.2 (May 1994): 323–26.

Wimsatt, W. K., and Monroe C. Beardsley, "The Intentional Fallacy." In Wimsatt, *The Verbal Icon: Studies in the Meaning of Poetry*, 21–39. Louisville: University of Kentucky Press, 1954.

Wong, Eva, trans. *Lieh-tzu: A Taoist Guide to Practical Living*. Boston: Shambhala, 1995.

Index

Abraham, Nicolas, 17, 76, 81–86, 92–95, 102, 111
Abrams, M. H., 26
Achtzehnte Brumaire des Louis Bonaparte, Der (Marx), 129, 131
Althusser, Louis, 70–74, 150
Amenhotep IV / Akhnaton, 37
American Translators Association, 1, 10, 188
Anarchy, State, and Utopia (Nozick), 184
anonymity of translator, 159–64, 175–77
Archilochus, 44
Aristeas, 48–51
Aristotle, 47, 100, 114, 117
Arnold, Matthew, 7
Arrojo, Rosemary, 142
Art of Translation, The (Savory), 171–72
Augustine, 48, 49, 51–53, 82, 160; and Heidegger, 100
authorial intention, 24–25, 123

ballistic speech acts (Dennett), 153–54
Balmary, Marie, 88–92
Bateson, Gregory, 91, 174–75
Beardsley, Monroe C., 24
Beginning of Mormonism, The (Tucker), 58
Benjamin, Andrew, 78–81, 102
Benjamin, Walter, 101
Berman, Antoine, 103

Bertola, Gisselle, 1–3
Beyond Good and Evil (Nietzsche), 91
Bible translations, 158; Erasmus' Latin, 5; King James, 56, 69–70, 82; Luther's German, 6; Rheims-Douai, 6; Septuagint, 5, 17, 48–54, 69–70, 101; Vulgate, 5–6, 49, 69–70, 82, 101
Boethius, 172–74
Book of Mormon, The (Smith), 7, 17, 49, 54–61, 69
Borges, Jorge Luis, 22
Bourdieu, Pierre, 102, 143
Bradley, A. H., 117
Burgundio of Pisa, 172–74
Burke, Kenneth, 31–32, 74, 75

cannibalism theory (de Campos brothers), 143
Cartesian Theater (Dennett), 147
Cayce, Edgar, 9
Cervantes Saavedra, Miguel de, 22
Chamberlain, Lori, 143
Channeling (Klimo), 37–39
Chesterman, Andrew, 72
Cheyfitz, Eric, 76, 143
Cicero, 42, 45, 104
Cixous, Hélène, 142
"Classical Theories of Translation from Cicero to Aulus Gellius" (Robinson), 42, 45

Colburn, Nettie, 43
Concept of Mind, The (Ryle), 152
Consciousness Explained (Dennett), 18,
     148, 194
Contemporary Translation Theories
     (Gentzler), 143
Cook, Florence, 43
Cratylus (Plato), 38–39, 151
crypt, 76, 81, 93–94; Heidegger's, 94–96,
     111–13, 115
cryptonomy (Abraham/Torok), 17, 82–
     88

Dante Alighieri, 24
Darwin, Charles, 182
Davis, Bette, 123
Daybreak (Nietzsche), 91
de Andrade, Oswald, 143
de Campos, Augusto and Haroldo, 143
De doctrina Christiana (Augustine), 51–53
Deleuze, Gilles, 142
Denham, John, 172–74
Dennett, Daniel, 8, 17–18, 74, 146–47,
     151–56, 157–58, 160, 164–65, 180,
     184, 190–91, 194–95
Derrida, Jacques, 11, 17, 28, 77, 83–84,
     101–2, 121, 128, 130–31, 136, 142, 157
"Des Tours de Babel" (Derrida), 142
Descartes, 146, 151
Descriptive Translation Studies, 75, 142
"Dialogue on Language" (Heidegger), 81
Diaz-Diocaretz, Myriam, 76, 142
"(Dis)Abusing Translation" (Robinson),
     11–12
disaggregated agencies (Nozick), 18,
     148, 165, 180, 184, 186–91, 193–95
Dogberry, Obadiah, 56
Don Quixote (Cervantes), 91, 93
double bind, 170–72, 174–79
Dreams and Occultism (Freud), 83

*Edgar Cayce on Channeling Your Higher
     Self* (Reed), 9–10
*Eighteenth Brumaire of Louis Bonaparte,
     The* (Marx), 129, 131
Elizabeth I, 116–17, 123
Enneads (Plotinus), 48
*Epistemological Problems in Translation
     and Its Teaching* (Pym), 143
Erasmus of Rotterdam, 5

Eriugena, Johannes Scotus, 172–74
Esau, 89
Euripides, 44
Even-Zohar, Itamar, 142
"Explanations" (Nozick), 183–84

Fichte, Johann Gottlieb, 103
fidus interpres (Horace), 65, 73, 151, 170,
     172–75
Findlay, Arthur, 40–41
Fiumara, Gemma Corradi, 8–9
Fliess, Wilhelm, 89
Forster, E. M., 146, 154
Foucault, Michel, 69, 73, 76, 142, 186
Fox, George, 43
Fox, John, 43
Franklin, Benjamin, 43
Freud, Jacob, 88–92
Freud, Sigmund, 8, 17, 76, 83, 86–93,
     111, 125, 146–48, 150, 170, 182, 185
*From Heaven to Earth: Shakespeare Re-
     turns* (Leichtman/Johnson), 118–19,
     123
functionalist theory (Nord), 142

Gadamer, Hans-Georg, 8
Geister (spirits/ghosts), 32, 131–38
Genealogy of Morals (Nietzsche), 70–71, 91
Gentzler, Edwin, 143
German Ideology, The (Marx), 31
Gespenster (ghosts), 32, 131–38
ghosts, 28–30, 32; logic of (Derrida), 11,
     121–22, 128, 130, 145, 157
Goethe, Johann Wolfgang von, 98
going doubled like a ghost (Schleier-
     macher), 133–35
Goneril (*King Lear*), 127
Graves, Robert, 89
Grotius, Hugo, 133
Guattari, Fèlix, 142

habitus theory (Bourdieu/Simeoni),
     143–44
Handlung theory (Holz-Mänttäri), 142
Harris, Martin, 58–60
Hegel, Georg Wilhelm Friedrich, 98, 182
Heidegger, Hermann, 94
Heidegger, Martin, 8, 17, 76, 94–115,
     132, 150; and the crypt, 94–96, 111–
     13; on machine translation, 95, 96,

108, 113–14; and the Nazis, 111, 115; and Petzet, 111–13; and revolutionary conservatism (Bourdieu), 102; his silence, 105–13; on spirit, 77–81; on technology, 106–9; and translation from Greek, 97, 99–104, 108, 115
Heraclitus, 38, 114
Herder, Johann Gottfriend, 104, 134–35
Hermans, Theo, 72, 76, 142
Hesiod, 44
hidden-hand explanations (Nozick), 184–86
Hildegarde of Bingen, St., 42
Hirsch, E. D., Jr., 26
History of Astronomy, The (Smith), 181
Hitler, Adolf, 99, 101, 111
Hofstadter, Albert, 77
Hölderlin, Friedrich, 95, 96, 98, 103–4, 157–58
Holmberg, Kalle, 116–17
Holmes, James, 142
Holz-Mänttäri, Justa, 142
Home, Daniel D., 43
Homer, 7, 24, 39, 44–47, 135
Horace, 65, 104, 161, 172
Humboldt, Wilhelm von, 134

ideology, 17, 186; channeled, 9, 11–12, 70–73, 123, 128, 193; as ideosomatics, 122; logology of, 74–76; in Marx, 130
ideoplasm, 76, 124, 127–29
"Intentional Fallacy, The" (Wimsatt/Beardsley), 24
interpreting, politics of, 125–29; as spirit-channeling, 61–65
"Intertextuality and Translation" (Littau), 142
Introduction to Metaphysics, An (Heidegger), 78–79
Investigations into the Method of the Social Sciences and Political Economics in Particular (Menger), 183
invisible hands (Smith), 8, 18, 74, 148, 180–83, 195
invisible subjects, 63, 156–66, 175–77
Ion (Plato), 17, 44–48
Ion (*Ion*), 39, 44–48
Irigaray, Luce, 142

Jacob, 89

Jacquemond, Richard, 76
James, William, 43
Jerome, 5–6, 64, 48–51, 157–58, 172
Jesus, 40–42
Joan of Arc, 43
John of Patmos, 40
John of the Cross, St., 43
Johnson, D. Kendrick, 118–19, 123
Jones, Ernest, 91
Joseph Smith the Prophet (Nibley), 59–60
"Joseph Smith and the Origins of "The Book of Mormon" (Persuitte), 55–56

Kant, Immanuel, 124, 157
King Lear (Shakespeare), 8, 17, 76, 116–24, 127–28, 134
King Lear (*King Lear*, "Kuningas/King Lear"), 116–29
"King Lear" (Rossi), 125–29
King Leir, 117
Klimo, Jon, 37–39, 43
Kristeva, Julia, 142
"Kuningas Lear" (Rossi), 125–29

Lacan, Jacques, 8, 142; on the mirror-stage, 157; on objects, 165; on the Other, 10–11, 122; on Schema L, 17, 75, 148–51, 156–57, 159, 170
Laing, R. D., 91
"Language" (Heidegger), 77
"language speaks us" (Heidegger), 77–81, 150
LANTRA-L, 1–2
Lectures on Rhetoric and Belles Lettres (Smith), 182
Lefevere, André, 17, 44, 76, 142
Leibniz, Gottfried Wilhelm, 94, 105, 109–10, 114, 133
Leichtman, Robert R., 118–19, 123
Levine, Suzanne Jill, 143
Lieh-tzu, 22–23
Life of Moses (Philo), 50
Lilly, Reginald, 94
Lincoln, Abraham, 43
Lips, Maarten, 5
Littau, Karin, 76, 142
logology (Burke), 30–35; of economic agents, 185–86; of ideology, 34, 74–76; of reason, 31–35; of the self, 145–48, 149–51; of spirit, 33

Lollards, 64
Lucan, 39
Lukacher, Ned, 88, 89
Luther, Martin, 5–6, 158
Lysis (Plato), 39

Macbeth (Shakespeare), 181
machine translation, 113–14, 166; for Heidegger, 95, 96, 108; as spirit-channeling secularized, 65; Urim and Thummim, 55
Macpherson, James, 54–55
Mahoney, Patrick, 22
Maier, Carol, 143
Marx, Karl, 17, 31–32, 119–20, 122, 128, 129–38, 182
Maxwell, Neal A., 57
Mayor, Carlos, 1, 3
Menard, Pierre (Borges), 22
Menger, Carl, 182
Merriam, Paul, 1, 3, 10
Metamorphoses (Ovid), 181
Miller, Alice, 92
Milton, John, 151
mirror-stage (Lacan), 157
Moses, William Stainton, Rev., 43
mysticism, 12–15, 25; in Heidegger, denied, 100

Napoleon Bonaparte, 103
Nathanson, Amalie, 89
Nazism, 94, 111, 115
Newbrough, John Ballou, 43
Newman, Francis, 7
Nibley, Preston, 59–60
Nietzsche, Friedrich, 70–71, 82–83, 85, 90–93, 104, 179
Niranjana, Tejaswini, 143
Noble, Joel K., 55–56
Nord, Christiane, 142
Norton, Glyn, 173
Nostradamus, Michel de, 43
Nozick, Robert, 18, 180, 183–84, 190–91

O., Anna, 90
Odile, St., 42
Odyssey (Homer), 39, 105–6
Oedipus complex (Freud), 87–89
Of Spirit (Derrida), 28, 77, 101–2
Oliver, Frederick S., 43

On the Way to Language (Heidegger), 77
"On the Different Methods of Translating" (Schleiermacher), 131
Ossian (Macpherson), 54–55
Other (Lacan), 10–11, 122, 144, 149, 151, 170–71, 174, 192
Other Side of Language, The (Fiumara), 8–9
Ott, Hugo, 111
Ouija board, 37, 39
Ovid, 181

Palladino, Eusapia, 43
pandemonium self (Dennett), 74, 146, 148, 151–56, 160–70, 184
Patai, Raphael, 89
Paul, 17, 40–41, 49, 50, 61–65
Persuitte, David, 55–56
Peters, Tom, 191
Petzet, Heinrich Wiegand, 111–13
Phaedrus (Plato), 38
Pharsalia (Lucan), 39
Philebus (Plato), 39
Philo Judaeus, 5, 17, 48–49, 53, 82
Pindar, 158
Plato, 17, 38–39, 44–48, 100, 114
Plotinus, 48
Poetics of Imperialism, The (Cheyfitz), 143
Poetics, The (Aristotle), 47
Poetry, Language, Thought (Heidegger/Hofstadter), 77
polysystem theory, 75, 142
Post, Isaac, 43
postrationalism, 13–16, 141–44
Praefatio in Pentateuchem (Jerome), 5
Principle of Ground, The (Heidegger/Lilly), 94
Psychic Stream, The (Findlay), 40–41
Ptolemy Philadelphus, 49
Pym, Anthony, 136–37, 143, 157–59
Pythagoras, 38–39

Rand, Nicholas, 83, 102
rationalism, 12–16, 25, 26–28, 141–42, 150–51, 185, 193–95; channeling of, 28; logology of, 31–35; and monotheism, 37; and mysticism, 12–15; of Romans for Heidegger, 100; of the self, 145–47
reader-response, 25–27, 124

Rebecca, 89
Reed, Henry, 9–10
Regan (*King Lear*), 127
Reich, Wilhelm, 122
Reiss, Katharina, 142
revolutionary conservatism (Bourdieu), 102
Ring Lardner and the Other (Robinson), 11, 171, 175
Robbe-Grillet, Alain, 35
Rockmore, Tom, 111
Rolle of Hampole, Richard, 42–43
Rose, Marilyn Gaddis, 143
Rossi, Matti, 76, 116–29, 134
Rothschild, Emma, 180–83
Rychlewski, Alex, 1–3
Ryle, Gilbert, 152

Samuel, 40
Santiago, Silviano, 143
Satz vom Grund, Der (Heidegger), 8, 17, 94–97, 100, 101, 105–6
Saul, 40
Savory, Theodore, 171–72, 174
Scandal of Translation, The (Venuti), 143
Schelling, Friedrich Wilhelm Joseph von, 98
Schema L (Lacan), 17, 148–51, 159–60
Schlegel, August Wilhelm and Friedrich von, 104
Schleiermacher, Friedrich, 17, 23, 32, 63, 99, 106, 129, 131–38, 184
seduction theory (Freud), 88–93
Selfridge, Oliver, 151
Sendbrief vom Dolmetschen (Luther), 6
Seneca, 104
Septuagint, legend of, 5, 7, 17, 48–54
sexual trauma (Freud), 88–93
Shakers, 43
Shakespeare, William, vii, 17, 76, 116–29, 127–28, 134, 181; channeled, 118–21, 123
Sherburne, Sir Edward, 173–74
Simeoni, Daniel, 143
Simon, Sherry, 143
Siting Translation (Niranjana), 143
skopos theory (Reiss/Vermeer), 142
Smith, Adam, 8, 18, 74, 180–83, 195
Smith, Joseph, 49, 54–61
Socrates, 38–39, 43–48, 99–100

somatics, 23, 82
Sophocles, 98, 103–4
Specters of Marx (Derrida), 11, 28, 31, 121, 130–31
spectrality, logic of (Derrida), 11, 17, 121–22, 128, 130, 145, 157
Speeches to the German Nation (Fichte), 103
Spiegel, Der (Heidegger interview) 94, 96, 98–101, 104, 111
spirit translates (Heidegger), 77, 80–81
spirit-channeling, as heuristic, 7–12, 16–17; and ideology, 11–12, 70–73, 130, 193; and interpreting, 61–65; and logology of reason, 31–35; and machine translation, 65
Spiritualism, 43
Steiner, George, 106
Steps to an Ecology of Mind (Bateson), 174
Stirner, Max, 31–32
Swedenborg, Emanuel, 43

"Task of the Translator, The" (Benjamin), 101
Tate, Nahum, 117
telepathy (Freud/Torok), 83–84
Teresa of Avila, St., 43
Theory of Moral Sentiments, The (Smith), 181–82
Torok, Maria, 17, 76, 81–86, 92–95, 102, 111
Toury, Gideon, 72, 76, 142
Trakl, Georg, 77
Translating Poetic Discourse (Diaz-Diocaretz), 142
translation, divine inspiration of, 4–7, 14, 36, 42, 44, 48–65 (denied), 69, 193; "free," 25–26; literal, 25–26; messianic, 80–81, 113; performative theory of, 124–27; sense-for-sense, 25–26; as spirit-channeling, 82; as writing, 1–4
Translation and Empire (Robinson), 76
"Translation and the Double Bind" (Robinson), 171
Translation and Literary Criticism (Rose), 143
"Translation and Normativity" (Hermans), 142
Translation and Taboo (Robinson), 7, 11,

Translation and Taboo (continued)
  14, 28, 32, 38, 49, 51, 63, 101, 122, 131,
  133, 143, 144, 147, 159, 160, 171, 172
Translation and Text Transfer (Pym), 143,
  157–59
"Translation in the Age of Postmodern
  Production" (Littau), 142
Translator's Invisibility, The (Venuti), 142
Translator's Turn, The (Robinson), 4, 7,
  11, 15, 25, 122, 124, 143, 147, 159, 164
translator-function (Diaz-Diocaretz),
  142
Tucker, Pomeroy, 58
Tytler, Alexander Frazer, 21

"Ueber die verschiedenen Methoden
  des Uebersezens" (Schleiermacher),
  131
*Untersuchungen über die Methode der Soc-
  zialwissenschaften und der politischen
  Oekonomie insbesondere* (Menger), 183

Unterwegs zur Sprache (Heidegger), 77
Urim and Thummim (Smith), 55, 57

Venuti, Lawrence, 63, 76, 137, 142–43
Vermeer, Hans, 142
Vieira, Else, 143
von Flotow, Luise, 143

Wang Ch'ung, 37
Wealth of Nations, The (Smith), 181–82
What Is Translation? (Robinson), 11–12,
  42, 76, 103
Wimsatt, W. K., 24
Wolf Man (Freud / Abraham / Torok),
  17, 81–88, 94, 111
"Wolf Man", The (Freud), 8, 86–93
Wolf Man's Magic Word, The (Abra-
  ham/Torok), 8, 81–86
Wong, Eva, 22–23
Wyclif, John, 64